MASTERS SCULLING

TECHNIQUE AND TRAINING

DR NANCY CHURCHILL

MASTERS SCULLING

TECHNIQUE AND TRAINING

DR NANCY CHURCHILL

The Crowood Press

First published in 2020 by
The Crowood Press Ltd
Ramsbury, Marlborough
Wiltshire SN8 2HR

www.crowood.com
enquiries@crowood.com

British Library Cataloguing-in-Publication Data
A catalogue record for this book is available from the British Library.

ISBN 978 1 78500 705 7

Dedicated to the athletes of the Masters Rowing Western Australia Development Teams 2016–2020.

Typeset by Kelly-Anne Levey
Printed and bound in India by Replika Press Pvt Ltd

CONTENTS

Acknowledgements...6

Preface 7

Introduction 9

1 MASTERS SCULLING FUNDAMENTALS.......................... 11

2 THE SCULLING SYSTEM: BOAT AND OARS.......................25

3 THE SCULLING SYSTEM: INTEGRATING THE ATHLETE 39

4 THE SCULLING SYSTEM: PROPULSION 53

5 DYNAMIC TECHNIQUE: PRE-DRIVE SEQUENCE 73

6 DYNAMIC TECHNIQUE: DRIVE SEQUENCE 91

7 ATHLETE ASSESSMENT 108

8 ASSESSMENT REVIEW AND INTRODUCTION TO TRAINING 130

9 CREATING THE INDIVIDUAL TRAINING PROGRAMME 145

10 RECOVERY STRATEGIES 169

11 RECOVERY SUPPORT ACTIVITIES 183

12 TRAINING EFFICIENTLY 193

13 COMPETITION AND RACE PLANS 213

14 RACING A SINGLE SCULL...226

Conclusion...236

Further Reading..238

Index...239

ACKNOWLEDGEMENTS

This book is the culmination of endless kindnesses and generosities from so many contributors that it is impossible to list them all. The greatest privilege has been their willingness to allow me to shape their gifts into a book and to pass on their goodwill.

My thanks to those whose research has appeared here, including: Australian Masters Rowing Commission and, in particular, Mark Mussared, who developed the 2013 Handicap Report and 2018 Review; Concept2 (US) and Meredith Breiland for the discussion on oars; Lorelle Klumpp for nutrition, hydration and osteoporosis; Chris and Carmel Lloyd for dental health; Dr Gavan White for the ageing athlete and cardiac event awareness; Marg Rhodes for her contribution to the development of the FMB assessment methodology; and Terry O'Neill, who made all of his work available, including the O'Neill test.

To others who have supported the work leading to this book: Joe Racosky and Nielsen Kellerman for their tremendous Masters support, including partnering on the Western Australian eRegattas; Ian Randall of Randallfoils for his collaboration on Masters performance development; Rowing Australia and the Australian Institute of Sport for their generosity in sharing high-performance, elite information through the coaching education programme; Valery Kleshnev for his BioRow newsletters and ready responses to biomechanical questions; Craftsbury Sculling Center for its generous sharing of information and ideas during my times visiting there; Troy Howell for answering rigging and other sculling questions; and Ric Ricci for providing the early methodology for measuring catch angles, as well as philosophical inspiration.

To all those who offered themselves as photographers and models, including Jen, Carmel, Plaxy, Susy, Chris, Diane, Andy, Terry, Pete and Phil.

To my readers Chris Lloyd, Sandy Ceriani, Phil House and Diane Stewart, whose time, suggestions, improvements, encouragement and advice were given with enthusiasm and thoughtfulness. Their handiwork appears silently throughout the book.

To the founders and selectors of Master Rowing Western Australia Incorporated who started us all on this journey: Jen, Nola, Plaxy, Pina and Darlene.

To Bunbury Rowing Club, Champion Lakes Boating Club and Fremantle Rowing Club, all of whom have provided a home base for the Masters Rowing Western Australia Development Teams.

At the heart of this book are the athletes of those Development Teams: Barb, Carmel, Chris, Mish, Susy, Kylie, Lorelle, Kimberley, Myra, Wendy, Gen, Sandy, Alex, Harvey, Diane, Phil and John (who contributed his race plan). With enthusiasm and persistence, these brave athletes explored the dynamic technique and the Masters development process described herein. Without them, this book would not have been possible.

Last, Pina – who introduced me to rowing (and officiating dragon boat races). Her devotion to the sport is legendary.

A sincere, heartfelt thanks to all.

PREFACE

Years ago I decided to compete seriously in a single scull. At that point, I had completed one 1X race with a time so slow it didn't register, in conditions that were cyclonic and with a skill level that took me seventeen strokes to get started. But, I beat someone. Delusional, I signed up for a three-day course at Craftsbury Sculling Centre in Vermont (US), far from Australia.

On returning, and guided by Jon Ackland's *Endurance Training*, I designed a meticulous cross training programme, based on elite methodologies that included a peak week of 170km. I diligently practised Rowing Australia's National Technical Model, sought the advice of coaches and implemented my new Craftsbury skills. Tapered and ready, I went off to compete at the Australian Masters Rowing Championships.

I did well. However, after reflecting on my training season and watching a video of my race, I realised something: there was no way I was going to improve significantly. I couldn't train any harder (or more thoughtfully) and was probably going to have serious future health consequences keeping up a 170km peak week training programme. I couldn't execute Rowing Australia's National Technical Model much better. I was puzzled by the gap between what I was experiencing at the club level and what I was seeing at the national and international level, including the fact that elite scullers didn't seem to be using any national technical model that I could find.

Adding to the above the insights gathered at Craftsbury, I began to think 'there has got to be a better way'. Especially for Masters who have a fifty-plus year career runway and who would, at best, get injured or, at worst, die young if they wholesale adopted an elite high-performance training methodology for decades.

I bought every book on rowing that was still in print. I searched websites and began to find the many threads that had yet to be woven into a system for those not on a national team. I discovered Valery Kleshnev's *BioRow Newsletters*, and his kindness and generosity in answering questions about them and, subsequently, his book *The Biomechanics of Rowing*. The journey took me to research, mainly in other sports because there is little rowing research, and to ancillary fields such as nutrition, hydration, sports psychology, training methodologies, physiology and so many others.

I returned to Craftsbury as both a sculler and for coaching education, gleaning information from many sources. When completing the Rowing Australia Level 3 performance coaching course held at the Australian Institute of Sport, a very large window opened as to what was possible for Masters. Rowing Australia and the Australian Institute of Sport were very generous in sharing national elite performance information, including leading edge research that applied to Masters.

The end result of all this questioning and investigation was a nascent system that looked to have a good possibility of being effective, efficient, safe and fun. It appeared to be a system that would improve performance, because it uses a dynamic technical model similar to that used by national elite performance scullers, modified for Masters. In addition, the system allows the Masters athlete to enjoy the experience, deciding how sculling will fit into his or her lifestyle with an expectation of continuous improvement and minimal injury risk.

Thanks to Masters Rowing Western Australia Incorporated, three Development Teams were formed. The team members pilot-tested this system of development, including the dynamic technical model. Their range of experience was from new learner to forty-plus years. Several years later, they were fitter, happier, rowing faster, injury free and thriving in their sculling practice, as am I.

This book shares that development system and the dynamic technical model. Whether you are sculling for pleasure or performance, the book provides the chance to explore the science and art of sculling. My hope is that by using the information contained in it, your sculling practice will be a journey of enrichment, longevity and joy.

INTRODUCTION

This book is about sculling with exquisite style, grace and speed. It incorporates evidence-based science while embracing the artfulness of the sport. It is about developing a feel, connection and partnership with the sculling system. This is a book for scullers of all ages, not just Masters. However, it does address the specific needs of Masters scullers in several ways.

First, this book begins to address the information needs of Masters scullers. The sport of rowing, including sculling, has a traditional oral legacy. As a result, historical experience is more available than the evidence-based. This is particularly so for Masters. A systematic approach based on contemporary, research-based information, as contained in this book, begins an informed pathway for Masters sculling development.

Second, Masters scullers have different opportunities with regards to the technical aspects of the sport. For example, the national technical models have been designed to homogenize the child, youth and junior development processes, facilitating the elite selection for these groups. Masters have the freedom to choose whatever technique reduces their injury risk and makes their boat go faster. By addressing Masters' long-term athletic runway and performance potential, this technique may be quite different. Here, it is.

Third, Masters' physical considerations are complex. These include aerobic/anaerobic development, sleep, nutrition, biomechanics and sports psychology amongst many others. Adult physiology changes over fifty-plus years. The ability to anticipate and manage these changes is beginning to demonstrate a marked improvement in performance for older athletes in many sports. This book begins to share that information with Masters scullers, too.

The challenge then becomes how to provide such a broad scope intelligently within one book. One strategy is to narrow the focus. By now, the use of 'sculling' versus 'rowing' is evident, a conscious decision to focus the book on sculling and, in particular, a single scull. A single scull is the boat through which an athlete can most quickly and comprehensively acquire sculling mastery. When there are stability and speed deficiencies in a single scull, only one person can correct them. Alternatively, when the platform is rock solid and the speed gripping, success is clearly individual, too. Single scull skills translate well to multi-seat sculling boats as well as sweep boats. The reverse is less clear. Thus, this book's focus is limited to a single scull.

Next is the issue of writing for the Masters sculling audience with its extraordinarily diversity. Aside from their ages, these athletes range from novices to past Olympians; from athletes who do not coach to those who coach extensively; from the fit to the unfit; from the recreational to the competitive. The strategy has been to provide content that evolves from less complicated to highly specific. The elementary, such as terminology, is not included. Many fine books already exist that cover the basics. They make excellent general reading and are listed in the Further Reading section at the end of the book.

Some topics will be abbreviated, highlighting specific information related to Masters scullers. For example, strength and conditioning is an enormous topic. It is very important for Masters athletes, both for general health and performance. It is not covered comprehensively here. Because space is limited, the book content will refer primarily to sport-specific information and then suggest additional resources.

The Masters national and international competitive 1,000m is the focus; its selection is not meant to exclude other distances, or the fact that some Masters do not wish to compete. The principles in this book extrapolate to longer and interpolate to shorter distances. Social and recreational sculling is likewise accommodated. Having a common distance allows for a coherent flow from concepts, to programme, training and racing.

The chapters are presented in a hierarchical order with each one building on information and concepts from the previous. Individual readers' skills, experience and interest may vary. For example, some readers may find the physics discussions enchanting. Others, not so. For those who seek a quick exit from a particular topic, a summary is available at the end of sections that lend themselves to that approach. Not all do. From a chronological perspective, the chapters are presented in the order of a training season.

Overall, the purpose here is to undertake a mutual journey with the reader towards sculling excellence understanding:

- each athlete is unique
- the journey will take us through a frontier where new discoveries are made every day
- and each individual sculler is indeed an explorer making discoveries of their own.

1 | MASTERS SCULLING FUNDAMENTALS

This chapter begins the journey of taking information and applying it to an individual's sculling practice. It is a chapter about experiments. First, about the experiments of others in the fields of aging and athletic performance. Then, recognizing the uniqueness of each athlete, about individual experimentation. It starts broadly, with a discussion of the sport, Masters, and research from other sports. Included is a summary of what is contemporarily known, as well as what appears to be possible. Masters sculling performance prognostics are introduced with initial guidance as to their use by the individual athlete. Last is the beginning of self-exploration for athletes, who now become researchers, guiding their own journey forward.

THE SPORT OF SCULLING

Whether you are a recreational sculler or a serious competitor, the sport of sculling provides a long athletic runway. Water, with its buoyancy, supports the torso. Sculling is physiologically kinder to the human body, with water's resistance softer than, say, a hockey ball or turf. When a sculler falls out of a boat, the landing is a splash, not a crash. Sculling can occur on many different water bodies and does not require an expensive sporting pitch or ground maintenance. For those who compete, FISA (World Rowing) is proactive in supporting Masters competition, regularly adjusting rules and age categories to accommodate changing needs. For example, in 2018 FISA (World Rowing) added three additional Masters rowing age groups (K, eighty-three to eighty-five; L, eighty-six to eighty-eight; M, eighty-nine-plus). Because of its longevity, its water-based focus and collegiality, the sport is growing, particularly for Masters.

WHO ARE MASTERS SCULLERS?

Depending on the country, Masters represent between 30 to 50 per cent of registered rowers in Australia, the US, UK and Canada. The majority of Masters are women. Their age is from twenty-seven to death! (The inclusive exception is the US, where Masters AA grade starts at twenty-one.) Independent Masters, rowing outside of the affiliated club system, swell these numbers.

Masters are the lifeblood of grass roots sculling. As well as being athletes, they are the committee members, coaches, officials, sweepers, cleaners, cake bakers and boat maintainers at the club level. Because of the significant support role Masters play, it is important to provide contemporary evidence-based information to this group not only for their own athletic development and retention in the sport. It is crucial to the long-term health of the sport as a whole.

CHARACTERISTICS OF MASTERS SCULLERS

Masters scullers have unique athletic needs. The typical child, youth or national/Olympic athlete has an average career trajectory of eight years. The structure and goals of their sculling experience is designed for that shorter participation period. By comparison, the career trajectory for a Masters sculler is measured in decades. A twenty-seven-year-old Australian Master sculler can expect to participate in the sport for forty-eight more years (male) and fifty-five more years (female).[1] With the increased longevity attributable to sports participation, even older Masters can expect to enjoy many decades of sculling. As opposed to achieving greatness in a four-year secondary school career, Masters athletes have the luxury of acquiring competencies slowly and well.

With the potential for such a long athletic career, retention is an issue. First, a primary training objective is injury and illness prevention. Another training objective is sport diversity. That is, training needs to include other sports or training modalities. These ensure the athlete develops physiologically and mentally in a balanced, robust way. That diversity provides a fall-back position when injury or illness does occur. An athlete may not be able to row, but they might be able to cycle or swim.

For Masters, the sporting experience needs to be rewarding and fun. Thus, the social environment that determines how athletes interact with other athletes, coaches and support personnel is important. Equally important for retention is a social environment where Masters athletes are validated and valued by the sport.

Masters scullers differ from their younger counterparts in other ways. They have a fully formed prefrontal cortex. They learn differently. They choose differently. They behave differently. Learning strategies that work for child, youth and younger elite rowers (primarily directive approaches used with a captive audience) either will not work or, as for new learner Masters, will work only for a short time. Skills acquisition strategies need to be different with a focus on independent learning. Few, if any, Masters scullers have the luxury of a full-time coach, a part-time coach or any coach at all. The challenge to their progressing athletically becomes how best to provide information to a skilled and experienced adult who can then apply that information effectively to their own sculling practice.

Masters scullers come to the sport with robust lives: families, children, aged parents, jobs, responsibilities, travel plans, needs and opinions. They do not receive full-time scholarships to participate in the sport they love. They are self-funded. Their life/sport balance changes over the decades and, oftentimes, within the week. Because they are grown-ups, they have acquired a level of self-management skills that they can bring to their sculling practice. This aggregate of skills, experiences and personal resources can be thoughtfully levered in the process of helping these athletes to succeed in a single scull. As adults, they are capable of defining what success is for themselves. It may not be winning regattas. It may be joyfully sculling with friends on a pristine river with a picnic lunch.

The Shifting Winds of 'Ageing'

With regards to Masters, the elephant in the room is that somehow 'ageing' is a term synonymous with 'middle-aged', 'old', 'elderly' or 'geriatric'. The latter tends to be pejorative, insinuating decrepitude, loss of mental capacity and need for assisted care. Ageing is a natural process that does not inherently incorporate any of these. The *true* ageing differentiator is 'sedentary' versus 'active'. Emerging research is confirming that the longer an athlete remains active, the more irrelevant the pejorative perspective becomes. The Coaching Association of Canada states that there is no noticeable decline in physical abilities until about the age of seventy, *as long as people stay active.*[2] And seventy is denoted only because there is so little research into the physical abilities of adult athletes beyond seventy. Realistic Masters athletic potential, particularly of older athletes, remains an unknown.

The Ageing Athlete

Still sound depressing? Be assured there is very good news following in the Emerging Research section below. For now, this section is an important first step in our journey so, please, soldier on. If an athlete does not understand the ageing process, the potential for injury and illness is high. This includes musculoskeletal injury as well as systemic injuries such as overreaching and overtraining.

Age-related change	Nutritional Implication
Decreased muscle mass	Decreased energy requirements
Decreased aerobic capacity	Decreased energy requirements
Decreased muscle glycogen (CHO) stores	Decreased energy requirements
Decreased bone density	Increased need for calcium and vitamin D
Decreased immune function	Increased need for vitamins B6, E and zinc
Decreased gastric acid	Increased need for vitamin B12, folic acid, calcium, iron and zinc
Decreased skin capacity for vitamin D synthesis	Increased need for vitamin D
Decreased calcium bioavailability	Increased need for calcium and vitamin D
Decreased liver uptake of retinol	Decreased need for vitamin A
Decreased efficiency in metabolic use of pyridoxal (one form of vitamin B6)	Increased need for vitamin B6
Increased oxidative stress status	Increased need for vitamins A, C and E
Increased levels of homocysteine (an amino acid related to heart disease)	Increased need for folate and vitamins B6 and B12
Decreased thirst perception	Increased fluid needs
Decreased kidney function	Increased fluid needs

Table 1 Major age-related changes that may influence nutrient requirements of Masters athletes. (Reaburn, P., 2019. *Masters Athlete.* Used with permission from www.mastersathlete.com.au)

A word to younger Masters, too. In the age brackets from twenty-seven to thirty-nine, younger athletes may find they can continue the excesses of youth with some impunity. However, by the time forty arrives, ageing is well and truly relevant. Disease research indicates the staging for eventual non-genetic Alzheimer's, bone density deterioration and cardiovascular disease amongst others begins in the late thirties and early forties. Some of these precursors are not reversible. They becoming ticking time bombs that explode decades later. Thus, good habits relating to sleep, nutrition, hydration, activity and stress are best formed as early as possible, as is an awareness of the ageing process.

Athletes who accept that ageing occurs are happier. This positivity gives them, on average, 7.5 more years of life.[3] Because these athletes manage their athletic careers more effectively, those careers are more rewarding. By developing an informed view of the ageing process with an eye to understanding and managing it, one can benefit from the performance improvements and good mental health that can result.

Ageing. Simplistically, as one ages, physiological processes change. They slow down. They do not repair as quickly. Their efficiency decreases. Then they stop. Table 1 provides some highlights of what to expect.

There is good news. For athletes actively engaged in sport, the situation outlined in the table either does not apply at all or applies in a different way. This begins the revelation that some broad, overarching research-based statements may be wrong when applied to the 'active' as opposed to the 'sedentary'.

Equally simplistically, but this time true, is that the human organism tends to sustain those patterns of behaviour that have got it this far in life. The primitive brain recognizes that doing things in a certain way has been evolutionarily successful for an individual. One has survived doing these things, no matter how annoying they are to family and friends.

The basal ganglia, deep in the brain, manages much of unconscious behaviour, which is 95 per cent of what is happening to the human organism. This is where habits come from. And autonomic behaviour. And why most of what one does in a day is unconscious behaviour. The longer one lives, the more these habits become entrenched and more difficult to change. This aspect of the human organism has implications for an athlete's self-coaching: how do I change that horrible wrist dropping at the release that I have just discovered and that has probably been there for ten years? If the athlete is lucky enough to have a coach, this habit-oriented behaviour has implications for them, too.

So, the body is deteriorating. The mind is on habit-driven autopilot. How does this affect an athlete's sculling career? The answer is a function of: how well does that athlete manage the journey? One way to manage is to become informed. Another way is to target, prioritize and proceed slowly, incrementally and hierarchically. A third is to play and experiment. But first, let us review some current information and develop a fundamental understanding of what is possible.

USING RESEARCH INTELLIGENTLY

Research provides evidence-based information that informs and guides. The role of research is not to replace critical thinking, of which much is required when analysing its results. Research conclusions need to be assessed intelligently, particularly in light of how they apply to an individual. An elite Masters athlete is one who competes successfully at the national or international level. Little research exists on elite Masters athletes. In any sport. There is a virtual information vacuum for non-elite adult athletes, most of whom are dedicated and serious. Research remotely related to the non-elite targets, primarily, the question of what changes occur when the sedentary become active. For a serious athlete, this information can be grossly misleading. Regardless, all of this research is for other sports, not sculling.

The first challenge is how applicable to sculling is research from other sports? With 1,000m race times in the three- to seven-minute range, comparisons with cycling and triathlon need scrutiny. Swimming, without its loads, may be comparative timewise but not from a musculature demand. Used thoughtfully, other sport-specific research does have value. It provides insight, raises questions to explore in sculling and is leading the way with investigating adult athletic performance.

The next issue is the sample size of research studies. Elite sports studies frequently use small sample sizes because of the shortage of an available elite athlete pool. For example, one study had thirty-two male cyclists, aged thirty-five to seventy-three years, assigned to three comparison groups of fourteen, ten and eight, with the smallest group representing the fifty-five or older age group.[4] This is not unusual. It does raise questions about validity and reliability.

The field of research compensates for this validity and reliability issue by building a body of studies that are confirmatory or negatory. However, because Masters research is such a new field, there are few comparable studies. Thus, one study's conclusions may, or not, be replicated in the future. In general, sports-related research for Masters athletes, especially scullers, is an absolute frontier.

This leads back to the enthusiastically optimistic Canadian Coaching Association statement that there is no noticeable decline in physical abilities until about the age of seventy, *as long as people stay active.*[5] This is an evidence-based statement, but the research supporting it is sparse. Thankfully, the increasing trickle of performance data and research on Masters athletes tends to support it.

The Emerging Research

The research for the general population, particularly the sedentary versus the active, is more available. Considered with a critical eye, it tells a different story than Table 1. For example, let's take the first item in Table 1: 'Decreased muscle mass'. A study questioning whether that conclusion was a result of using sedentary ageing adult subjects, as opposed to active ones, decided to use 'masters athletes' instead.

> This study contradicts the common observation that muscle mass and strength decline as a function of aging alone. Instead, these declines may signal the effect of chronic disuse rather than muscle aging. Evaluation of masters athletes removes disuse as a confounding variable in the study of lower-extremity function and loss of lean muscle mass. This maintenance of muscle mass and strength may decrease or eliminate the falls, functional decline and loss of independence that are commonly seen in aging adults.[6]

That is, decreasing muscle mass is not a function of age. It is a function of chronic disuse.

Next, decreased aerobic capacity. One study across age groups for Masters-Level cyclists determined that maximal oxygen uptake, maximal heart rate, the first and second ventilatory thresholds and power output were significantly lower among subjects fifty-five and older.[7] However, this is the study with only eight subjects in the fifty-five and older group. Also, these eight subjects were training 359km per week and 15.4 hours per day as compared with 283km and 9.5 hours for the forty-five to fifty-four year age group, raising the question of whether the recovery period for the older athletes was sufficient and provided an accurate comparison.

Another study compared Masters records in athletics, swimming, rowing, cycling, triathlon and weightlifting for ages thirty to the nineties and determined that record performance did decrease with age over longer distances. Rowing showed the least decline. For sprint events there was no greater decline with age.[8]

A comparison of athletic performance in older Masters athletes investigated performance in running and swimming at shorter distances. The findings were that all Masters age group records improved significantly over time.

> While younger athletes' performance has stagnated, Masters athletes improved their athletic performance significantly and progressively over the years. The magnitude of improvements was greater in older age groups, gradually closing the gap in athletic performance between younger and older participants.[9]

Some cardiovascular age-related effects are to be expected, but Masters athletes are impacted differently from sedentary peers.

> Masters athletes who perform endurance training-based activities demonstrate a more favourable arterial function-structure phenotype, including lower large elastic artery stiffness, enhanced vascular endothelial function and less arterial wall hypertrophy. As such, they may represent an exemplary model of healthy or 'successful' vascular ageing.[10]

As for decreased muscle glycogen (CHO) stores, the issue may be more complicated. Protein synthesis becomes less efficient as athletes age. Protein synthesis affects the recovering of muscles damaged during training. Research indicates a need for increased protein intake, particularly immediately after exercise, with protein amounts for older athletes exceeding those of younger athletes.[11] Coincidentally, muscles that are damaged may retard glycogen synthesis. Thus, insufficient protein to repair muscles may result in insufficient glycogen stores.[12] That is, the issue may not be capacity to store muscle glycogen but, rather, the need to increase post-exercise protein to augment the glycogen synthesis process.[13] Additional protein intake after exercise is relevant to the retention of muscle mass.

How about bone density? An article in the Journal of Bone and Mineral Metabolism investigated bone mass and bone metabolic indices in male master rowers of mean age forty-five years, comparing them to non-athletic body mass index matched controls.

> ... rowers also had significantly higher values of total and regional (left arm, trunk, thoracic spine, pelvis and leg) BMD [Bone Mineral Density], as well as higher BMD values for the lumbar spine and the left hip ... In conclusion, the systematic training of master rowers has beneficial effects on total and regional BMD and may be recommended for preventing osteoporosis.[14]

The authors concluded that the metabolic findings supported the prevention of lifestyle-related diseases for the subjects.

Another study of 560 athletes recruited from the 2005 National Senior Games in Pittsburgh (US) analysed the bone mineral density of its participants, average age 65.9 years. Participants were grouped by high-impact sport or non-high-impact sport (rowing was not included). The study concludes that high-impact sports are a significant contributor to bone mineral density in Masters athletes.[15] Athlete bone density does not necessarily decrease as a result of age alone, either.

The problem, however, is determining whether sculling is osteogenic (relating to the formation of bone). The study of rowers above would indicate ... possibly. But with a mean age of forty-five and all men, questions remain. Osteoporosis Australia lists seated rowing as a resistance exercise but rowing, as a sport, at the same level of cycling, which has no osteogenic properties at all.[16]

Table 1's remaining items can be grouped into (a) need for vitamin and mineral supplementation and (b) management of hydration, both topics that will be covered more extensively in Recovery in Chapters 10 and 11.

Ageing brings with it changes. It is unrealistic to believe that at ninety an athlete will

have the same performance capabilities as at thirty. But how will those changes unfold? What the research is telling us is that participation in sport has significant protective factors and the rate of change can be attenuated by being active.

SUMMARY OF EMERGING RESEARCH

As an adult athlete, sport participation is a huge protective factor and contributes to some of the following:

- Prevention of one type of Alzheimer's disease and delay of the onset of genetically related Alzheimer's[17]
- Reduced risk of cardiovascular disease[18]
- Lower risk of diabetes[19]
- Improved cognitive abilities[20]
- Improved sex life [21,22]
- Better mental health[23]
- Reduced risk of osteoporosis[24,25]
- Reduced brain tissue loss[26]
- Longer lived with better quality of life[27]

The single biggest result of adult sports participation is a significant delay in the ageing process, with 'use it or lose it' a fair characterization.

Thus, the research conclusions related to active adults, generally, as well as elite adult performance are that:

- Being active provides a cornucopia of benefits with 'active' defined in Australia as (a) 150 to 300 minutes of moderate-intensity or (b) 75 to 150 minutes of vigorous-intensity aerobic physical activity per week – or a combination of the two. That's the minimum.[28]
- Aerobic physical activity should be accompanied by two resistance training sessions per week, be that high-impact sports, resistance weight training, or combined with the aerobic activity above;

with basketball, impact aerobics, tennis and jumping rope being some of the highly osteogenic examples.
- To accrue long-term benefits from aerobic and resistance physical activity that can slow age-related decline, this aerobic and resistance activity needs to be in place lifelong. That is, from twenty-seven to death for all Masters scullers, with emerging research indicating an increased urgency at forty and beyond.
- The research on adult athletes in all sports is showing significant performance improvements, particularly for older athletes.
- It appears that with age, endurance-based performance over long distances decreases. However, over shorter distances, the same does not appear to be true.

PERFORMANCE IMPLICATIONS FOR MASTERS SCULLING

Performance implications for adult athletes are less well understood, particularly with a dearth of research for Masters scullers (or rowers). Fortunately, robust Masters performance data exists from sanctioned regattas. It's time to begin investigating whether the performance improvements observed in other sports are also happening in sculling. That is exactly what Rowing Australia has done.

The Rowing Australia Masters Commission, Handicap Sub-Committee studies

In 2013 the Rowing Australia Rules handicaps were twenty years old. Accompanied by diverse and intensifying discourse, older rowers seemed to be gleefully dominating the handicapped competitions. In 2013 Rowing Australia (RA) through its Masters Commission, Handicap

Sub-Committee responded, observing that:

There has been increasing evidence in recent years that, while performance of masters crews in the younger A and B grades has been relatively consistent, performance in the middle age grades, C to G, has been steadily improving ... The apparent improvement in performance in the middle grades has increasingly meant that racing between younger and older crews using the RA handicaps is not as close as originally intended. Younger crews seem to find it

increasingly difficult to make up the time allowances in the RA tables.[29]

This observation coincides with the research into Masters performance over short distances in running and swimming.

FISA (World Rowing) maintains detailed performance records for its annual World Masters Rowing Championships. These events are well attended by elite athletes from many countries, providing an excellent pool of data for analysis. Using that data, the RA Handicap

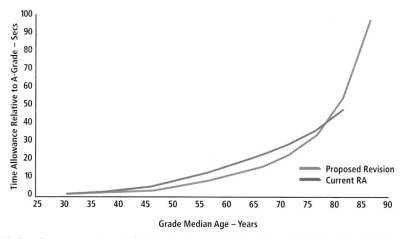

Fig. 1 W8+ handicap comparison study. (Rowing Australia Masters Commission Handicap Sub-Committee November 2013 Report and Recommendations, Mark Mussared, 31 October 2013, published by Rowing Australia)

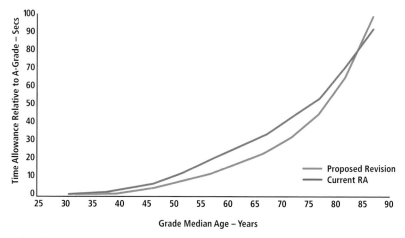

Fig. 2 M8+ handicap comparison study. (Rowing Australia Masters Commission Handicap Sub-Committee November 2013 Report and Recommendations, Mark Mussared, 31 October 2013, published by Rowing Australia)

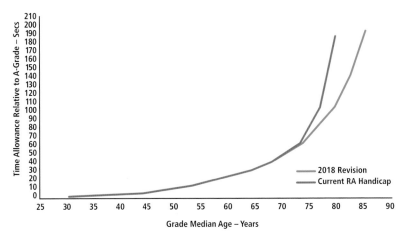

Fig. 3 W1X comparison of 2013 and 2018 handicaps. (Rowing Australia Masters Commission Handicap Sub-Committee July 2018 Review and Recommendations, Mark Mussared, 31 July 2018, published by Rowing Australia)

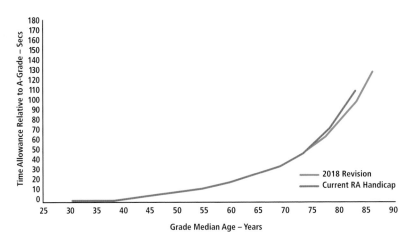

Fig. 4 M1X comparison of 2013 and 2018 handicaps. (Rowing Australia Masters Commission Handicap Sub-Committee July 2018 Review and Recommendations, Mark Mussared, 31 July 2018, published by Rowing Australia)

Sub-Committee undertook a comprehensive analysis using the FISA World Masters Regattas of 2011, 2012 and 2013 for the purpose of determining changes needed in RA Rules Masters handicapping. The final report recommended substantial changes in Australian handicaps that were quickly adopted in 2014.

In 2018 the WA Handicap Sub-Committee undertook a follow-up study. The primary motivator was to provide handicaps that aligned with the new FISA grades: J (80–82), K

(83–85), L (86–88) and M (89–91). However, a review of the performance data from the FISA World Masters Regattas of 2015, 2016 and 2017 disclosed that the performance of rowers eighty and older continued to improve.

... since 2014, more data for older rowers has become available. The evidence was that rowers in age grades over 80 were achieving times better than the prognostics derived from the 2013 analysis and that therefore

their time allowances (handicaps) were a little generous.... These categories require close observation in coming years to ensure the handicaps appear fair.[30]

Somewhat surprisingly given only five years between studies, the performance times for men's grades E through K and women's grades D through K were improving as well.

These studies have two important dimensions. First is the conclusion that older Masters are indeed getting faster. Figs 1 and 2 from the 2013 study provide a comparison of the M8+ and W8+ times, with analysis across all boat types and grade showing similar improvements.

The 2018 study provides a new comparison of M1X and W1X handicap as revised between 2013 and 2018 (Figs 3 and 4). Both figures show decreasing handicaps, a function of improving performance times.

The second dimension of the studies is that the RA Masters Commission Handicap Sub-Committee's studies provides contemporary FISA (World Rowing) Masters prognostic speeds by boat class, age grade and gender. That is, the speeds that represent the best winning time for still conditions. (Although the report observes that times do not tend to vary more than 10 per cent even in stiff headwind or fast tailwind conditions.) The 2018 study also added an inaugural 1,000m mixed prognostic speed table derived mathematically.

Tables 4, 5 and 6 contain the winning prognostic speeds by boat class, age and gender (Table 6 is an average of 4 and 5). The information about other boat classes is presented here because Masters rarely compete in only a 1X. However, from this point forward in the book only the 1X times will be discussed.

The times within the tables are in metres per second (mps), a speed value that will be used throughout this book because, quite simply, it is easier to average and analyse a number (X.XXX) than a time (XX:XX:XX). Table 2 shows a sample of how to convert between time and metres per second (mps) over 1,000m. Table 3 shows a sample of the reverse process.

Distance (m)	1,000
Time	4:40.6
Convert time to seconds	280.6
Calculation	1,000/280.6
Metres per second (mps)	3.564

Table 2 Sample calculation for converting 1,000m time (minutes: seconds) to metres per second (mps).

Distance (m)	1,000
Metres per second	3.564
Calculation	1,000/3.564
Seconds	280.584
Convert time to minutes	04:40.6
Metres per second (mps)	3.564

Table 3 Sample calculation for converting 1,000 metres per second (mps) to time (minutes: second).

Developing prognostics by rating

This prognostic information is incredibly useful for self-assessment and training. Assume that the time of 3.564 mps in Table 2 is for an H grade woman in a 1X. She is sculling only slightly slower than the World Masters Championship Regatta prognostic winning time for her age grade (3.564 versus the 3.607 in Table 5). Her training programme is working well. Alternatively, if that time is for an experienced D grade man, his training programme may need refinements. Later chapters will guide the reader through assessment and training that uses this information including, if the athlete competes, how to adjust the prognostics for their country of interest.

The problem is, of course, that the speeds in Tables 4, 5 and 6 are the winning speeds. What about lower ratings? The prognostics speeds have allowed for the calculation of extrapolated prognostics, by rating, for single scull (1X) performance by Masters grade. That is, by

	Relative Speed	A	B	C	D	E	F	G	H	I	J	K	L	M
M8+	100.0%	5.750	5.712	5.621	5.511	5.397	5.258	5.087	4.872	4.598	4.325	4.082	3.800	3.473
M4X	97.0%	5.578	5.541	5.453	5.346	5.235	5.100	4.934	4.725	4.460	4.196	3.960	3.686	3.369
M4X+	93.3%	5.363	5.328	5.244	5.141	5.034	4.905	4.745	4.544	4.289	4.035	3.808	3.545	3.240
M4-	94.0%	5.405	5.369	5.284	5.181	5.073	4.943	4.781	4.579	4.322	4.066	3.837	3.572	3.265
M4+	90.5%	5.204	5.169	5.087	4.988	4.884	4.759	4.603	4.409	4.161	3.915	3.694	3.439	3.143
M2X	90.5%	5.204	5.169	5.087	4.988	4.884	4.759	4.603	4.409	4.161	3.915	3.694	3.439	3.143
M2-	85.5%	4.916	4.884	4.806	4.712	4.615	4.496	4.349	4.165	3.932	3.698	3.490	3.249	2.970
M1X	84.0%	4.830	4.798	4.722	4.630	4.534	4.417	4.273	4.092	3.863	3.633	3.429	3.192	2.918

Table 4 Men's prognostic speeds by boat class, age and gender. Numbers in metres per second (mps).

	Relative Speed	A	B	C	D	E	F	G	H	I	J	K	L	M
W8+	100.0%	5.100	5.066	4.988	4.894	4.795	4.670	4.508	4.294	4.007	3.709	3.437	3.115	2.736
W4X	97.0%	4.947	4.914	4.838	4.748	4.651	4.530	4.373	4.165	3.886	3.598	3.334	3.021	2.654
W4X+	93.3%	4.757	4.726	4.653	4.565	4.473	4.356	4.205	4.005	3.737	3.460	3.206	2.906	2.552
W4-	94.0%	4.794	4.762	4.689	4.601	4.508	4.390	4.238	4.036	3.766	3.486	3.230	2.928	2.572
W4+	90.5%	4.616	4.585	4.514	4.429	4.340	4.227	4.080	3.886	3.626	3.357	3.110	2.819	2.476
W2X	90.5%	4.616	4.585	4.514	4.429	4.340	4.227	4.080	3.886	3.626	3.357	3.110	2.819	2.476
W2-	85.5%	4.361	4.332	4.265	4.185	4.100	3.993	3.854	3.671	3.426	3.171	2.938	2.663	2.340
W1X	84.0%	4.284	4.256	4.190	4.111	4.028	3.923	3.787	3.607	3.366	3.116	2.887	2.617	2.299

Table 5 Women's prognostic speeds by boat class, age and gender. Numbers in metres per second (mps).

	Relative Speed	A	B	C	D	E	F	G	H	I	J	K	L	M
Mix8+	100.0%	5.425	5.389	5.305	5.203	5.096	4.964	4.797	4.583	4.302	4.017	3.759	3.457	3.105
Mix4X	97.0%	5.262	5.227	5.146	5.047	4.943	4.815	4.653	4.445	4.173	3.897	3.647	3.354	3.012
Mix4X+	93.3%	5.060	5.027	4.948	4.853	4.754	4.630	4.475	4.275	4.013	3.747	3.507	3.225	2.896
Mix4-	94.0%	5.100	5.066	4.986	4.891	4.790	4.666	4.510	4.308	4.044	3.776	3.534	3.250	2.919
Mix4+	90.5%	4.910	4.877	4.801	4.709	4.612	4.493	4.342	4.147	3.894	3.636	3.402	3.129	2.810
Mix2X	90.5%	4.910	4.877	4.801	4.709	4.612	4.493	4.342	4.147	3.894	3.636	3.402	3.129	2.810

Table 6 Mixed prognostic speeds by boat class, age and gender. Numbers in metres per second (mps).

(Tables 4–7 from Rowing Australia Masters Commission Handicap Sub-Committee July 2018 Review and Recommendations, Mark Mussared, 31 July 2018, published by Rowing Australia)

% Speed	Rating (spm)	ME1X	WE1X
75	16–18	3.40	3.02
76	18–19	3.45	3.06
80	21–23	3.63	3.22
83	24–26	3.76	3.76
86	27–29	3.90	3.46
93	33–34	4.22	3.75
96–100	34–36	4.534	4.028

Table 7 Prognostic speed by rating for E grade 1X calculated using Tables 4 and 5 prognostic speeds as 100 per cent.

using a formula that estimates the approximate speed for various stroke ratings, the athlete can incrementally measure their progress through the ratings against an international standard. Even at low ratings. Thus, if one is sculling for fitness and not competition, a lower rating may provide a more useful target. For competition, the highest rating provides the FISA (World Rowing) winning time.

Table 7 is a sample of a set of these extrapolated prognostics for ME1X and WE1X. That is, an E grade man sculling at 23 strokes per minute (spm) at 3.63 metres per stroke (mps) is performing at the prognostic for that rating. At 3.63mps, an E grade woman would be performing significantly better than the 23spm prognostic (3.22) for E grade.

These prognostics speeds will reappear in the chapters on self-assessment, training and performance assessment. By way of caution, while these prognostics by rating have proven extremely useful for training and performance development, they are not inviable. For example, if a performance sculler cannot rate 34–36spm efficiently, the assumed rating for that winning speed, that sculler will need to recalculate the required speed at their optimal rating.

A debate may ensue about the precision of the rate of speed drop-off due to drag. The meticulous scientists will advocate for a better level of precision in how these lower rating speeds are calculated. The data and methodology are provided so that the scientists can refine as needed. Given the current alternatives, though, this approach is a good starting point. In addition, the prognostics are for 'still' conditions meaning: not applicable to 99 per cent of real world conditions. But useful, nonetheless.

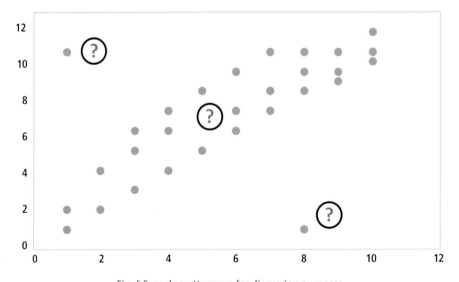

Fig. 5 Sample scattergram for discussion purposes.

An Experiment of One

A healthy level of suspicion about the conclusions of research studies, performance reports, the blanket statements of others or book content (including this one) is a good protective characteristic in an adult athlete. The primary reason is: no matter what, each athlete is an experiment of one.

Refer to the sample scattergram of Fig. 5. The data show results for thirty mythical athletes. The data demonstrate a distinct upward trend and a statistically significant result. But, which one of those little dots is you? Is it the dot that showed a negative change? Or is it the dot that showed a large significant positive change? The conclusions of the study will be aggregated into a summary conclusion based on the statistics and trends, a conclusion that may not apply at all to that little individual dot that is you.

Thus, research and someone else's personal experience have a place. They provide information or new ideas to try. However, how research or someone else's experience applies to an individual athlete is an enduring question. The responsibility falls to the adult athlete to navigate these troubled waters and, first and foremost, to conduct their own experiment of one as they progress along their sculling journey.

Conducting an Experiment of One

This book is all about individual experimentation. Each athlete is so unique that blanket directive statements (do this, do that) are unhelpful. The strategy contained herein is a lifelong learning approach (try this, try that). Because even if an approach works this year, five years from now and with the same athlete, it may no longer work.

For example, the information about the nutritional needs of adults is indicating that those involved in activity, particularly new activities, need more protein. (The needs for beginners often outweigh that of experienced athletes because the beginner's metabolic processes are not attuned to the demands.)[31] This information presents the question: how much protein does a unique individual athlete need? The answer is best answered by individual experimentation. In this case a simple experiment might be to try, for two weeks, various post-workout nutrition and hydration strategies that target protein.

The experiment: what works best for the athlete in terms of compliance and reduction in post-workout symptoms such as fatigue and muscle pain? Is it a 600ml carton of chocolate milk? Or, is a tuna sandwich on white bread more appealing? But the milk helps hydrate, too. Does that make hydration easier or more complicated because the athlete just drank 800ml of diluted electrolyte at the end of the training? When answered, an appealing aspect of individual experiments is that if an approach works, an athlete is more inclined to integrate it into their sculling practice. This as opposed to telling a group of adults they *must* all do the *same* thing in an *identical* way, an approach doomed to failure.

Then, five years (or months) later when a food allergy to milk (or bread) unexpectedly presents itself, the athlete now has the experience to replicate the previous experiment and develop a new tactic. Perhaps their more mature palate decides: fruit, soy yoghurt and nuts. The available research information can guide, experienced information can inform, but only the athlete can decide what truly works for them, especially in changing conditions.

This model of experimentation carries through rigging, technique, training, assessment, performance, nutrition, supplementation and so many other topics in this book. The expectation is that each athlete is empowered to explore and learn. When incredibly diverse individuals aged twenty-seven and onward consider information that may apply to them, the hope is they will do it with a critical mind. Their discoveries will add to the body of knowledge about the sport with everyone joining this journey into the frontier of possibilities.

Endnotes

1 Australian Bureau of Statistics. *3302.0 – Deaths, Australia, 2010*. www.abs.gov.au/ausstats/abs@.nsf/Products/57E4ADF3F2034BCECA-257943000CEE0B?opendocument

2 Coaching Association of Canada. *Coaching Masters Athletes*. www.coach.ca/files/Coaching_Master_Athletes_FINAL_EN.pdf.

3 Levy, B.R., Slade, M.D., Kunkel, S.R., Kasl, S.V., 'Longevity increased by positive self-perceptions of aging', *J Pers Soc Psychol*. 2002 Aug; 83(2): pp.261–270. PubMed PMID: 12150226.

4 Peiffer, J.J., Abbiss, C.R., Chapman, D., Laursen, P.B., Parker, D.L., 'Physiological characteristics of masters-level cyclists', *J. Strength Cond Res*. 2008 Sep; 22(5): pp.1434–1440. doi: 10.1519/JSC.0b013e318181a0d2. PubMed PMID: 18714246.

5 Coaching Association of Canada. *Coaching Masters Athletes*, www.coach.ca/files/Coaching_Master_Athletes_FINAL_EN.pdf.

6 Wroblewski, A.P., Amati, F., Smiley, M.A., Goodpaster, B., Wright, V., 'Chronic exercise preserves lean muscle mass in masters athletes', *Phys Sportsmed*. 2011 Sep; 39(3): pp.172–178. doi: 10.3810/psm.2011.09.1933. PubMed PMID: 22030953.

7 Peiffer, J.J., Abbiss, C.R., Chapman, D., Laursen, P.B., Parker, D.L., 'Physiological characteristics of masters-level cyclists', *J Strength Cond Res*. 2008 Sep; 22(5): pp.1434–1440. doi: 10.1519/JSC.0b013e318181a0d2. PubMed PMID: 18714246.

8 Baker, A.B., Tang, Y.Q., 'Aging performance for masters records in athletics, swimming, rowing, cycling, triathlon, and weight-lifting', *Exp Aging Res*. 2010 Oct; 36(4): pp.453–477. doi: 10.1080/0361073X.2010.507433. PubMed PMID: 20845122.

9 Akkari, A., Machin, D., Tanaka, H., 'Greater progression of athletic performance in older Masters athletes', *Age Ageing*. 2015 Jul; 44(4): pp.683–686. doi: 10.1093/ageing/afv023. Epub 2015 Mar 8. PubMed PMID: 25753790.

10 DeVan, A.E., Seals, D.R., 'Vascular health in the ageing athlete', *Exp Physiol*. 2012 Mar; 97(3): pp.305–310. doi: 10.1113/expphysiol.2011.058792. Epub 2012 Jan 20. PubMed PMID: 22266948; PubMed Central PMCID: PMC3303941.

11 Doering, T.M., Reaburn, P.R., Phillips, S.M., Jenkins, D.G., ,Postexercise Dietary Protein Strategies to Maximize Skeletal Muscle Repair and Remodeling in Masters Endurance Athletes: A Review', *Int J Sport Nutr Exerc Metab*. 2016 Apr; 26(2): pp.168–178. doi: 10.1123/ijsnem.2015-0102. Epub 2015 Sep 24. Review. PubMed PMID: 26402439.

12 Murray, B., Rosenbloom, C., 'Fundamentals of glycogen metabolism for coaches and athletes', *Nutr Rev*. 2018 Apr 1; 76(4): pp.243–259. doi: 10.1093/nutrit/nuy001. PubMed PMID: 29444266; PubMed Central PMCID: PMC6019055.

13 Betts, J.A., Williams, C., 'Short-term recovery from prolonged exercise: exploring the potential for protein ingestion to accentuate the benefits of carbohydrate supplement', *Sports Med*. 2010 Nov 14 40(11): pp.941–959. doi: 10.2165/11536900-000000000-00000. Review. PubMed PMID: 20942510.

14 liwicka, E., Nowak, A., Zep, W., Leszczy ski, P., Pilaczy ska-Szcze niak, Ł., 'Bone mass and bone metabolic indices in male master rowers.', *J Bone Miner Metab*. 2015 Sep; 33(5): pp.540–546. doi: 10.1007/s00774-014-0619-1. Epub 2014 Sep 16. PubMed PMID: 25224128.

15 Leigey, D., Irrgang, J., Francis, K., Cohen, P., Wright, V., 'Participation in high-impact sports predicts bone mineral density in senior olympic athletes', *Sports Health*. 2009 Nov; 1(6): pp.508–513. doi: 10.1177/1941738109347979. PubMed PMID: 23015914; PubMed Central PMCID: PMC3445153.

16 Osteoporosis Australia. *Exercise*. www.osteoporosis.org.au/exercise.

17 Chen, W.W., Zhang, X., Huang, W.J., 'Role of physical exercise in Alzheimer's disease', *Biomed Rep*. 2016 Apr; 4(4): pp.403–407. doi: 10.3892/br.2016.607. Epub 2016 Feb 22. PubMed PMID: 27073621; PubMed Central PMCID: PMC4812200.

18 Carnethon, M.R., 'Physical Activity and Cardiovascular Disease: How Much is Enough?', *Am J Lifestyle Med*. 2009 Jul; 3(1 Suppl): pp.44S–49S. doi: 10.1177/1559827609332737. PubMed PMID: 20419076; PubMed Central PMCID: PMC2857374.

19 Aune, D., Norat, T., Leitzmann, M., Tonstad, S., Vatten, L.J., 'Physical activity and the risk of type 2 diabetes: a systematic review and dose-response meta-analysis', *Eur J Epidemiol*. 2015 Jul; 30(7): pp.529–542. doi: 10.1007/s10654-015-0056-z. Epub 2015 Jun 20. Review. PubMed PMID: 26092138.

20 Gomez-Pinilla, F., Hillman, C., 'The influence of exercise on cognitive abilities', *Compr Physiol*. 2013 Jan; 3(1): pp.403–428. doi: 10.1002/cphy.c110063. Review. PubMed PMID: 23720292; PubMed Central PMCID: PMC3951958.

21 Stanton, A.M., Handy, A.B., Mestoncm. 'The Effects of Exercise on Sexual Function in Women', *Sex Med Rev*. 2018 Oct; 6(4): pp.548–557. doi: 10.1016/j.sxmr.2018.02.004. Epub 2018 Mar 30. Review. PubMed PMID: 29606554.

22 White, J.R., Case, D.A., McWhirter, D., Mattison, A.M., 'Enhanced sexual behavior in exercising men', *Arch Sex Behav*. 1990 Jun; 19(3): pp.193–209. PubMed PMID: 2360871.

23 Penedo, F.J., Dahn, J.R., 'Exercise and well-being: a review of mental and physical health benefits associated with physical activity', *Curr Opin Psychiatry*. 2005 Mar; 18(2): pp.189–193. PubMed PMID: 16639173.

24 Borer, K.T., 'Physical activity in the prevention and amelioration of osteoporosis in women: interaction of mechanical, hormonal and dietary factors', *Sports Med*. 2005; 35(9): pp.779–830. doi: 10.2165/00007256-200535090-00004. Review. PubMed PMID: 16138787.

25 McMillan, L.B., Zengin, A., Ebeling, P.R., Scott, D., Prescribing Physical Activity for the Prevention and Treatment of Osteoporosis in Older Adults. Healthcare (Basel). 2017 Nov 6; 5(4). doi: 10.3390/healthcare5040085. Review. PubMed PMID: 29113119; PubMed Central PMCID: PMC5746719.

26 Colcombe, S.J., Erickson, K.I., Raz, N., Webb, A.G., Cohen, N.J., McAuley, E., Kramer, A.F., 'Aerobic fitness reduces brain tissue loss in aging humans', *J. Gerontol A Biol Sci Med Sci*. 2003 Feb; 58(2): pp.176–180. doi: 10.1093/gerona/58.2.m176. PubMed PMID: 12586857.

27 Lear, S.A., Hu, W., Rangarajan, S., Gasevic, D., Leong, D., Iqbal, R., Casanova, A., Swaminathan, S., Anjana, R.M., Kumar, R., Rosengren, A., Wei, L., Yang, W., Chuangshi, W., Huaxing, L., Nair, S., Diaz, R., Swidon, H., Gupta, R., Mohammadifard, N., Lopez-Jaramillo, P., Oguz, A., Zatonska, K., Seron, P., Avezum, A., Poirier, P., Teo, K., Yusuf, S., 'The effect of physical activity on mortality and cardiovascular disease in 130,000 people from 17 high-income, middle-income, and low-income countries: the PURE study', *Lancet*. 2017 Dec 16; 390(10113): pp.2643–2654. doi: 10.1016/S0140-6736(17)31634-3. Epub 2017 Sep 21. PubMed PMID: 28943267.

28 Australian Government Department of Health, *Australia's Physical Activity and Sedentary Behaviour Guidelines for Adults (18–64 years)*. www.health.gov.au/internet/main/publishing.nsf/content/health-pub-hlth-strateg-phys-act-guidelines#apaadult.

29 Mussared, M., *October 2013. Rowing Australia Masters Commission Handicap Sub-Committee November 2013 Report and Recommendation*. Rowing Australia: Canberra.

30 Mussared, M., *July 2018. Rowing Australia Masters Commission Handicap Sub-Committee July 2018 Review and Recommendation New Masters Age Grade Brackets Above Age 80, and Revised Handicaps*. Rowing Australia: Canberra.

31 Phillips, S.M., Van Loon, L.J., 'Dietary protein for athletes: from requirements to optimum adaptation', *J Sports Sci*. 2011; 29 Suppl 1: pp.S29–38. doi: 10.1080/02640414.2011.619204. Review. PubMed PMID: 22150425.

2 | THE SCULLING SYSTEM: BOAT AND OARS

Sculling on a lake above the Arctic Circle, on the Blackwood River in Western Australia, or on a buoyed course at a regatta, most scullers pursue the sport because it involves the joy of being on the water. This requires equipment. The equipment acts as an extension of the athlete, whose purpose is providing propulsion. To scull well means understanding the systematic relationship between that equipment and the athlete.

The sculling system includes three components: a single sculling boat (1X), oars and the athlete. Each component of the sculling system has its own individual characteristics, which differ at rest and in motion. The working relationship amongst the static components, with the later addition of propulsion, reveals a highly complex system. The athlete who understands each component at rest and in motion, as well as how the components interrelate, will be able to make an intelligent assessment of how best to optimize their sculling system.

This chapter discusses the single scull and oars. It introduces concepts that will be used in later chapters to explore technique. It begins the discussion of how the sculling system works, with underpinnings of physics and fluid dynamics. The focus is on how this information can be more easily understood and practically used.

THE SINGLE SCULLING BOAT

A boat is designed by balancing two factors: stability and speed. Boat designers pay special attention to a boat's purpose when engineering to these factors. For example, an ocean-going barge needs to carry large loads in rough weather. It is designed to be stable. The design trade-offs are that hull efficiency and speed are reduced. In comparison, a scull is designed for speed, while stability is reduced. Designers explore the limits of how to achieve speed. One result is a narrow, long boat. Scull design is further refined based on the skill level and weight of the intended athlete. Novice boats are designed to be more stable. They are wider than elite boats and sometimes shorter. Boats for heavier athletes are wider and/or longer. World Rowing (FISA) provides additional design limits stipulating a 1X minimum weight of 14kg and minimum length of 7.2m (Rules 39 and 41).[1] The weight includes all essential items: rigger, stretchers, shoes, slides and seat.

The design of a single scull has not changed substantively in decades. The materials used to construct the scull have been more influential. Nothing on the horizon indicates that significant performance improvements through boat

Fig. 6 Single sculling boat (1X) without its rigger showing stability of hull design.

Fig. 7 The effect of adding the rigger to the single sculling boat (1X) and the effect of the higher centre of mass and change in centre of gravity.

design are in the offing. The current reality is that scull designs are only slightly nuanced. The most realistic way of improving sculling performance is not through the equipment but through the athlete's fitness and technique.

The single sculling boat at rest

Stability is a function of a boat's width, height and depth of hull. An optimally stable vessel will have a ratio of width to length closer to 1.00, almost square, and a hull depth that supports the design load, much of that load being below the waterline. A boat designed to go fast, such as a 1X, will have a much lower ratio of width to length, closer to 0.05. This means the vessel is long, narrow and less robust in its load-carrying characteristics. The low width to length ratio means that, when loaded, the boat is less stable.

Without wind or waves, a scull (without its riggers) will float comfortably in the water (Fig. 6). It is buoyant because of its concave shape, which displaces an equivalent weight in water. This is because the centre of mass of the 1X is in the same place as the centre of gravity. With wind and waves, the 1X may roll a bit, but even in this rolled position will resume its original position when the wind and waves abate.

The boat will not remain flat and balanced when the rigger is added. The rigger raises the centre of mass and, because the rigger extends out from the hull, gravity becomes a factor. Assume the 1X has no decking and is only the hull. The centre of mass is that point at the bottom of the hull where the boat could be balanced on a single point. When decking is added, the centre of mass is raised. When the rigger is added, the centre of mass goes up again. However, because both the rigger and decking are only small proportions of the mass of the hull, the total effect of these additions to the hull on the centre of mass of the athlete-less system is small. The boat rides a little lower in the water, but not much.

Then a small ripple or breeze comes up. The boat moves and the centre of mass and the centre of gravity, which were in perfect alignment before, shift. Because the centre of mass and the centre of gravity are not the same, gravity attracts the rigger on the side of the boat to which the centre of mass has shifted. The rigger on one side lowers and, because it is attached to the boat, the boat rolls (Fig. 7).

The effect of adding an athlete is not small. An athlete of 75kg in a boat of 14kg comprises 84 per cent of the total mass. This 75kg sitting on a seat raised above the deck means: the centre of mass of the system has been raised by orders of magnitude. The boat plus athlete, without oars, is now inherently unstable. When the mass of the athlete is in perfect alignment, and the centre of mass and gravity are the same, the boat will ride in the water the same as if it had no athlete or rigger (albeit lower). If the centre of mass shifts, gravity takes

over. With such a high centre of mass, and with a mass that shifts because humans are mobile, it is very difficult to sit in a 1X without oars and not capsize.

Gates: the connecting point with oars

The gates (oarlocks) at the end of the rigger are the sculling system connection point for the boat and the oars. Gates provide several functions. Even though they swing, gates provide a stable connection point. To facilitate this, the gate is laterally flat on its inboard side. The oars are likewise flat at the button (collar). The two surfaces are flush when connected, requiring a small amount of outward pressure to make that connection. When the oars are connected at the gate/button interface, the scull characteristics change from those of the boat alone to that of a boat with, essentially, outriggers. The increase in system stability is significant. A gentle outward thumb pressure on the oar handles achieves this connection, allowing the hand and fingers to remain loose on the handles.

Fig. 8 Thumb position with slight outward pressure and relaxed hands.

The single sculling boat in motion

Speed is a function of drag and gravity. In a magical world where there is no resistance, a push on the single scull's stern would cause it to continue onwards forever, much as if it were in outer space. In the real world after that single push, drag causes the boat to slow then stop.

Drag

The three important types of drag are skin, form and wave. The most influential type of drag on a scull is skin drag. Skin drag is the friction between the hull of the boat and the water. Skin drag contributes between 85 and 90 per cent of the scull's total drag on a calm, windless day. Form drag is the least significant type of boat drag because a single scull is specifically designed to minimize it. An ocean-going barge has a very broad and tall presentation to the water and this 'form' creates a much higher degree of drag than the narrow, pointed bow of the scull with its small form drag.

Wave drag results from the boat breaking the surface tension of the water and passing through that water. Wave drag describes the energy required to push the water out of the way of the hull. The sharp, narrow bow of the scull and its length are designed to reduce resistance as the boat moves through the water. On a calm, windless day, wave drag is minimal. On days that are not calm and windless, or with tide and currents, the boat becomes less efficient as the total drag increases.

A major loss of efficiency to the sculling system is attributable to the athlete's effect on the boat. The athlete's mass causes the boat to sink. A larger area of the hull's surface is now in contact with the water, increasing skin drag. In motion, the wave drag is increased because of the additional energy required to push water out of the way. Thus for the same scull, the drag with a large athlete will be greater than for a smaller athlete. For that smaller athlete,

the wetted surface area is less. Therefore, the skin drag is less, too.

One performance question becomes whether the larger athlete will be able to provide sufficient power to overcome that drag differential. In a 1,000m race, the physics suggests the answer is: slightly but not overwhelmingly.[2] That is, in a short race the size of the athlete is far less important than for a longer race where size does matter.

What is the ideal weight of the boat for an individual athlete? That ideal boat weight may not necessarily be 'as light as possible'. Considering the asynchronicity of propulsion (resulting in uneven changes in surface area and wave drag), the boat oscillates. This oscillation is greater for lighter boats and requires extra power to maintain an average speed. Thus, an argument can be made for an optimum boat weight of 28 per cent of the athlete's weight.[3]

Constant velocity

Velocity has two elements: (a) speed and (b) direction. Boats are optimally efficient at a constant velocity where the power is applied consistently and is directionally even. That is, no roll, pitch or yaw (discussed below). To achieve optimal boat performance based on the design characteristics of the scull, the speed should be constant and the direction straight.

The difficulty arises in that force is applied to a scull unevenly, not like a boat engine. In sculling, force is applied cyclically and, even in the most technically proficient athlete, inconsistently. If power is applied by a boat engine where constant velocity is achieved, the drag factor is consistent. In sculling due to power fluctuations and changes in velocity, the drag factor can be very inconsistent. The greater the speed variation, the less efficient the boat's performance.

The asynchronicity of the application of power creates directional inefficiencies in boat performance. Oars uneven at the catch, one hand preceding another during the stroke and changes

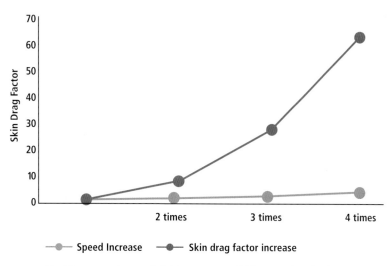

Fig. 9 Increases in speed yield an exponential increase in skin drag.

in the athlete's position in the boat all contribute to changes in roll, pitch and yaw. These changes affect drag, speed and directionality, too.

Skin drag increases exponentially, not linearly. Skin drag is proportional to the square of the velocity of the boat (Fig. 9). For example, if the speed of the boat is doubled, the skin drag is eight times greater at constant velocity. If the speed of the boat is quadrupled, the skin drag factor increases to sixty-four (2^4). For the athlete, this means an exponential amount of increase in work to achieve these incremental speed gains because of the increased skin drag. It highlights the advantages of an efficient technique that minimizes drag.

Effect of speed variation

Constant speed matters. Two athletes scull for four minutes each. Athlete A sculls for two minutes at 3.2 metres per second (mps), then increases speed to 3.8mps for an additional two minutes. The total distance covered by Athlete A is 840m (Table 8). The average speed for the piece is 3.5mps. Athlete B covers the same 840m but sculls at a constant 3.5mps for the entire 840m (Table 9).

Did one athlete need to produce more power to cover the same distance in the same time? The answer is yes. Athlete A needed to produce considerably more power to cover the same distance at the same speed as Athlete B because of the influence of drag.

Increases in speed require exponentially more power, a factor of three times: Power (P) = a (drag factor) × V^3 (velocity cubed). (For both samples, the drag factor has been set at 1kg/m to simplify the calculations.) Thus, to double the speed in a scull, the athlete must provide 2^3 or 2 × 2 × 2 = 8 times more power, measured in watts. (Watts describe the rate at which work is done or energy transferred. One watt is equal to one joule of work done in one second.)

Table 8 first calculates the work in Joules required from variable speed Athlete A or 12,203 Joules. One joule is equal to the energy used to accelerate a body with a mass of one kilogram using one newton of force over a distance of one metre. A joule is also equivalent to one watt-second.

Table 9 calculates the work in Joules required from constant speed Athlete B or 10,290 Joules.

The average power (in watts) for the two athletes shows 16 per cent fewer watts needed for Athlete B to complete the same piece in the same time (Table 10).

	Seconds	MPS	Distance
Distance @ 3.2mps	120	3.2	384
Distance @ 3.8mps	120	3.8	456
Total Distance			840

Work	Seconds	Drag Factor	Velocity cubed	Joules
@3.2mps	120	1	3.2^3	3,932
@3.8mps	120	1	3.8^3	8,271
Total Work (Joules)				12,203

Table 8 Athlete A work calculations for 840m with half at 3.2mps and half at 3.8mps, average 3.5mps.

	Seconds	MPS	Distance
Distance @ 3.5mps	120	3.5	420
Distance @ 3.5mps	120	3.5	420
Total Distance			840

Work	Seconds	Drag Factor	Velocity cubed	Joules
@3.5mps	120	1	3.5^3	5,145
@3.5mps	120	1	3.5^3	5,145
Total Work (Joules)				10,290

Table 9 Athlete B work calculations for 840m at constant speed of 3.5mps.

	Work	Time	Watts
Athlete A. Variable Speed	12,203	240	51
Athlete B. Constant Speed	10,290	240	43

Table 10 Comparison of the effects of power (watts) required for constant and variable speeds.

Thus, constant speed is desirable not only for optimizing the hydrodynamics and drag reduction of the boat. Constant speed is desirable because it results in comparably less work for the athlete. Human physiology performs best at constant levels of effort, too. Thus, constant speed becomes a crucial element of performance strategies.

Effects of roll, pitch and yaw

Roll, pitch and yaw describe the position of the boat hull in relationship to the water. Each has an effect, due to drag, on performance with the least being roll, the most being yaw.

As designed, the scull without riggers will sit level with the water surface. Pushing down on one side of the scull causes it to 'roll' (Fig. 10). One gunwale is now higher than the other. The fin on the stern bottom provides a very small resistance to this rolling action. The fin minimally acts as ballast such that when the pressure on the gunwale is released (riggers off the boat), the hull will resume its level design position. Because the hull is rounded, the effect of roll on drag is minimal.

Pitch has greater performance implications. In motion, the single scull is designed to minimize all drags when the boat is level from bow to stern and moving in a straight

Fig. 11 Scull level not pitched.

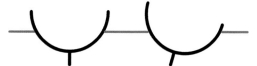

Fig. 12 Scull pitched.

direction. The design has considered the combined reduction of all the drag factors: skin, form and wave. However, under way, the scull is not always level. It pitches. The bow may rise and fall during the stroke. The greater the bow to stern variation from level, the greater the effect of drag. A number of factors can result in pitch changes.

For example, the athlete's position affects the boat's pitch. When the athlete moves to the catch position, the compressed athlete changes the sculling system's centre of mass, moving it sternward (Figs 12 and 13). This change in centre of mass alters the pitch, making the boat less level, increasing drag and reducing speed. For some techniques the result can be a significant slowing of the boat prior to the catch. (The dynamic technique

Fig. 10 Scull hull level and rolled.

Fig. 13 Effect of the sculling system's change in centre of mass at the catch.

Fig. 14 Effect of the sculling system's change in centre of mass at the release.

described in this book compensates for this effect by accelerating the boat prior to the catch.) Minimizing the athlete's time at the catch will improve the efficiency of the boat.

The boat will pitch at the release. However, because the athlete's legs remain in the stern, the centre of mass moves only slightly forward, having less effect on the boat's pitch. Thus, the bow drop will be small, as will the stern lift. The boat will usually be at a more level position.

In motion, the bow of that same boat may rise due to hydrodynamic lift. This lifting is accompanied by a concurrent lowering of the stern, due to negative pressure of water passing the hull. The result can be an overall increase in the boat's pitch. At lower speeds, the degree of hydrodynamic lift is trivial. At higher speeds it may be considerable.

Yaw describes the sideways alignment of the boat and has the greatest impact on performance because of its effect on directionality. Yaw means the boat is not moving straight. Consider the boat moving through the water at a constant speed and straight as an arrow.

Then imagine a change in direction where the boat deviates from its straight path. This change can result from an uneven application of force, environmental factors such as wind and waves, or simply because the sculling technique may require asynchronicity in, for example, one hand preceding the other.

This 'twisting' from the straight direction impacts performance. The most immediate is that the side of the hull presents itself to the water as not a narrow, sharp bow but as a broad and flat object. We now know this is form drag. Where before the form drag was

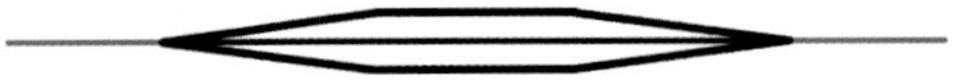

Fig. 15 Scull travelling straight.

Fig. 16 Scull yawed.

inconsequential, it is now considerable. Boat speed drops. In order to resume a straight path the yaw has to be corrected, compounding the decrease in speed.

Gates in motion: the dynamic connecting point with oars

In motion, preserving a stable connection between the gate face and the oar collar is vital to maintaining overall stability of the sculling system. A decrease in stability, usually exhibited through excessive rolling and yawing, diminishes the conveyance of the athlete's propulsive force. Maintenance of a good collar/gate connection is required for good performance.

Gates swivel and can be adjusted to alter both the blades' presentation to and extraction from the water, a term known as 'pitch'. Because the gate has four degrees of pitch formed into the plastic (look at the inside of the gate to see the slight angle built into the plastic), bushings are required to restore the gate position to zero degrees. Bushings of four degrees/four degrees (4/4) accomplish this. Other bushings are available as well, including 1/7, 2/6 and 3/5, altering the pitch from one degree to seven. Modern blade designs are resilient. It is unusual to require bushings other than 4/4, a pitch of zero.

Lateral pitch is another traditional consideration where the pin or rigger holding the gate is bent to change the presentation of the oar to the water. A lateral pitch of other than zero is rarely necessary, with technique improvements the first solution to try. To determine whether gates have a lateral pitch, measure the distance between the bottom centre of the pins as well as the top centre of the pins. With no lateral pitch, the distance should be the same. A difference indicates either lateral pitch or damage.

Gates may have a raised ridge on the bottom face. This raised ridge is subject to wear, as are the pitch bushings. An annual check is advised and both replaced as a unit when required.

Summary: the single sculling boat

In summary, when the scull is in motion it operates most efficiently at a constant velocity (constant speed and straight direction) and level (zero pitch). An athlete's technique is crucial to achieving both. Below are the main points of this section:

- Without its rigger, oars and athlete, the single scull is inherently stable
- Instability increases as each component (rigger, oars and athlete) is added, raising the centre of mass
- Gravity has a greater effect on stability as the centre of mass rises
- Skin drag contributes between 85 and 90 per cent of all drag on a calm, windless day
- The boat performs best at constant velocity, velocity being speed and direction
- Speed variation requires more work and power from the athlete than constant speed
- Roll, pitch and yaw affect the performance of the scull, with roll having the smallest effect and yaw, the greatest
- The connection between the boat (through its gate) and the oar is optimized by a gentle outward pressure of the thumb.

Oars

Oars have two primary purposes: providing stability and conveying propulsion. The addition of the rigger to the scull allows the oars to act as pontoons or balancing poles, much like those used by a high-wire artist. Oars are engineered to take the athlete's propulsive force and translate it into forward movement of the boat. While oars look simple, their design is very sophisticated. Understanding their intrinsic design capabilities will provide insight into oar selection that allows the athlete to avoid injury and optimize performance.

FISA has limited requirements for oars. Scull blades must not be less than 3mm thick as measured 2mm from the outer edge (Rule 39). The colour and design must be the same on both sides (Rule 51).

Oars at rest

Oars float. They have handles with multi-sized grips of varied shape and composition, all intended to optimize their connection to the athlete. They have blades with different purposeful shapes that connect to the water in different ways. Oar shafts, connecting the handle and blades, vary in size, composition and sup-

Fig. 17 The inherently stable scull plus oars, with oar handles free.

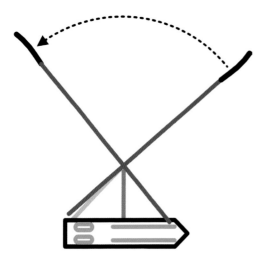

Fig. 18 The assumed blade path while observing the oar motion when the sculling system is at rest. (Adapted and used with permission from Concept2, Inc.)

pleness. The oar connection at the rigger gate is adjustable to allow for flexibility in loading. All of these are crucial considerations to an athlete when selecting oars.

The biggest contribution of the oars at rest is: they allow the athlete to sit in the boat without capsizing. This monumental improvement in system stability is achieved because the oars act as an extension of the hull. Properly connected to the boat at the gates, the oars expand the lateral stability of the boat to the extent of their length. From an effective design perspective, the scull plus oars (minus the athlete) now take on the stability characteristics of the ocean-going barge with its width to length ratio of 1.0.

For an experiment in the stability of the scull and oars, tie the two handles of the oars together (a sock will do). Notice that the blades will tend towards lying flat on the water rather than perpendicular. This is a function of surface tension and blade design. Blades flat on the water provide a large area of resistance between the blade and surface, improving stability. Standing outside the

boat, pick up one blade and try to capsize the boat. What happens? Grasp the boat across the gunwales and try to capsize the boat. What happens? Now assess the scull and oar combined stability for future consideration when the athlete is added.

Oars will seek their design level. Oars have a pitch, too, that describes how the blade is connected by the manufacturer to the shaft. Most oars have a pitch of zero (blades perpendicular when squared). When perpendicular to the water and under load, blades will tend to stay perpendicular. However, when the loading connection to the water diminishes significantly, say at the end of the stroke, the blades will 'release'. The implication here is that the athlete can interfere with these design characteristics or utilize these characteristics for performance benefits. The perpendicular blades will rest in the water at the point where the oar shaft connects to the blade, approximately the ideal position for efficient sculling.

When the boat and oars are at rest, the blade squared and the oar, lightly loaded, moved through the water, the blade travels in a continual arc. However, this assumed blade path (Fig. 18) gives a false impression of what happens when the sculling system is in motion. With the oar loaded and boat in motion, something entirely different occurs.

Oars in motion

When loaded, the typical blade path is as in Fig. 19. The blade moves slightly forward, outward, backward and inward somewhat, around a point. Instead of the blade moving, the boat moves.

This typical blade path presents opportunities for improved blade design. The less the blade 'slips' in the water at perpendicular, the better the transmission of force. The improved blade would be more efficient and able to rotate in the water, with the point of rotation

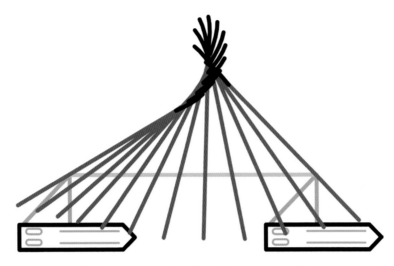

Fig. 19 The typical blade path during the drive. (Adapted and used with permission from Concept2, Inc.)

defined as the point where the blade and shaft join.[4] (See Developing a New Blade Path and Blade box.)

Slip and wash

In the absence of the ideal blade, or the ideal athlete, slip and wash occur. Both describe the connection of the oar to the water. Slip occurs in the time between blade entry and when the form drag provides sufficient resistance for the boat to move forward. For example, assume the boat is tied to a dock and a very light stroke is taken. The blade path would look like that in Fig. 18 with the slip being 100 per cent of the total arc. Untie the boat, insert the blade into the water and apply force. A strong, dynamic force will create form drag and the blade will slip considerably less. From a technique perspective, the less slip, the greater the efficiency and effectiveness of the oar in the water. The transmission of power is greater.

Wash describes the connection of the blade with the water at the end of the stroke. Most modern oar blades are designed to release from the water when the connection ceases to provide propulsion. Indeed, some blades will 'pop' out at the effective end of the stroke. This requires that the oar and boat be connected through the gate, that strong propulsion is being delivered and that light hands allow the oar to operate as designed.

Oar tracking

Oars are designed to track optimally through the water. This tracking is horizontal. Sitting in a scull, a simple experiment is to use two fingers very lightly to move the handle of an oar towards the athlete. The resting squared blade will float with its top surface slightly above the water. Pulling the blade lightly with one or two fingers towards the athlete will cause the blade to sink slightly below the surface and track horizontally level until finger pressure is released. This is the optimal blade depth and tracking.

Other oar considerations

When perpendicular, the blade presents a large surface area to the water. The shape and size of the blade determines how much it 'slips' in the water, with 'slip' being a descriptor of energy lost during the stroke. For example, Concept2's Fat2 blades provide a sharper grip at the entry and heavier loading at the initiation of the

Developing a New Blade Path and Blade

Exploring the difference between the typical blade path and an 'ideal' blade path presents several opportunities for oar design improvements.

Observation 1: Shorter Outboard Length
Using the same boat speed as for the typical blade path, the new ideal blade and oar are shorter.

Observation 2: Slower Rotation at Beginning of Drive
They also travel a different blade path. Because the blade slips less, the point of rotation does not move sternward but remains more forwards throughout the stroke. As a result, at the initiation of the drive, the ideal blade and oar rotate more slowly at the beginning of the drive and then speed up in the second half of the drive.

To the athlete, this means the ideal blade will feel heavier early in the drive and feel lighter after the oar reaches perpendicular. From a physiological standpoint, it makes sense to maximize blade efficiency at the same point of the stroke when the athlete is using his or her large muscles to power the drive. From the perpendicular to the finish,

only the upper body and arms are engaged, so it makes sense that the load becomes lighter and handle speed increases in this phase of the drive.

Observation 3: Less Work Required to Move the Same Speed
Because the outboard lever is shorter in the ideal blade path, the force on the handle is less, which means that less work is required to move the boat the same speed. This means that if the same force is applied on the handle, the force on the end of the shorter oar will be greater. In other words, the athlete will get more speed for equal effort.

Observation 4: Less Slip
The ideal blade slips less by definition. Comparably, the typical blade slips more during the first part of the drive and doesn't slip enough during the last part of the drive. The insufficient slip at the last part of the drive creates a backwatering condition where the part of the blade near the shaft produces some negative thrust or drag. This is created by the combination of blade rotation and forward movement of the boat.

drive. Blades described as smoothies provide a softer feel and lighter loads at the initiation of the drive. During the last part of the drive, Fat2 blades move more quickly towards the finish. Smoothies provide a heavier load and slower handle speed toward the finish.[6] Thus, different blades will prove more advantageous for different techniques.

Shafts are designed with various characteristics, one being the degree of suppleness. Stiffer shafts transmit force more directly. Their loading characteristics need to be considered in relationship to the physiology and fitness of the athlete. A stiffer shaft means the load is transmitted more quickly to the athlete than

the more biomechanically forgiving softer shaft. Softer shafts have the benefit of transmitting more force later in the stroke because of the energy stored in that bend.[7]

Oars, both blades and shafts, need to be considered in relationship to the technique being used and the individual characteristics of the athlete. A technique that is front-end loaded with the maximum degrees of force applied early in the drive, like the dynamic technique described in later chapters, will benefit from an oar that loads up early. A technique that is back-end loaded will benefit from a blade that loads up later in the stroke. That is not to exclude the use of any oar type for any technique.

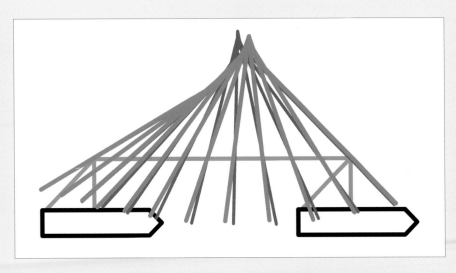

Fig. 20 Comparison of typical blade path (purple) and ideal blade path (green).
(Adapted and used with permission from Concept2, Inc.)

Characteristics of Blade that Approaches the Theoretical Ideal

• Surface area – Increased surface areas tend to resist slippage perpendicular to the blade surface.
• Curvature/hook – Flatter blades generate a heavier feel earlier in the drive, allowing for slower rotation.

• Tip characteristics – Vortex generating features reduce slippage perpendicular to the blade surface.
• Tip shape – Tapered blade edges create a force on the back of the blade, increase lift and reduce slip, much like the delta wing effect in aeronautics.[5]

(Adapted and with permission from Concept2, Inc.)

A wise athlete will try many types of oars to determine the best fit. Rigging plays a part, too. This includes span, outboard and inboard oar length, all to be discussed later. Thus, oars and their loading should be less a matter of local culture and past preference and more a considered decision about an athlete's (a) physical characteristics and (b) preferred technique.

Summary: oars

The complexity of oars provides opportunities for exploring 'best fit' scenarios, with athlete characteristics and the technique being as primary considerations. Below are other main points of this section:

• Together, the scull and oars are inherently stable
• Oars are designed to seek their design level, both at rest and in motion
• The blade path changes with the oar in motion, the loaded blade generally rotating around a single point

- Slip describes the time between blade entry and when the blade significantly connects with the water
- Wash describes the time between when the blade releases from the water and blade exits the water.

SUMMARY: THE SCULLING SYSTEM – BOAT AND OARS

While the boat and oars are inherently stable, they cannot move without a source of propulsion. Propulsion is provided by the athlete. To do this, the athlete integrates with the boat and oars. The integration of a flexible, thinking athlete can be done haphazardly, resulting in instability and suboptimal performance of the system. Or, it can be done thoughtfully and well, particularly with consideration for individual differences in athletes. The next chapter explores this athlete integration, resulting in a connected, stable, effective and efficient unit – the optimal sculling system.

Endnotes

1 World Rowing Federation. *FISA Rules of Racing and Related Bye-Laws. 2017. Bye-Laws to Rule 39 – Boats and Equipment and Rule 41 – Weight of Boats*. www.worldrowing.com/mm//Document/General/General/13/58/39/FISArulebookEN2019web_Neutral.pdf.

2 Dudhia, A., *Physics of Rowing, 5. Relationship between Weight and Boat Speed*. http://eodg.atm.ox.ac.uk/user/dudhia/rowing/physics/weight.html.

3 Dudhia, A., *Physics of Rowing, 9. Effect of Boat Weight on Boat Speed*. http://eodg.atm.ox.ac.uk/user/dudhia/rowing/physics/weight.html.

4 Concept2, Inc. Blade Path and the Ideal Blade. www.concept2.com/oars/how-made-and-tested/blade-path.

5 Concept2, Inc. Blade Path and the Ideal Blade. www.concept2.com/oars/how-made-and-tested/blade-path.

6 Concept2, Inc. Blades Overview and Loading Profile. www.concept2.com/oars/how-made-and-tested/blade-path.

7 Kleshnev, V., *The Biomechanics of Rowing* (Marlborough: The Crowood Press Ltd, 2016) pp.156–17.

3 | THE SCULLING SYSTEM: INTEGRATING THE ATHLETE

The boat and oars change when in motion. The boat oscillates. The oar shaft bends. Yet, the overall effect of this on the sculling system is small. By comparison, integrating the flexible athlete creates enormous changes. In exchange for gaining a biological propulsive force, the sculling system now must accommodate mass, human plasticity and a brain operating 95 per cent on unconscious habit.

This chapter will explore the biomechanical aspects of integrating the athlete into the sculling system. The discussion will include rigging for injury prevention, stability and performance. Initial aspects of the dynamic technique are explored. Topics such as propulsion, technique, performance and the brain with its subliminal, primitive priorities will follow in later chapters.

The primary objective of integrating the athlete into the sculling system is *connection*. A well-connected athlete results in the sculling system's components acting as a single entity. A poorly-connected athlete has the same characteristics as a sack of potatoes sitting on the boat seat. The sack of potatoes system is unstable, because the boat, oars and sack are independent. With the athlete connected through the feet, hands and all the biome-chanical components in between, the system will be stable. The components (boat, oars and athlete) are interdependent.

With the athlete's well-connected body, the sculling system achieves a direct flow-on effect from oar blades to boat run. In this system the athlete works *with* the equipment. The pleasure and performance of the sculling system acting as a single entity are glorious.

THE MASS OF THE ATHLETE

The addition of the athlete changes the sculling system's centre of mass. It rises from below the decking to approximately the athlete's mid-chest level. The athlete's percentage of body weight above the seat from head, trunk and arms is 67.8 per cent (Table 11), potentially overwhelming the stability of the system.

This higher centre of mass is flexible. The athlete 'swivels' laterally, side to side around the centreline of the boat, affecting roll. The athlete 'swivels' horizontally, forward and aft, affecting pitch. The impact of the additional mass on horizontal stability is small because the change in pitch of a long, narrow boat is small. The boat is designed to accommodate it. Laterally, the stability of the boat becomes a

	% Body Mass
Head	7.3
Trunk	50.7
Arms	9.8
Legs	32.2
Sum	100

Table 11 Percentage of mass by body component. (Clauser et al. Weight, Volume and Center of Mass of Segments of the Human Body. Air Force Systems Command, Wright-Patterson Air Force Base, Ohio (US). August 1969. https://apps.dtic.mil/dtic/tr/fulltext/u2/710622.pdf)

function of the connectedness of the system. If the centre of mass shifts left or right to either side of the centreline, and the athlete is not well connected with the boat and oars, the boat rolls. The high centre of mass overwhelms the inherent stability of the system. Gravity acts more substantially. The athlete either recovers connectedness or falls laterally off the seat into the water.

What size boat?

The mass of the athlete is an integral component in deciding what size boat. Boat hulls come in shapes that are less rounded, with a flattish bottom. These less-rounded hulls provide a more stable platform for novices, sacrificing performance. The alternative is a rounded hull, which provides less stability but better performance.

Boats come in different sizes (length, width and weight), as evidenced by the manufacturer's specifications and design weight found on each boat's FISA production plaque (Rule 39 2.3).[1] The problem is manufacturers may provide design weight ranges that are quite large or that make comparison between two boats challenging.

The way to determine the best boat size is for the athlete to explore various makes and models, starting with a boat in the athlete's design range. Athletes should try boats slightly larger or slightly smaller. On-water trials of various boats will provide valuable information that is not available from the production plaque and manufacturer's specifications. Several trials in each boat size are recommended. The boat size should see the fin remaining in the water throughout the stroke and pitch variations moderated.

A final boat consideration is rigger placement. Both the weight of the athlete and the speed of the boat will affect the trim, which describes how level the boat is under way. Some riggers come with multiple holes allowing them to be mounted more fore or aft. The initial recommendation is to mount the rigger using the middle holes. Then, observe the boat at rest with the athlete in the seat, moving through the stroke with blades flat on the water. The pitch of the boat should be relatively similar, fore and aft. Next, observe the boat under way. The boat should be trim, level, at performance speed. At higher speeds (assume over 4.0mps), the boat may need to be trimmed more bow down, at rest, in order to achieve level, at speed. The objective in trimming is: after release, boat horizontally level at the desired speed.

THE FLEXIBLE ATHLETE

Simplistically, the human body is comprised of solid elements, primarily bones, and soft tissue including muscles, tendons, ligaments and cartilage. Joints are those locations in the body where bones connect. While bones are rigid, joints are not. Movement results from the interaction of muscles and tendons on bones and joints. In some body parts, like the hands, feet and spine, a series of small bones are connected with soft tissue and are ultra-flexible. Muscles become more important in supporting these ultra-flexible components. With all this flexibility, describing

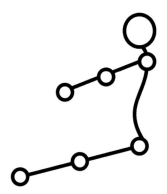

Fig. 21 Basic diagram of bones and joints.

the optimal connection of the athlete to the rest of the sculling system is complicated. Fig. 21 is a simplistic diagram showing key areas of connection for the athlete.

Based on the rigid bony structures of the body, this chapter will investigate the flexible athlete in three major groups: (1) feet, legs and hips, (2) seat, spine and head, and (3) shoulders, arms and hands. The two major transition points at the pelvic and shoulder girdles will be discussed individually. Each section will consider biomechanics, rigging and connection.

Human bodies are unique, between each other and within themselves. For example, there is a difference in length between left and right leg for 95 per cent of athletes. The same for arms and hand sizes. For most, the differences are small. When the differences are large and affect how propulsion is delivered to the sculling system, for example causing yaw if leg length is significantly different, that difference needs to the addressed, in this example through a shoe wedge.

To be well connected, the boat and oars need to be optimized for the athlete's body. That is, properly rigged. Rigging a boat for a particular athlete is a long-term evolutionary exercise. As an athlete changes in terms of flexibility, fitness and age, the rigging will need adjustment. Also, when one component of rigging is changed, inevitable follow-on impacts on other rigging parameters occur. For example, changing the span may require a change in the position of the footstretcher and a change in the inboard. When the athlete is well integrated into the sculling system, comfort, effectiveness and efficiency will be the outcome.

GROUP 1: FEET, LEGS AND HIPS

Connection at the feet

When the feet are well connected, the athlete and boat become a single unit. Assuming the oars are well organized, our single unit is ocean-going barge-like. Very stable. If the feet are not well connected, the athlete resembles the sack of potatoes and, with a slight shift in mass around the lateral, capsizes. The foot connection with the boat is the most overlooked element of integrating an athlete with the sculling system. The issue is that from outside the boat, the feet are hidden. What goes on in the foot well of the boat is a mystery to observers and often to the athlete, too.

The feet are connected to the sculling system through the shoes, shoe plate and footstretcher. The footstretcher is then

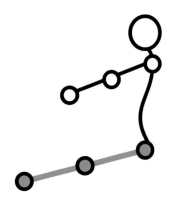

Fig. 22 Group 1: feet, legs and hips with joints shown in circles.

attached to the boat. Aside from the foot-stretcher's ability to move fore and aft, it can be angled to suit the athlete. This angle is called 'rake' and is a particularly important consideration for Masters.

Shoes

In order to achieve an effective connection with the boat, the shoes must fit. Bozo the Clown shoes, purchased to fit the largest feet in the club, will not do. In the dynamic technique to be described later, the athlete will be both pushing *and pulling* on the shoes. If the shoes are too large, feet will slip out. If feet are sloppy in the shoes, boat control and stability will be sloppy. Clogs are similarly suboptimal.

Why is this foot connection so important? First, a good foot connection avoids the sack of potatoes effect. It draws the centre of mass down because the mass of the unified system (boat, oars and athlete) has one centre point. It is lower than the mass of a disunified system with two components (1: boat and oars, 2: athlete). The disunified system has two separate centres of mass that gravity can affect differently. Since in the disunified system the athlete's centre of mass is higher (and total mass greater), the effect of gravity is more persuasive on the athlete.

Once well connected, feet are active. They propel the boat. They draw the boat in. Feet steer the boat. Feet correct for the effects of roll and yaw. In rough weather, feet can help counteract crosswind by levelling the boat. Feet are dynamic connectors to the boat and achieve stability as well as propulsive effectiveness, for example direction.

Safety is important. Shoes must have heels tied to the boat to ensure, in an emergency, the heels remain in place. Also required is a handhold that, when pulled, releases the shoe straps or laces (FISA Rule 39, 2.4). FISA has additional requirements with regards to the dimensions, materials and specifications for the quick release equipment (FISA Rule 39, 8.6).[2]

For some, the idea of feet held snugly in shoes may be intimidating because, in the past, their boat control was tenuous. While capsizing is unpleasant, the thinking may be that capsizing with feet tied snugly into shoes and upside down in the water may be even more so. Be assured, boat control will be less tenuous with shoes that fit. Because of the unified system, stability will improve. Shoe straps should be tight or laces tied. However, in the initial stages of using properly sized and fastened shoes, a capsize drill with shoes fitted snugly is recommended for athletes. One should ensure the heel ties are in place before every outing. Another tactic at the end of each workout is to use the handhold to release the shoe straps, thus creating a good motor habit in the event of capsize.

Shoe plate

Shoes connect to the shoe plate, which usually has four small screw holes per shoe. Athletes are encouraged to consider purchasing their own shoe plate and correctly sized shoes to use in shared boats. Another commercial option for shared boats is the BAT Logic quick release system,[3] which lends itself to a club-wide approach. For athletes who find a significant difference in leg length affecting the equal transmission of force through the shoe heel to the footstretcher, BAT Logic system offers a set of shims, placed between their shoe and shoe plate, that can be helpful in compensating for these leg length discrepancies. Other options are available, such as orthotic inserts, with the objective being properly sized shoes, well connected in such a way the athlete can push *and pull* with the feet.

The biomechanical considerations for shoe plates are (a) width between the feet and (b) splay. Splay describes the angle of the feet outwards from centreline. Because the shoe plate is rigid, the width of the feet and splay are almost universally fixed in a one size fits all configuration. While this uniform arrangement might be acceptable for younger athletes who have flexible soft tissue, athletes who have stiffer tissue or limitations from past injuries will find themselves at risk of injury.

Fig. 23 At the catch, the shoe plate height should result in the athlete's knees being at or just below armpits.

The first issue has to do with the narrow alignment of the foot position. The closer the feet are to the centreline of the boat, the less stable the athlete's position because the boat is more likely to roll. For most athletes, this narrow foot position is not biomechanically optimal. For example, stand and do a comfortable squat. Next, put feet approximately the same width apart as normal sculling shoes attached to the shoe plate. Perform the same squat and observe. For some, the narrowness will feel very awkward because in a conventional squat, the natural tendency is to align legs with the shoulders. Some shoe connection systems allow for customization of the shoe placement. Ideally the feet should be positioned as wide apart as possible to mimic a comfortable, conventional squat. This improves the biomechanics as well as stability.

The second issue is splay, the outward angle of the toes. Shoe plates are designed with men in mind, and the splay, or direction of the feet, is only slightly toe outwards. An athlete can determine whether the splay in a given shoe plate is biomechanically adequate by standing, with shoes on and connected to the shoe plate. Perform the same comfortable squat as before. If the knees go naturally forward and/ or outwards, the splay is adequate. If the knees go inward and clash, it is inadequate. The latter happens most often for women, whose pelvic

alignment is different from men's. The problem with the inward movement of the knees is that this creates instability in the boat because the legs are now at the centreline, or interfering with one another. It places a great deal of stress on the knee joint. Ideally the knees should come out slightly and provide a slight balancing effect when under way (Fig. 23).

Inadequate splay is an injury risk issue. The wear on the pelvic girdle, knees and ankles because of improper foot and leg alignment is a recipe for a repetitive stress injury (RSI). Inexpensive solutions are limited. One is to physically force the heels inward and toes outward in the shoes, and even consider a slightly larger shoe size if the problem is significant, understanding that stability may be sacrificed for joint longevity. A better solution is to organize a custom shoe plate, which will involve a local machinist.

Footstretcher: Shoe plate height and rake

First, it is oddly true that some manufacturers do not provide footstretchers with adjustable rakes. Because of the biomechanical alignment of the foot, with its subsequent effect on leg alignment, a footstretcher without a rake adjustment should be replaced.

The footstretcher is the first major opportunity to explore how rigging adjustments are inter dependent, particularly shoe plate height

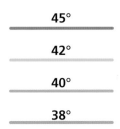

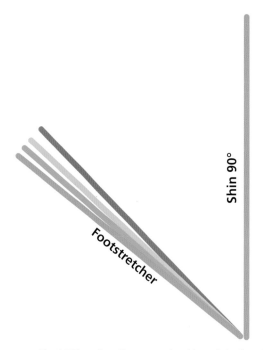

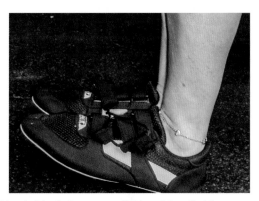

Fig. 24 The rake adjustment should result in the athlete's shins being perpendicular while still able to retain floor connection both at the catch and release. The photo shows the athlete's natural ankle flexion without compression.

and footstretcher rake. The shoe is connected to the shoe plate, which is connected to the footstretcher. But where does the shoe plate go?

The first adjustment is shoe plate height. Biomechanically, a good rule of thumb is: at the catch, for the knees to be slightly at or below the armpit. Thus, the shoe plate should be installed on the footstretcher at the relevant height to achieve this. The degree of flexibility of the athlete's ankle and knee has an effect on how comfortable this will be. A shoe plate that is higher or lower may be more comfortable, although substantially higher or lower may cause stability problems. The height of the shoe plate affects the rake because the biomechanics of the foot are now intertwined with ankle, knee and hip.

The next adjustment is rake. As the athlete comes sternward and compresses, the heels have a tendency to rise and the toes go down. As the athlete moves towards the bow, the heels go down and the toes rise. This motion is a rocking

of the foot within the shoe as well as a bending of the shoe. The issue is, given the shoes are fixed, what is the optimal rake of the footstretcher? With connection being the objective, the answer is: a rake that will allow for the maximum foot connection throughout the athlete's stroke. This maximum foot connection needs to be made both with the flat of the foot, particularly the heel, as well as the top of the foot.

There are technique considerations here. Is the athlete on the ball of the foot or toes at the catch? This is a technical position with several problems. The first is that this foot position raises the centre of mass and begins to disconnect the foot from the boat. The effects may not be immediately obvious at the catch, but the resulting drive is likely to be initially unstable, with an uneven transmission of power. In addition, the muscles of the foot and shin, which are notoriously weak, are the muscles that bring the heel down to the footstretcher.

Fig. 25 Athlete well connected through the feet (and core) at the catch.

The capacity of these muscles to drive the boat are very limited. The general effective action of the foot then becomes one of the heel moving downward in space and nothing, or very little, happening at the oar handles. Thus, the recommended distance between the heel and the footstretcher at the catch is 1cm or less.

The other technique consideration is the location of the athlete's heel at the release. The heel should be driving the boat until the oars release. The heel is low in the heel cup. The top of the foot comes up to solidify the foot connection.

Thus, shoe plate height becomes an experiment. The guidelines are: knees at or just below armpits with heels no more than 1cm off the footplate. The experiment is: at what location are the heels connected both at the catch and release? This experiment will need to consider rake.

Rake is a place where athletes who are less flexible at the ankle and/or knee should feel comfortable using a flatter footstretcher, with 38 degrees or less not uncommon in Masters. The 'normal' advertised adjustment ranges for youth scullers, often 42 degrees or more, are very misleading. The issue with the flatter footstretcher is that unless the technique compensates by driving through the heel horizontally, the drive is likely to put energy into vertical as opposed to horizontal action. Technique and awareness can compensate for this.

For the rake adjustment, start with the foot flat on the footstretcher. Come to the catch, heels no more than 1cm off the footstretcher and preferably flat. Adjust the rake to where the shins are approximately perpendicular to the boat. The shins should not be forward of perpendicular because of the resulting knee

Fig. 26 Athlete well connected through the feet (and core) at the release.

joint stress. Shins slightly behind perpendicular is acceptable in cases where flexibility is very limited. (Flexibility is measured in a later chapter and an inflexible athlete should work towards improved ankle, leg and hip flexibility.)

The next rake adjustment is at the release. At the release the heels should still connect to the footstretcher with the toes up. It is almost guaranteed that this will not work the first time because adjusting the rake is a balancing act between the foot connection at the catch and the foot connection at the release. Since the dynamic technique drives through the heels horizontally for the entire stroke, it is important to achieve the best connection possible for as long as possible. To do so may require a further adjustment in the height of the shoe plate.

The end result is connection through the heels for the entire stroke, shins approximately perpendicular to the boat at the catch, knees at or below the armpits at the catch and stability. Comfort is required, too.

Special footstretcher rigging considerations

Athletes come in all sizes, including some with large abdomens. The guideline for the shoe plate height adjustment is: the knees at the catch are at or slightly below the armpits. This guidance fails if the athlete cannot get fully to the catch. For athletes with large abdomens, it is important to *estimate* the catch and where the athlete's knees would be in relationship to their armpits without the large abdomen. The danger of not so doing is putting the feet too high. Err on the side of lower. Rake is less of an issue.

Forward and aft position of the footstretcher

This measurement will be reviewed briefly here and more fully in the next chapter because the position of the footstretcher has propulsion implications. Its location is integral to setting the catch and release angles.

With the adjustments made above, the entire athlete now moves fore and aft as a unit. At the catch the footstretcher can move towards the stern and the biomechanics will remain constant. The same holds true for the athlete if the footstretcher moves towards the bow. Thus, the footstretcher can go anywhere and the biomechanics of the athlete, from the hips and below in the boat, remain the same. The next consideration is: the athlete's performance objectives and position of the oar handles. Later, the goal will be to achieve a 60 degree catch angle and 40 degree release angle by adjusting everything above the seat, both technique and equipment, but primarily the span and oars.

At this point in time, the feet, legs and hips are now connected to the boat through the footstretcher, shoe plate and shoes. Where exactly the footstretcher assembly is positioned is not yet answered, but a topic to be covered in the next chapter.

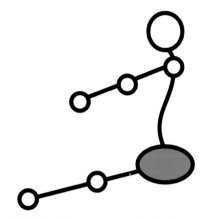

Fig. 27 Pelvic girdle transition point linking Group 1 and Group 2.

TRANSITION POINT: PELVIC GIRDLE

The boat is now rigged so that the athlete can maintain optimal connection through the feet to the hips (32 per cent of total body mass). How do these lower limbs connect to the rest of the athlete and sculling system? The connection is through the pelvic girdle, which denotes the link between Group 1 (feet, knees and hips) as it attaches to Group 2 (seat, spine and head). The gluteus maximus (buttocks) is the most significant muscle in the pelvic girdle. During the drive it provides stability and power.

The dynamic technique achieves a distinct separation of movement in the groups. Group 1 moves and flexes. It, along with the gluteus maximus, provides muscular power and propulsion. Group 2 remains as a relatively unmoving unit, a monolithic transmitter of power and propulsion that simultaneously moderates stability. Group 2 adds to power and propulsion through the application of body mass, 57 per cent of the athlete's total. This will be achieved technically by driving the body mass

through the feet by, essentially, 'standing up' horizontally during the drive while hanging, not pulling, on the oar handles. The pelvic girdle allows for this effective use of body mass, linking the very different functions of these two groups to operate as part of the whole.

Thus, the pelvic girdle is crucial in sustaining the connection between Group 1 and Group 2. The glutes as well as the many smaller pelvic girdle muscles need to be actively engaged during various parts of the stroke, especially the drive sequence, to achieve optimal power and stability.

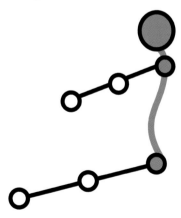

Fig. 28 Group 2: seat, spine and head showing connections with pelvic girdle, shoulder girdle and head.

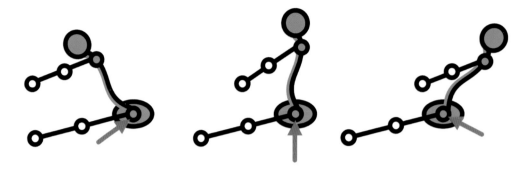

Fig. 29 The pelvic rock showing identical Group 2 alignment, rotating on hip joints, with weight shift (red arrow). The Group 2 alignment is identical in each illustration, although an optical illusion may indicate otherwise. The hands also travel level.

GROUP 2: SEAT, SPINE AND HEAD

Connection at the seat

One might think gravity would take care of this. However, the connection at the seat is complicated by the Group 2 objective: retain the same natural seat (pelvis), spine and head alignment throughout the stroke. This objective targets retention of the natural curvature of the lower back. It targets natural thoracic spine and head alignment. The purpose of this alignment retention is back preservation and injury prevention. This alignment provides connectedness and a strong pathway for transmission of power throughout the sculling system.

Back problems comprise the majority of sculling injuries. Once the back is injured, the likelihood of a reoccurrence increases.[4] With an athletic career measured in decades, preservation of back health is paramount. Research evidence indicates that for younger elite subjects the lumbar spine constitutes 51 per cent of all rowing injuries, with more than half of subjects in some studies reporting a back injury in the past twelve months.[5] Masters scullers are

arguably more at risk because of the lack of technical advice regarding back preservation strategies and complementary techniques. The injury risk factor increases with fatigue as well as with ergometer sessions longer than thirty minutes.

The first and foremost back preservation strategies are:

- Rock (swing) from the pelvis around the hip joints
- Retain the natural spinal alignment at all phases of the stroke, including head alignment
- Fatigue management
- Muscle strengthening of core muscles and all supporting torso musculature
- Glutes engagement
- Improved flexibility

All of these preservation strategies are integrally woven with connectedness. An athlete with a sloppy spine and poor core musculature will be unable to retain a natural Group 2 alignment under sustained loading conditions. The resulting disconnectedness means that the link between feet and hands, and boat and oars, will be broken. Stability deteriorates with this loss of connection, as does performance.

To remain connected, the first consideration is the seat and pelvis. Fig. 29 shows the recommended alignment of seat, spine and head. These do not change throughout the stroke. While an optical illusion may indicate elsewhere, in all three figures the seat, spine and head (Group 2) are aligned exactly the same, with feet and legs in the same position. With a small articulation at the shoulder joint, the hands travel level. What changes is the location of the pelvis, which rocks slightly forward and backwards from the hip joints. The pelvis remains connected with the spine and in the same position throughout. The entire group 2 assembly rolls forward and back around the hip joints. The feeling is of weight on the front of the pelvis to weight on the back of the pelvis, while the back stays in its same natural position. The head follows to retain the alignment of the thoracic spine and to facilitate the function of the shoulder girdle, discussed later.

A simple way to determine if this is happening is to put one hand on the lumbar spine region, feeling the natural concave curve. Next, rock forward with that hand in place ensuring that the natural concave nature does not change. That is, the lower back does not bow out and resemble a 'C'. 'S' is the operative letter. Alternatively and sitting tall with the hand in place, bend forward and create a 'C'-shaped back where the lumbar region pushes back against the hand. Then repeat the rock forward motion to feel the difference. The head should remain over the shoulders.

This rocking motion allows for excellent connection through Group 1, the pelvic girdle, and Group 2 since the only change is articulation around the hip joint. It is ideal for back protection provided the athlete has developed the torso musculature to provide spinal support and retain the Group 2 position. Thus, for athletes for whom this is a new technical approach, it is critical that this core musculature be well developed before high loads and speed are introduced into the training programme.

The Group 2 unit is strong and static. It serves as a link in the sculling system, transmitting power from the oar blades to hands, to feet, to boat. This is a different technical approach, designed for athletes with long careers, but an approach with performance advantages.

Finally, the actual boat seat. All seats are not equal. Men tend to have narrower hips. Women tend to have broader hips. One seat size does not fit all comfortably and most seats are designed for men. Mis-sized seats can lead to problems with boat balance. If a seat is uncomfortable, consider changing it. Gel pads are not ideal solutions since they undermine the connection. Closed cell foam pads, the thinner the better and permanently affixed to the seat, are the preferred option.

Last, before setting out, a final check about the location of the athlete's body on the seat and alignment of the torso over the centreline of the boat is helpful. Through habit, it is possible for the body to believe it is centred on the seat when it is not. A simple test is to centre the torso on the seat and then, with very light hands, see if the handle heights differ. A large difference in handle heights, not due to the gate height, is a good indicator that the athlete needs to shift laterally on the seat.

TRANSITION POINT: SHOULDER GIRDLE

In comparison to the pelvic girdle's strong, almost rigid bony structure, the shoulder girdle is the exact opposite. The shoulder girdle is comprised of the shoulder blades, the collarbone, and a substantial amount of soft tissue including the rotator cuff. These collectively provide a relatively unstable connection to the upper arm. The shoulder girdle structure trades the benefits of strength and stability for flexibility. An arm can 'windmill' in a 360 degree arc. Try that with a leg.

In order to transmit power, the shoulder girdle connection needs to be stable and

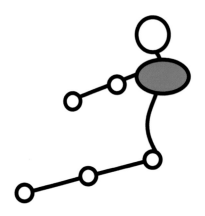

Fig. 30 Shoulder girdle transition point linking Group 2 and Group 3.

system, a strong shoulder girdle increases system stability and performance.

This position of the shoulder blade engaged on the torso at the catch reduces the forward reach of the arms. This is not a problem for two reasons. The first is that with the shoulder blades 'latched', the chest cavity is larger. Sit in a chair and move your hands forward as far as possible, releasing the shoulder blades. Take a deep breath. Next, engage the shoulder blades on the torso and move your hands forward as far as possible. Take a deep breath. The amount of lung capacity is different, favouring the engaged shoulder blade position.

Second, while the catch distance will be shorter with the shoulder blades on the torso, the effective catch distance will not. That is, by disengaging the shoulder blades, the athlete will rely on the weak muscles of the hands, arms and shoulders during the initial stages of the drive. The result is slip in the stroke, because the powerful leg muscles are driving while the hands, arms and shoulders are trying to get to an engaged position. The result is instability. And, time taken to, essentially, reach too far. Thus, with shoulder blades engaged, the stroke will be more effective with the additional opportunity for higher ratings.

strong. The only way to achieve this strength and stability is through muscular support of the shoulder blades in such a way that the shoulder blades lie flat on the upper torso, throughout the entire stroke. This requirement is similar to the one discussed in Group 2 where the flexible spine needs to be supported by strong musculature. With the shoulder musculature engaged and the shoulder blade flat on the back of the ribcage, the shoulder girdle becomes strong and stable.

Sitting in a chair, move the shoulders forward and feel the flexibility in the shoulder connection. Arms move loosely and fluidly. Now, 'latch' the shoulder blades down against the back using primarily the latissimus dorsi muscles. This will feel quite strong because the shoulder blades have formed a connection through their musculature to Group 2. However, in this strong shoulder position, the arms will be less mobile. Try putting one hand on the head with shoulders forward and loose. Then try with the shoulders 'latched'. There is a loss in shoulder flexibility. Because sculling takes place with the arms below the collarbone, this loss in flexibility is irrelevant. To reduce the risk of injury, technique must ensure shoulder girdle stability before applying load. Because an engaged shoulder girdle improves the sculler's connection within the

GROUP 3: SHOULDERS, ARMS AND HANDS

Connection at the shoulders and hands

Stand with arms by your side. Relax the shoulder joint. Loosen the shoulder blades. Now look at your hands. Are your fingers pointed straight down? Or, are they curved gently inward similar to the position used to hold an oar? Are the thumbs approximately at the end of the imaginary handle? For most athletes, the natural position of the fingers at rest is curved. Birds' feet are designed this way. When a bird lands on a branch, it does not spend the night with muscles engaged, gripping. Its natural anatomy causes the feet to curl around the branch without active muscle engagement.

The same is true for humans. However, because humans are so hand dependent, the natural impulse is to try to control the boat with hands instead of the feet, with which boat control is truly achieved. Hands are small and relatively weak. In the sculling system, they have three purposes. First, gentle thumb pressure to engage the oar collar to the gate, ensuring the entire system is connected. Second, is for the upper palm/knuckle/first finger joint to assist with the blade feathering and squaring, most of which will occur naturally with soft hands because the equipment is designed to achieve this. The last purpose of the hands is to complete the connection between oar handle and the rest of Group 3. This connection is made always with wrists flat so that the connection from hands to arms is straight and strong. Light, sensitive hands using a correct handle size complete the connection.

The correct handle size is one that allows the sculler to roll the handle easily when feathering and squaring the blade, maintaining

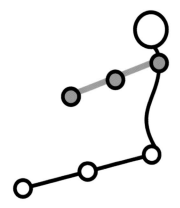

Fig. 31 Group 3: hands, arms and shoulder with joints shown in circles.

a flat wrist throughout. Oars handles that are too large will be difficult to roll and will encourage a 'death grip', increasing injury risk in the hand and forearm. Croker Oars provides a useful handle grip size chart on their website.[6] It is not definitive. The athlete should try different handle sizes, multiple times, to obtain a fair assessment of what works best for him or her. Oar handles are varied in shape, for example some have interdigital ridges. Oar handles are varied in composition: soft, firm,

Fig. 32 A light pressure from the thumbs keeps collars against the gates at the catch.

tacky and any number of options. The objective should always be achieving the grip that allows the lightest, best connection between the hand and the oar.

The muscles of the hands and arms are small. They are designed primarily to be versatile. The bones are comparatively small, too, and all the joints from hand to elbow to shoulder are designed to articulate. Group 3 is not designed for power or strength. Because the anatomy of Group 3 is so intricate, the risk of injury here is quite high due to overuse injuries. Such as, using Group 3 for tasks for which it was not designed, 'pulling' large loads being one of those.

'Hanging onto' large loads is a nuanced but important difference from 'pulling' and one that translates into technique. The difference between 'pulling' and 'hanging onto' involves the position of the shoulder girdle. In order to pull effectively, the shoulder girdle needs to extend and then reconnect. As we know, this introduces a large degree of instability into the sculling system. However, if the sculler 'hangs onto' the oar handle, hands gripping lightly, arms extended straight, and shoulders latched, then Group 3 acts as a connected unit.

Even extended straight, the arms can articulate. Put a hand flat on the wall or table top. Rotate the inner elbow so that it faces up and down. Notice this involves motion in the shoulder rotator cuff. Rotate the inner elbow to face downward and hold it in that position.

Notice the position of the shoulder blade, which is disconnected from the torso, and the arm, which can bend. The whole effect is one of flexibility.

Next rotate the inner elbow up and hold it in that position. Notice that the elbow is semi-locked and the arm held in a more rigid position. In addition, the shoulder blade is positioned on the torso. The whole effect is one of stability. The preferred position of the elbow when the arms are loaded is 'inside elbow up'.

SUMMARY: THE SCULLING SYSTEM – INTEGRATING THE ATHLETE

In order for the sculling system to work optimally, the system must be stable. To be stable, the athlete must be connected. Because the human body is incredibly versatile, awareness of how to achieve this connectedness is the first step. The next is to internalize this connectedness as a habit. Simple experiments for exploring connectedness (and improving stability) are included in Chapters 5 and 6. Of course, the equipment needs to be rigged for the athlete and to this point only the foot adjustments and athlete have been discussed. Additional adjustments are needed to achieve the final objective, propulsion.

Endnotes

1 World Rowing Federation. *FISA Rules of Racing and Related Bye-Laws. 2017. Rule 39 3.4 – Flotation.* www.worldrowing.com/mm//Document/General/General/13/58/39/FISArulebookEN2019web_Neutral.pdf

2 FISA World Rowing rules World Rowing Federation. *FISA Rules of Racing and Related Bye-Laws. 2017. Rule 39 3.6 – Quick release foot stretchers.* www.worldrowing.com/mm//Document/General/General/13/58/39/FISArulebookEN2019web_Neutral.pdf.

3 Bat Logic. https://batlogic.net/.

4 World Rowing. *Back pain in rowing – update on current understanding.* 2 May 2016. www.worldrowing.com/news/back-pain-rowing-update-current-understanding.

5 Rowing Ireland. Wilson, F., 'Back Pain in Rowing; An Evolution of understanding', *Rowing Ireland.* www.worldrowing.com/mm/Document/General/General/12/17/32/Lowbackpaininrowinganevolutionofunderstanding_Neutral.pdf.

6 Croker Oars Australia. https://docs.wixstatic.com/ugd/128a41_a9a5a0d0f96347b095f98121c5b1e48b.pdf.

4 | THE SCULLING SYSTEM: PROPULSION

Performance and reduced injury risk depend on proper rigging. An athlete can optimize their sculling experience by understanding how to rig their equipment optimally. We begin here assuming the athlete has made the initial rigging adjustments described in Chapter 3.

It is not unusual for there to be a lack of clarity about individual rigging at this point. Shins will not be perpendicular and, in order to get the shins perpendicular at the catch, the rake is so flat that the feet cannot stay engaged at the release. There is only one seat available, and it doesn't fit. Clarity will come as the athlete makes further adjustments and puts the sculling system in motion.

OAR AND ATHLETE CONNECTION

The sculling system connects with the water in only two places: the boat hull and oar blades. It is now clear that when the oar is loaded and the boat is in motion, the oar rotates around a point. Once the oars are square and fixed, propelling the boat can be accomplished in a number of ways, some stable and efficient, others not. When this propulsion occurs, the athlete will move the entire weight of the system, equipment plus athlete, from one point to the next. Our objective is for that propulsion to occur systemically. That propulsion needs be efficient and effective, too: the minimum amount of effort for the greatest propulsive force.

With the oar blade fixed in the water, the oar and gate/pin relationship changes. The pin becomes the point where force is applied, driving the boat forward. In order for this to occur optimally, Group 3's role (the hands, arms and shoulders) is, essentially, to hang on and stay connected through the initial stages of the stroke. The Group 3 bones and muscles are not strong enough to contribute to propulsion in a meaningful way at the beginning of the stroke (or the end, for that matter). In fact, their participation may interfere with the leg drive because the system connection will be broken. At the beginning of the drive, the hands and arms remain straight and, through a shoulder girdle that is engaged at the catch, provide a strong stable connection to the rest of the system. With Group 3 connected properly, the drive from the legs is transmitted efficiently through the entire sculling system, driving the boat forward decisively.

Later in the drive when the body rocks back, the hands and arms remain straight, connected solidly through the shoulder girdle and continue to hang on. The connection between the boat, feet and blades is continuous.

As the body rocks back further and the leg drive continues, the athlete will notice a subtle change. The legs are fully extended, the body is back. And then, if arms remain extended, the connection with the water is broken. If the athlete is light or off the seat, as they should be, this broken connection is signalled by their falling to the seat before the stroke is completed. To preserve the connection, two technical actions must occur. The first is that the hips that should have been off the seat the entire way through the stroke need to be lifted to continue to stay off the seat, still driving the boat through the feet. The feeling should be one of standing up.

Second, the handles migrate towards the body to help maintain this connection. The athlete will 'hang' on the handles. The drive will be horizontal through the feet, preferably heels, while extending the body. (If the athlete pulls their arms, that connection will be broken early, the effective stroke length truncated and performance diminished.) The slack that occurs as the stroke ends needs to be regulated by Group 3, like shock absorbers

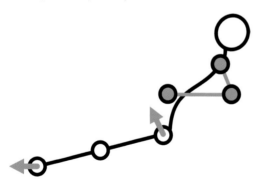

Fig. 33 The last stage of the stroke with the feet driving through the foot plate, the hips elevated slightly and light off the seat and the hands modulating the connection until the oars release (hanging off the handles).

in a car. The connection remains stable and solid by Group 3 modulation, bringing in the arms evenly to maintain blade connection. This allows a continued strong propulsion to be transmitted through the feet. When the oars reach their design limit, they will release naturally from the water. The athlete will come down into the seat. The stroke ends.

To facilitate this drive sequence, the boat and oars must be rigged properly. Chapter 3 has described the rigging for the hull to foot connection. This chapter investigates the oars themselves as well as how they are connected to the boat in relationship to the athlete.

RIGGING FOR PROPULSION

There are three fundamental dimensions to rigging for propulsion: technical theory, the athlete and equipment adjustments. Technical theory includes technique. Load and effort are asynchronous throughout the stroke. Technique will determine how load and effort change during the stroke; it will determine the priority and specifications of rigging.

For example, the dynamic technique is a front-end loaded technique. (The reference point for 'front end' is from the athlete's perspective. That is, looking sternward.) Theoretically, the dynamic technique recognizes that the leg muscles are the largest and most powerful. Using these muscles effectively early in the stroke will optimize propulsion. The athlete is placed forward in the boat. The dynamic technique intends to capitalize on the theoretical opportunities inherent in an ideal blade path. A front-end loaded technique can be further enhanced by the oars selected, particularly the oar length and blade type, resulting in more speed for less effort.

The next theoretical objective of the dynamic technique is to apply the athlete's effort throughout the entire stroke. That is, as opposed to a disproportionately large application of force at one point in the stroke, that

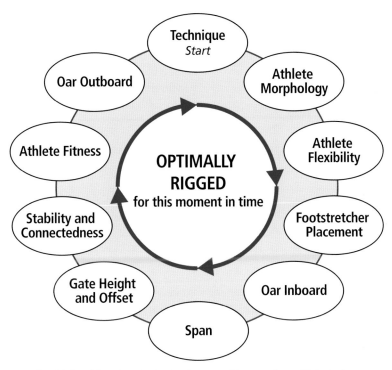

Fig. 34 Considerations in rigging for propulsion starting with technique.

force is delivered for the longest time possible and as continuously as possible during the stroke. This approach involves the use of the body mass smoothly during the stroke. One practical rigging consideration then becomes whether the heels connect with the shoes and footplate from the catch all the way to the end of release, while hanging off the handles. If they do, the athlete can drive the boat during the entire stroke.

The second dimension to rigging is the athlete whose infinite variability needs to be catered for in the rigging process. Athlete characteristics such as morphology, fitness, flexibility, experience, technique, injury history and sculling objectives are important considerations. While these characteristics differ amongst athletes, more importantly they differ within an athlete over time. An athlete whose fitness improves, who becomes more flexible, remediates a lingering injury, or changes their performance objectives needs to review their rigging.

The third dimension has to do with propulsion-related equipment adjustments. That is, how to rig the boat and oars in such a way that

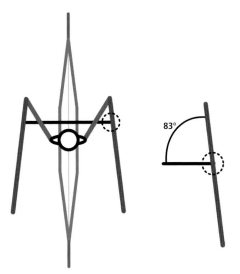

Fig. 35 Very steep catch angle example of 83 degrees.

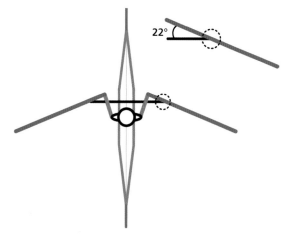

Fig. 36 Very shallow catch angle example of 22 degrees.

the potential for propulsion is optimized. The decisions are not static. Rigging at the beginning of the season, or a sculling career, will need changes along the way. Rigging adjustments can be interdependent. Moving the shoe plate height on the footstretcher usually results in a forward, or backward, footstretcher adjustment. Moving the rake has a similar result.

Thus rigging is an iterative process. It involves both art and science. Fig. 34 provides a range of considerations, presented roughly sequentially with regards to the propulsion rigging process. This sequential sequence starts with technique and proceeds clockwise, although jumps and backtracks are normal. A minimum annual review of each athlete's rigging is recommended.

THEORETICAL AND PRACTICAL OBJECTIVES

The theoretical objective is to achieve the best performance for the least effort. Practically, this is achieved through the optimal utilization of the equipment, with its limitations, coupled with the athlete and the athlete's limitations.

For example, the oar can rotate around the pin only as far as the athlete can hold onto the handle. Athletes with long arms have an advantage in one regard: they can rotate the oars further (Fig. 35). However, that athlete's limitation may be that with long arms come a long torso and long legs. It may take these athletes longer to complete the stroke. Or, their stroke may be so long that the slip and wash are quite large if the boat is not rigged properly.

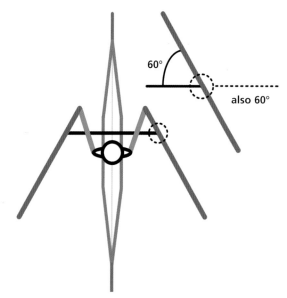

Fig. 37 Catch angle of nominal 60 degrees.

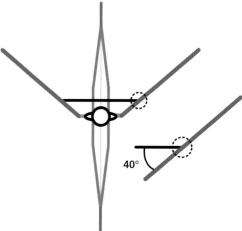

Fig. 38 Release angle of nominated 40 degrees.

This happens when oar blades cannot achieve the form drag for which they are designed because the angles of the blades are too acute.

Conversely, athletes with shorter arms may intially find their catch angle stroke is very shallow (Fig. 36).

Because of their design and the way they function, oars perform well within certain parameters. For example, in Fig. 35 with the 87-degree catch angle, the oars will not perform well. They will slip in the water until the form drag creates the desired resistance and the blade begins to rotate around a point. They will generate increased wash at the end of the stroke. In short, the 87-degree stroke arc is too long. In Fig. 36, the oars will perform well but the athlete will not achieve optimal propulsion because the catch angle is too shallow. The release angle will probably be shallow as well. For this athlete, the effective stroke arc is too short.

Why is the effective stroke arc important? Sculling is not about how long the oars are in the water; it is about how long the oars are in the water generating propulsion. The total stroke arc is the combined angle of the catch and release, and measures the arc when the oars are in the water. The *effective* stroke arc, however, is a function of how much slip and wash is introduced into the stroke. That is, the arc in degrees when the oars are in the water generating propulsion.

First, a description of how to calculate the total stroke arc. Fig. 37 shows a catch angle of 60 degrees. Compare that catch angle with 22- and 83-degree catch angles in the previous figures. At 60 degrees, the face of the oar blade enters the water at a point where it can quickly engage. While athletes with proportionately longer arms may be able to benefit from a slightly larger catch angle, for most athletes 60 degrees is a good place to start. (Later in this chapter a protocol and table will assist the athlete with determining their own catch angle.)

Next, a release angle of 40 degrees is nomi-nated. Again, this is a good starting point but

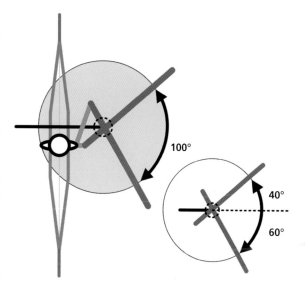

Fig. 39 Total stroke arc of 100 degrees catch angle (60 degrees) plus release angle (40 degrees).

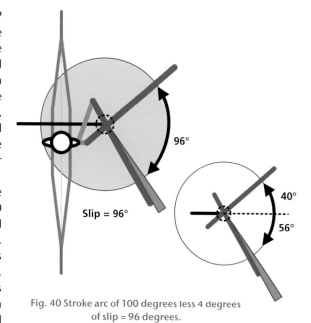

Fig. 40 Stroke arc of 100 degrees less 4 degrees of slip = 96 degrees.

completing all the rigging steps will define what each athlete's release angle is.

The stroke arc describes the degrees when the oars are in the water. The nominated

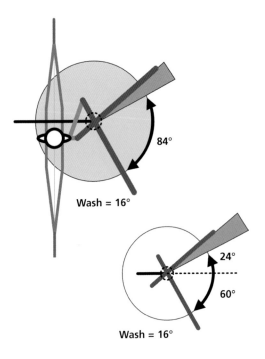

Wash = 16°

Wash = 16°

24°

56°

12°

40°

Fig. 41 Stroke arc of 100 degrees less 16 degrees of wash = 84 degrees.

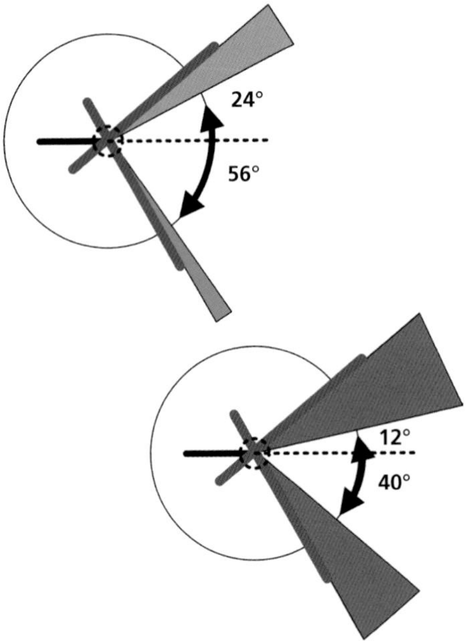

Fig. 42 Comparison of the results of lesser and greater slip and wash.

60-degree catch angle plus 40-degree release angle equals a stroke arc of 100 degrees (60 + 40 = 100).

The *effective* stroke arc is different. It describes the arc in degrees when the oars (and athlete) are generating propulsion. The effective stroke arc is a function of slip and wash. Ideally, slip and wash would each be zero degrees. In reality while the oar design may contribute a small amount of slip or wash, the predominant contributor is technique. For example, the design of some blades (smoothies) may cause them to slip more at the catch but provide a heavier load and slower handle speed during the last third of the drive. Other blades (Concept2 Fat2) slip less at the catch with a lighter load and faster handle speed during the last third of the stroke.[1] But how the athlete uses either of these oars will be the dominant factor in the total slip and wash in their stroke. Thus, the technical quest for slip and wash reduction is an important one.

Fig. 40 introduces a slip of 4 degrees into the stroke arc. This 4 degrees may be due to oar design, technique, or a combination of both. It is normal to have some slip. In this case, the slip has reduced the effective catch arc for the catch from 60 to 56 degrees (60 – 4 = 56) and the total stroke arc to 96 degrees (100 – 4 = 96).

Wash reductions are calculated in the same way. Fig. 41 displays the same 100-degree stroke arc with a wash of 24 degrees. The effective release stroke arc is calculated as total release arc less wash (40 – 16 = 24). The total stroke arc has also been reduced by 16 degrees of wash, resulting in a stroke arc of 84 degrees (100 – 16 = 84). It is not unusual for the degrees of wash to be greater than the degrees of slip, particularly if the technique is front-end loaded. However, for both slip and wash, less is preferred.

Fig. 42 provides a comparison of two identical stroke arcs, both 100 degrees. One exhibits the slip and wash described above (4 degrees slip; 16 degrees wash). The other example shows a different stroke (20 degrees slip; 28 degrees wash), which is not unusual for a new athlete or one with an inefficient technique. The comparison effective stroke lengths are 80 degrees (100 − 16 − 4 = 80) versus 52 degrees (100 − 20 − 28 = 52). Thus, even though the oars are in the water the same amount of time for both strokes, the propulsive result is significantly different. While rigging plays a role, the primary contributor to this difference is almost always technique.

All the angles discussed above (catch, release, slip and wash) can be measured using Nielsen-Kellerman's Empower Wireless Oarlock and other electronic measuring systems. Barring that, observation is helpful. Is the oar blade fixed in the water at the catch and the athlete able to rise totally off the seat at the initiation of the leg drive? Is the time between catch (blade placement) and leg drive initiation simultaneous or almost so? Are there splashes forward or backward on blade entry? Does the water form a vortex at the release of the blade and how much further does the blade travel after that vortex is released? Does the wake break at the catch or release? Most important, though, is does the athlete feel connected through the entire stroke? How long can that athlete stay light or off the seat?

RIGGING CONSIDERATIONS AND STEPS

The suggested order of rigging below is somewhat flexible. Certain steps require one or more predecessor steps to have been completed. Others do not. For example, determining the oar outboard rigging is a linked process that should be a function of the athlete's fitness as well as the inboard, as determined previously by the span, as determined previously by athlete morphology. Athlete morphology is a given.

The first time, the athlete should proceed through the steps in order. Fig. 34 starts with 'Technique' at the top and moves clockwise

through the rigging steps. Done properly, this will not happen in one day; it may take weeks. When future rigging opportunities appear, the wise athlete will complete a status review of the predecessor elements first.

Some initial rules of thumbs for rigging changes in both Chapters 3 and 4 are:

- One change at a time. Because the changes are interdependent, and because sometimes a change made needs to be modified or undone, it is more efficient to approach the process slowly and experiment with one change before moving on to the next. A nominal three on water trials to assess each change is recommended.
- Feet first, then hands. The foot connection is crucial to system stability. Start there (Chapter 3) before moving on.
- Incremental versus big changes. Depending on how well the athlete was rigged before, some of the proposed changes have the potential to be quite significant. For example, large changes in the placement of the footstretcher can result in the athlete's current oar rigging presenting difficulties. Big changes increase injury risk.
- Iteration. Small iterative changes should become part of each athlete's toolkit. As the athlete changes, the rigging will change, too. Assessing rigging on an ongoing basis, and exploring different options, is important.
- Each athlete is different. How that athlete feels about comfort, performance and what they expect to achieve is unique. Equipment is adjustable for that reason.

Technique

The first rigging consideration is technique. The dynamic technique is front-end loaded. The nominal catch angle is 60 degrees, with

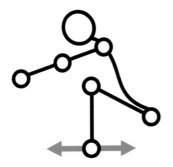

Fig. 43 The footstretcher can be moved forward and back with the athlete remaining in the same catch position (trunk on thighs, shoulder blades on torso, knees at or slightly below armpits and shins perpendicular).

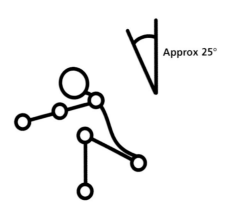

Fig. 44 Catch position with a nominal 25 degrees of pelvic rock.

recovered closer to mid-stroke when the shaft straightens out. Wash of 15 degrees or less is encouraged and a function of the drive being smoothly executed and the boat being driven through the feet horizontally until the oars reach their design limit and release.

Athlete morphology

Athlete morphology describes the physical characteristics of the athlete, primarily in terms of their shape and structure. Morphology is a given, with the understanding that adults shrink with age, athletes generally shrinking less. Two athletes that are 161.8cm tall and weigh 71.1kg, the average-sized woman in Australia, are probably built very differently. One may have a very short torso, long legs and long arms. The other may have a very long torso, shorts legs and short arms. Because of their morphology, each athlete's rigging will be different.

Athlete flexibility

Athlete flexibility in this specific instance describes his or her ability to assume the catch position. The broader aspects of flexibility, mobility and balance will be explored as part of each athlete's assessment in Chapter 7. An athlete who is not flexible in the pelvic area, hamstrings, knees or ankles is going to be limited. If the limitation is due to injury, the rigging objective will be to achieve the best compromise while maintaining comfort. If the limitation is reversible through stretching, mobility and balance training, the rigging objective will be the same in the short term, understanding that said rigging will need to be revisited as the athlete's flexibility improves.

Flexibility is important in injury prevention. Athletes who are 'tight' are prone to make technical and positioning leaps in the boat that increase their injury risk, overextending at

the understanding that some athletes may morphologically be able to achieve a greater angle comfortably. The nominal release angle is 40 degrees, with little or no performance advantage in the dynamic technique for a release angle much greater than that.

For a 100-degree stroke arc, experienced athletes are encouraged to achieve an 80-degree effective stroke arc or more. Slip degrees of 4 or less are the objective at the pre-elite level. Observation has shown that the soft shafts on oars, which are well-considered for Masters, tend to introduce a small degree of slip at the catch. However, that energy is

the catch being a common culprit. Flexibility is important in performance. An athlete with a limited effective stroke arc is going to need to produce more effort to compensate for that shortness. It is better in the early stages to rig the boat for the athlete's current level of flexibility, understanding there are flexibility, mobility and balance improvement opportunities. Capitalizing on these opportunities will take time, recommending once again a continued review of an athlete's rigging.

Footstretcher placement

The first rigging task is to achieve the optimal catch position. Optimal means that position that can be achieved with the best foot to hull rigging connection. Critically, it means not overextending at the catch (or lifting the heels more than 1cm off the footplate – a finger width). The arms should reach forward while the shoulder blades remain engaged on the torso. The athlete's trunk should be on their thighs. The spine should be aligned as shown in Fig. 44 with the natural concave lumbar region preserved.

The degree of forward rock differs based on athlete morphology and flexibility. An alignment of approximately 25 degrees is the preferred nominal starting point. The issue is ensuring that the shoulder blades are engaged

and that the rest of the biomechanical alignment for the athlete are catered for first (perpendicular shins, knees at or under armpits and comfortable).

Fig. 45 shows a common issue in taking catch angle measurements (and under way) where an athlete may, in the quest to get a larger catch angle, tend to pull their seat under them at the front end. Proprioceptively, the athlete feels as though they are going further forward because the seat truly *is* going further up the slide. However, this action creates a backward rotation on the pelvis, cantilevers the body upwards and takes the hands further back. The backward rotation of the pelvis puts the lower back in a position of taking up too much load too early in the stroke. Ensure the athlete is in the correct, and same, position when taking the catch angle measurements and making adjustments.

The first rigging objective is a 60-degree catch angle with the best catch position the athlete can achieve, using the oars and oar rigging (inboard and outboard) the athlete currently uses. Refer to the *Measuring the catch angle* text box for the protocol to obtain the athlete's current catch angle. Because the athlete's foot to hull rigging has been set, the footstretcher can be moved forward and backward along the tracks with the athlete maintaining the same physical trunk-on-thigh alignment shown in Fig. 44. If the catch

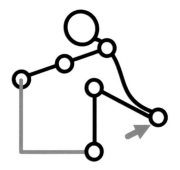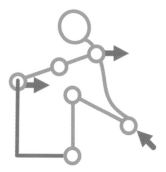

Fig. 45 Forcing the hands forward frequently leads to the athlete cantilevering upwards, rotating back on the pelvis, raising the torso, with the catch angle reduced.

Measuring the catch angle

The athlete and an assistant first measure the span (distance from centre pin to centre pin). Check and verify no lateral pitch has been introduced by measuring the distance both from the bottom and top centre of the pins. The athlete should then warm up for at least five minutes on the water, using their current rigging, oars and equipment. Flexibility will improve with the warm-up, allowing for a more accurate catch angle measurement.

Fig. 46 Measuring the distance between handle grips at the catch to determine catch angle.

With an assistant straddling and holding onto the boat, the athlete comes to the catch position from mid-drive or release. The athlete and assistant should ensure that overextension does not occur, shoulder blades are on the back and the spine is correctly aligned (no slumping). Blades can be flat on the water for increased stability.

The assistant measures the distance between the centres of the handle grips. The athlete repeats the stroke several times, with the assistant measuring. The objective is, through a relaxed, fluid stroke, an accurate measurement of the distance between the handles.

Table 12 provides the catch angle for a particular span, inboard and handle measure.

angle is less than 60 degrees, try moving the footstretcher forward.

The next consideration is the release angle. In the dynamic technique and because the athlete is driving the boat through their heels until the oars release, the nominal release angle is 40 degrees, as shown in Fig. 38. The position of the body is 25 degrees behind vertical. That is, approximately the same body rock forward and backward. While it is possible to do trigonometric calculations for the release angle, it is less helpful to do so. This is because the accurate placement of athlete's body at release is a function of when the oars themselves release. How to determine this is described in Chapter 6.

The larger question is: has the footstretcher been moved so much that the inboards on the handles are no longer functional? For those athletes for whom the footstretcher placement and inboards are optimal, it is time to explore how that new rigging feels on the water. For other athletes, let's discuss the inboards.

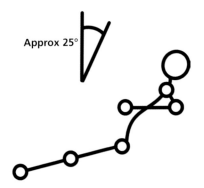

Fig. 47 Release angle with a nominal 25 degrees of pelvic rock.

Inboard (cm)	Catch Angle (degrees)	Distance Between Grips (cm)				
		161cm Span	160cm Span	159cm Span	158cm Span	157cm Span
86.5–87.5	70	101	100	99	98	97
86.5–87.5	67.5	95	94	93	92	91
86.5–87.5	65	87	86	85	84	83
86.5–87.5	62.5	81	80	79	78	77
86.5–87.5	60	75	74	73	72	71
86.5–87.5	57.5	67	66	65	64	63
86.5–87.5	55	61	60	59	58	57
86.5–87.5	52.5	55	54	53	52	51
86.5–87.5	50	49	48	47	46	45

Inboard (cm)	Catch Angle (degrees)	Distance Between Grips (cm)				
		161cm Span	160cm Span	159cm Span	158cm Span	157cm Span
87.5–88.5	70	101	100	99	98	97
87.5–88.5	67.5	95	94	93	92	91
87.5–88.5	65	87	86	85	84	83
87.5–88.5	62.5	81	80	79	78	77
87.5–88.5	60	73	72	71	70	69
87.5–88.5	57.5	67	66	65	64	63
87.5–88.5	55	61	60	59	58	57
87.5–88.5	52.5	55	54	53	52	51
87.5–88.5	50	47	46	45	44	43

Inboard (cm)	Catch Angle (degrees)	Distance Between Grips (cm)				
		161cm Span	160cm Span	159cm Span	158cm Span	157cm Span
88.5–90.5	70	101	100	99	98	97
88.5–90.5	67.5	93	92	91	90	89
88.5–90.5	65	85	84	83	82	81
88.5–90.5	62.5	79	78	77	76	75
88.5–90.5	60	73	72	71	70	69
88.5–90.5	57.5	65	64	63	62	61
88.5–90.5	55	59	58	57	56	55
88.5–90.5	52.5	53	52	51	50	49
88.5–90.5	50	47	46	45	44	43

Table 12 Measuring the catch angle from the distance between grips (cm) at the catch position.

Oar inboard

Inboard lengths that worked before may now be too long or too short. The inboard of the oar should be sufficient to allow for, nominally, a 40-degree release angle as well as a 60-degree catch angle. Since the rigging has been set from the front end, the limiter may be the release angle because the athlete's body may restrict the handle motion. Or the athlete may discover too much room.

The first consideration is to ensure the athlete is rocking back sufficiently on his or her pelvis to achieve the nominal 25-degree pelvic rock. At the 25-degree release, the oar handles should be about one hand width apart when approximately a fist width from the body. This distance prevents clothes from getting caught in the thumbs. The objective is to be able to rock back and forth, +/- 25 degrees or so, feeling comfortable and unrestricted. The inboard can be shortened or lengthened as needed to achieve this.

The longer the inboard is in proportion to the outboard, the less effort will be required from the athlete. So, a longer inboard is desirable. However, a shorter inboard may allow the athlete to move the footstretcher forward

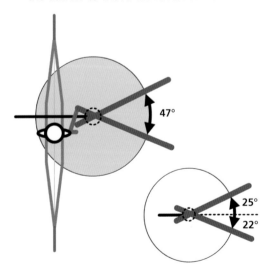

Fig. 48 Shallow catch angle of 22 degrees and stroke arc of 47 degrees.

and gain more degrees of catch angle. The outboard will then need to be reduced proportionately as discussed below. In addition, some athletes are more comfortable with less handle room at the release, others prefer more.

General rules for inboards are:

- A reduction in inboard length will result in approximately a two to three times proportional increase in reach at the catch, meaning small changes in the inboard will generate larger changes at the front end because the footstretcher can be moved forward.
- Inboards of 85cm to 88cm are not unusual for the average Masters sculler.
- After adjusting the inboard and footstretcher as needed, and if the rigging at the moment is optimal, it is time for a trial. If suboptimal, read on.

Span

For other athletes, the footstretcher placement and inboard adjustment sections above may not yield the desired (approximately 60/40 degree) result. This is common and not a cause for concern. Here is what is most likely happening: athlete morphology and flexibility.

An athlete with shorter arms, a shorter torso and/or legs or flexibility limitations may find they are restricted in both their catch and release angles, or the boat is rigged for the largest people in the club. Fig. 48 shows the same boat as in Fig. 39 but with a more diminutive morphology, including shorter arms. Fig. 48 is an extreme example to facilitate discussion.

To increase the catch angle for this athlete, the span – the distance between the pins – needs to be reduced. Refer to Fig. 49. The span has been reduced to allow the athlete to come further forward. By reducing the span for this athlete, the preferred 60-degree catch angle can be achieved.

The opposite is true for athletes with long arms, torso and/or legs, or for athletes with

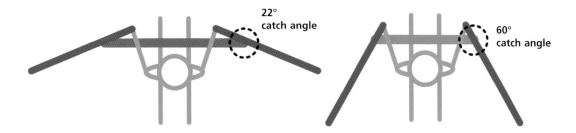

Fig. 49 Example of how reducing the span increases the catch angle to 60 degrees.

boats rigged for the smallest person in the club. Fig. 50 is also an extreme example.

In this case to achieve a 60-degree catch angle, the span is made wider – the distance between the pins increases. In this circumstance, a catch angle of greater than 60 degrees may be possible if the athlete is taller than average. The determining factor is the athlete's catch position in the boat. If the athlete can comfortably achieve a catch angle greater than 60 degrees, while still retaining a release angle of approximately 40 degrees, then the span can be adjusted to take advantage of that opportunity. However, the degree of pelvic rock should be similar, forward and backward.

One of the advantages to smaller, incremental span changes is that the athlete can use their same oar rigging in the initial stages. However, if the changes are large, or the oars were not rigged properly for the athlete in the first place, the inboard may need to be adjusted – yet again.

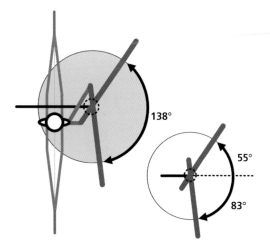

Fig. 50 Long catch angle of 83 degrees and stroke arc of 138 degrees.

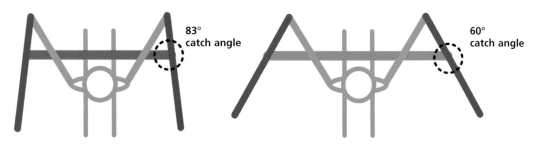

Fig. 51 Example of how increasing the span achieves a 60 degree catch angle.

General rules of thumb for span changes:

- Don't shy away from making span changes. Span changes are simple to make and undo. They can improve performance.
- Try small, incremental span changes as opposed to one large change. Row at least three times to assess the result.
- Coloured tape on the rigger to denote the original (or new) pin position is helpful.
- Ensure that the pins are equidistant from the centreline of the boat, more easily measured from the seat rails. As long as the pins are both equidistant from the centreline, even if the distance between pins is, say, 158.1 instead of the objective of 158, that will suffice.
- Reduced span may initially feel less stable; increased span may feel more stable. This is because the oars take up less/more space laterally from the hull and the stability of the sculling system is indeed changed. But not much.
- Spans of 158 to 159 are very normal for the average Masters sculler, men and women. A span of 156–158 would not be unusual.

Gate height and offset

Because changing the span involves loosening the pins, this is an ideal time to do a gate height adjustment. (This is also a good time to look for wear on the gates and bushings, replacing both together if either is worn.) Gate height should allow the forearms to be parallel to the water at release (Fig. 33) with shoulders relaxed, shoulder blades on torso and chest open. That being said, gates and oars that are slightly lower tend to be hydrodynamically more efficient. Gates that are higher are required in bad weather and, sometimes, for wider blades. Thus, the athlete should be comfortable with different gate heights and use the correct one for the conditions and equipment.

Oar offset is a thorny topic. The putative reason for oars to be offset (one gate higher than the other) is so that the hand crossover during the stroke minimizes boat roll. With this end in mind, many boat manufacturers build a misalignment into their riggers such that one side of the rigger is higher than the other. Some do not, though, so measuring is required.

Which gate is higher is technically irrelevant. Whole nations scull with right hands over left, others with left over right. One argument is that because most athletes are right handed, a right hand over left rigging benefits from this dominance. Especially in a 1X, the athlete should explore which provides the best result for them.

What is rarely discussed is equal offset. The argument for equal gate height is that while the boat is more prone to roll at the hand crossover, the athlete can execute a catch and release with hands aligned at the same height. More important, the oars will behave similarly at the crucial catch and release positions. As athletes become more proficient, it is usual for their gate offset to reduce.

Gates that are offset will cause the oars to behave differently from one another, particularly at the catch and release unless the athlete adjusts their hand height to compensate. Meaning, the shoulder arms and shoulders will need to be aligned differently. This may introduce yaw, which creates greater drag than roll.

Each athlete should explore what offset allows them to execute the stroke consistently well. Some scullers may prefer a larger offset to differentiate hand height during the stroke. Others might want to explore small/no offset or reverse hand offsets.

Stability and connectedness

The sculler's feeling of security in the boat is usually a direct reflection of system stability. Stability is a function of connectedness, which describes the unification of the athlete, boat and oars into a sculling system. When a sculler is connected through the stroke, the boat and oars are stable. When a sculler becomes disconnected during a stroke, the boat wobbles, the oars waggle and stability decreases. Connectedness includes an element of propulsion, with a well-connected athlete generating more of it.

Rigging can assist with stability, connectedness and propulsion. For example, longer oars and a larger span will take on a larger space, like the ocean-going barge, increasing stability. When a new sculler is learning the art of connection, longer oars and a larger span may help. Athletes who are connected can benefit from rigging that optimizes their performance, such as shorter oars. Rigging changes, even small ones, can initially contribute to instability. This instability is almost always a function of the athlete learning new connections. That's why data, multiple tries and an open mind are needed.

Athlete fitness

Athlete aerobic fitness is the key determinant of propulsive capacity. Muscular fitness, flexibility and strength play roles, too. A primary objective through rigging is to allow the athlete to optimize their propulsive capacity. For those who compete, this means lasting the whole race with a quality stroke throughout. Rigging is a trade-off. A sculling system that is not rigged properly will take more athletic effort and go slower than one that is rigged properly. The critical question is: how fit is the athlete and what rigging will allow that athlete to achieve the maximum speed for their available capacity? These will change throughout the training season and the decades of their athletic career. Thus, experimenting with rigging should be an ongoing tool, particularly for competitive athletes. Oar outboards are a good place to start that experimentation.

Oar outboard

Oars are levers. They behave differently when lightly loaded versus heavily loaded. They behave differently at different times during the stroke, for example during slip and wash versus propulsion. The athlete has the ability to manipulate how oars behave through technique, with some stroke techniques undermining propulsion and others enhancing it. Thus, how to rig an athlete's oars is a function of a number of factors: how oars behave under light and heavy loads, the technique the athlete is using and the athlete's physical capacity.

Oars as levers

Lightly loaded, the oar acts as a Class 1 level. It's the same as a teeter-totter or seesaw: push down, the load goes up. Heavily loaded, the oar acts as a Class 2 lever. It's the same as a wheelbarrow: pull up, the load goes up.

Oar rigging decisions are about loads. Let's confirm what is happening during the lightly

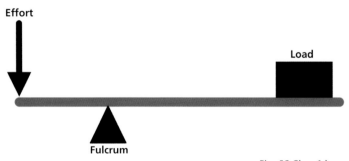

Fig. 52 Class 1 lever.

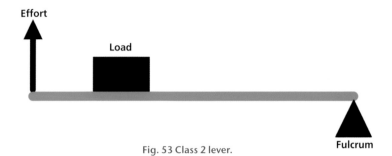

Fig. 53 Class 2 lever.

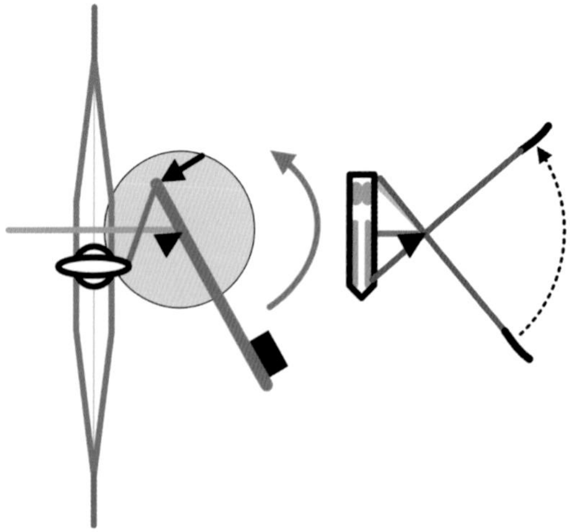

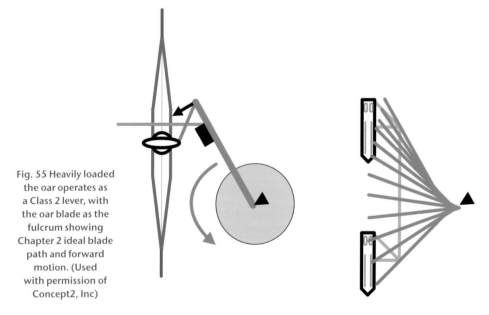

Fig. 54 Lightly loaded the oar acts as a Class 1 lever.

loaded and heavily loaded sculling stroke. The determinant for this is whether the load is sufficient to create form drag on the blade.

Sitting in the boat, the athlete can move the oar lightly and slowly with one or two fingers through its entire arc with the boat not moving much. Instead, the blade is moving water and generating little or no propulsion. In this case, the lightly loaded oar acts as a Class 1 lever. The same is true during slip or wash.

When the oar load is sufficient to create maximum form drag, the blade rotates along a virtual point. This oar acts as a Class 2 lever with the fulcrum at the blade. The load is at the gate where the athlete's effort drives the load (equipment + athlete) forward. (The Class 2

Fig. 55 Heavily loaded the oar operates as a Class 2 lever, with the oar blade as the fulcrum showing Chapter 2 ideal blade path and forward motion. (Used with permission of Concept2, Inc)

lever in Fig. 55 has been flipped for illustration purposes but operates in the same way.)

For the purposes of moving the boat forward, the Class 2 lever is superior to the Class 1 lever. The objective for the dynamic technique is: Class 2 lever through as much of the stroke as possible, limiting slip and wash, to gain the most efficient propulsion.

Oar outboard rigging

Where the load is located in relationship to the fulcrum is important. For the Class 1 lever and the same effort, moving the fulcrum further from the load makes it harder to move the load. Moving the fulcrum closer to the load makes it easier to shift.

So why not move the fulcrum as close to the load as possible? The practical answer for sculling is: the limitations of the equipment and the athlete. The gate is fixed with only very small adjustments possible (span). The inboard at this point in the rigging process is fixed with the inboard set to allow the athlete to achieve the desired catch angle. Thus, the only adjustment remaining is to shorten or lengthen the outboard.

Imagine Fig. 57 is operating as a Class 1 lever. Lengthening the outboard moves the blade (load) further from the gate (fulcrum). This requires more effort to move the load than for a shorter outboard.

The same holds true for a Class 2 lever. Moving the load closer to the fulcrum increases the mechanical advantage (makes it easier). In our Class 2 oar, this means shortening the outboard to gain a mechanical advantage.

Shorter oars are more efficient. In an article of the same name in the *Journal of Biomechanics*, Volker Nolte describes the evolution of oars and the biomechanical advantages of shorter oars.[2] The original theory, now disproved, was that longer oars would allow the blade to travel in the water and create larger blade forces. As we now know, the blade is not moving through the water unless it is operating as a Class 1 lever, the most inefficient use. For peak propulsion, the blades are rotating around a point and moving the load at the gate. This 'load moving' translates into propulsion, recommending shorter oars.

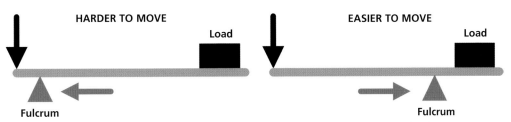

Fig. 56 Effort changes as the fulcrum is moved closer to or further from the load.

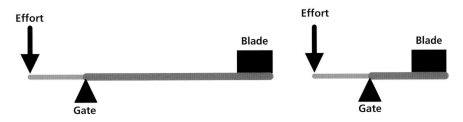

Fig. 57 Because the gate position and inboard are relatively fixed, a way to change the effort required to move a load is to shorten or lengthen the oar outboard.

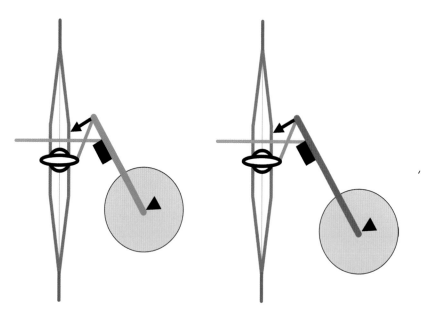

Fig. 58 Shorter oars have a greater mechanical advantage.

Blade development has seen increases in blade area to accompany shorter oars, as in the evolution from macon blades to smoothie blades. Concept2 has explored shorter oars with their Fat2 blades, which have a greater blade area to capitalize on the ideal blade path opportunities discussed in Chapter 2. To accommodate this larger blade area, a total oar length for Fat2 blades is a recommended 4–8cm shorter than their Smoothie2 Plan Edge.

How short?

This question has yet to be answered conclusively. Following the logical argument of lever loading, the extreme result would be a specific inboard (say 87cm) and a total oar length as close to the boat as possible with the blade remaining in the water. The problem is: stability.

Longer oars provide stability. Remember the ocean-going barge? The wider the boat, the more stable. Oars as pontoons and extensions of the sculling system act in the same way. Thus, total oar length is a trade-off

between stability and performance. A general guide is newer scullers may prefer longer oars. However, the more connected an athlete is with the sculling system, the shorter their outboards can be. More speed and/or less effort.

In keeping with the 'small incremental changes' and 'one change at a time' theme, the first task in outboard rigging is to determine whether the inboard has been changed due to the previous rigging sections. If so, it is important to rig the oars so that they provide the same load for the athlete. To do this a simple ratio is followed: length of the outboard divided by length of the inboard.

Say the athlete's original outboard was 200cm and their inboard was 88cm for a total oar length of 288cm. Our athlete has reduced the span and now finds that an 87cm inboard is comfortable. What should the new outboard be to retain the same effort required to move the same load?

The original oar gearing ratio is 200/88 = 2.273. Multiplying that ratio by the new 87 inboard (87 × 2.273) = 197.7. This is the new outboard required to retain the same gearing (Table 13).

	Outboard (cm)	Inboard (cm)	Oar length (cm)	Gearing ratio
Old oar rigging	200.0	88.0	288.0	2.273
New oar rigging	197.7	87.0	284.7	2.273

Table 13 The new outboard and oar length to achieve the same gearing after reducing the inboard distance.

	Outboard (cm)	Inboard (cm)	Oar length (cm)	Gearing ratio
Old oar rigging	199.0	87.0	286.0	2.287
New oar rigging	198.0	87.0	285.0	2.276

Table 14 The change in gearing ratio for a reduction in outboard, retaining the same inboard.

If an athlete decides to experiment with shortening the current oar length, the calculation is similar but this time, assuming the other rigging is optimal, the inboard remains the same. This athlete has decided to shorten the outboard from 199 to 198, achieving a total oar length of 285 and a gearing that is less than before. This change will affect stability and performance, but to a degree than can be easily accommodated by a connected athlete.

Words of caution are in order here: gearing ratios do not provide valid results across dissimilar oar manufacturers and oar types. The gearing ratio is relative and applies to a particular oar, with the sole exception being two oars that are identical in every way. The gearing ratio is not an absolute measure and invalid for comparisons. For example, Concept2 Fat2 blades are used with considerably shorter oar lengths, by 4–8cm, and gearing comparisons with longer-shafted smoothie oars will be invalid.

After an athlete has validated the previous rigging changes, experimentation with shorter outboards can be conducted, advisably starting with a one centimetre reduction in outboard. Athletes who scull with smoothie blades and who are having success with shorter outboards are encouraged to try Concept2 Fat2 blades, which provide a larger blade area, allow for an even shorter oar and give performance opportunities.

OTHER CONSIDERATIONS

Comfort and injury prevention

The human body has an amazing capacity to protect itself. Thus, body messages communicating tightness, joint stress, or discomfort are important. Pain is a red flag to stop or undo. Rigging changes put stress on new parts of the body, a good reason for not making precipitous, large changes. The older an athlete, the more inflexible soft tissue becomes. Thus, more time should be given to adjusting to changes, and the smaller those incremental changes should be.

The human body also has an amazing capacity to resist change. Thus, brain messages communicating dislike, resistance and opposition are important, too. At least three tries (and an open mind) with anything new is recommended, preferably focusing on measurable results.

Slide placement

The slides should be positioned so that the athlete can execute a complete stroke unimpeded. However, the slides can be used as a proprioceptive cue to address the problem of athletes who continue too far up the slide and cantilever their bodies back (Fig. 45). Adjusting the slides so that the athlete must stop at a certain position is a clever way to provide cuing and facilitate undoing the habit.

Optimal rigging, for this moment in time

Chapters 3 and 4 have referred to 60-degree catch angle, 40-degree release angle, shins perpendicular, knees at or slightly below armpits, +/- 25-degree body rock and other objectives. These are guidelines, not requirements, and need to be explored for each sculler. Many scullers can't, at this moment in time, achieve them. Old injuries, stiff joints, personal preferences to have less catch angle or longer oars (and more stability), as well as a host of other factors may intervene. This is not a cause for concern.

The objective here is to rig the equipment optimally for each athlete, today. An athlete cannot rig their way to greatness. Aerobic fitness, flexibility, strength, training, recovery strategies and technique are far more important.

SUMMARY: THE SCULLING SYSTEM – PROPULSION

Comfort, stability and connectedness are the initial steps to achieving optimal propulsion. At this point in time the athlete has achieved the best partnership by rigging the boat and oars to suit. Rigging is an evolutionary process. As the athlete changes, the rigging will change, too. Now it is time to explore how to actually move the sculling system forward.

Endnotes

1   Concept2, Inc. *Blades Overview and Loading Profile*. www.concept2.com/oars/oar-options/blades.
2   Nolte, V., 'Shorter oars are more effective', *J. Appl Biomech*. 2009 Feb; 25(1): pp.1–8. PubMed PMID: 19299825.

5 DYNAMIC TECHNIQUE: PRE-DRIVE SEQUENCE

The dynamic technique is so named because the pre-drive sequence, from release to pre-catch, is dynamic – as is the front-end transition. The actively connected sculler works *with* the boat to gain acceleration and speed prior to the catch, comparable to a running start. Stability is improved through this connectedness and dynamism, setting up the catch and drive to be more consistent. The legs are used in a pull in, push out cycle that transitions the athlete from pre-drive to drive in a continuous, smooth, fluid motion. The elasticity of the large leg muscles is recruited, adding power. Done properly, the boat velocity is increased prior to the catch. The resulting fluidity of the motion requires less effort from the athlete, while achieving more speed.

To begin exploring the dynamic technique, the first step is to define its terms and reference points. The stroke sequence steps, which are naturally continuous and fluid, have unique characteristics and are broken down for the purpose of analysis. The concepts in previous chapters, such as stability, connectedness and fluidity are integral to the functioning stroke. These concepts are described from the perspective of how the sculling system can respond, particularly when the sequence timing is precise. The outcomes of each sequence element and key points offer the answer to the 'why' of each sequence step. Finally, a 'try this' experiment or two are available for the sculler to explore and determine for themselves how this technique might apply to them.

FUNDAMENTAL CONCEPTS

This section introduces a common language and terminology. It explores the use of hands and arms during the stroke, including the finger roll, because these need to occur competently, lightly and automatically in order for the sequence steps to be successful.

Terminology

The dynamic stroke has two major components describing directionality: pre-drive and drive. The viewpoint for both is from the perspective of the sculler, seated in the boat. The pre-drive describes the stroke sequences from release to pre-catch (Fig. 59). The drive sequence includes catch to pre-release (Fig. 60). Together these two directional components encompass the entire stroke.

73

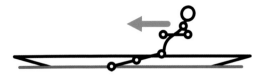

Fig. 59 The pre-drive sequence begins at the release and ends at the pre-catch position.

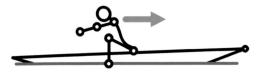

Fig. 60 The drive sequence begins at the catch and ends at the pre-release position.

The dynamic stroke has two major components describing transition: front-end transition and back-end transition (Figs 61 and 62). The front-end transition includes the sequence steps immediately before and after it. The same for the back-end transition. The execution of those changes in direction, the application and release of power through the oars (catch and release) and the timing make these transitions extremely important in achieving optimal propulsion. Their complexity makes transitions challenging to execute.

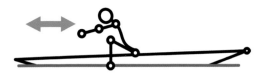

Fig. 61 The front-end transition involves changing direction in a way that optimizes speed from the front end.

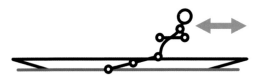

Fig. 62 The back-end transition involves changing direction in a way that optimizes speed from the back end.

The individual dynamic technique sequence steps are:

- Pre-drive
  - Release
  - Body flip
  - Hand launch
  - Pre-drive transition
  - Boat gathering
  - Pre-catch
- Front-end transition, including: boat gathering, pre-catch, catch and initiate leg drive
- Drive
  - Catch
  - Initiate leg drive
  - Initiate body
  - Early mid-drive
  - Mid-drive transition
  - Pre-release
- Back-end transition, including: pre-release, release and body flip

Stability, connectedness and fluidity

The boat and oars are inherently stable, the athlete is not. In order to operate optimally, the sculling system needs to be stable. For the purposes of this chapter and discussing the dynamic technique, stability is defined as: all the components of the sculling system being where they should be at that specific point in time in the sequence, particularly in relationship to gravity. Indications that the system is not stable are that it is pitched, rolled or yawed; that it wobbles; or is capsized.

Stability is achieved through connection, primarily through the feet-to-hull connection and the hand-to-oar connection, assuming that the athlete, between the feet and hands, is also connected internally through the appropriate muscles and joints. The athlete being internally connected from feet to hands is a significant technique step. It means the sculler is connected with the equipment throughout the entire stroke, resulting in a stable sculling system.

Being efficient in achieving stability requires the sculler to develop connectedness through the correct muscles, activating those that need to be engaged while relaxing those that do not. Learning this oppositional activation and relaxation, while staying connected through the active muscles for each particular moment in the sequence, is important for performance. An athlete that develops this muscular awareness uses less oxygen, experiences less muscle fatigue and has the opportunity to optimize the application of power.

Fluidity begins to describe the art of sculling where the stroke becomes a continuous, purposeful, almost effortless-looking endeavour that is a combination of stability, connectedness and the equipment working at its peak design. Fluidity achieves the highest level of efficiency, both from the athlete and equipment.

The position of hands and arms

Without the appropriate hand mechanics and hand/forearm alignment, it will be difficult to achieve a consistent stroke. The front-end transition, including the catch, is quick for the dynamic technique. Hand mechanics and hand/forearm alignment require a particular focus to ensure the front-end transition is smooth.

While the feet are connected snuggly to the boat through shoes, the hands and arms are not. Thus, many variations on how to use the hands and arms can creep into a sculler's technique and suboptimize the equipment, the athlete and the system as a whole. For the dynamic technique, the position of the hands and arms is crucial (as is the position of the shoulder blades, nestled on the torso). The guidelines for hands and arms are as follows:

- The wrists should be flat, always, and in a straight line with the forearms. Wrists cocked at the catch destabilize the catch. Wrists cocked at the release destabilize the release.
- At the catch, the articulation for the hands comes from the shoulders. The arms remain straight, as do wrists, and the entire arm group pivots around the shoulder joint.
- At the release, the articulation of the hands comes from the shoulders and elbows. The wrists and forearms are flat with the pivot occurring at elbow and shoulder.
- Flat wrists and forearms, as well as shoulder blades on the torso, allow the chest to maintain its maximum capacity throughout the stroke. Cocked wrists and dropped forearms tend to pull the shoulders forward, collapse the chest and reduce lung capacity.
- Flat wrists and forearms tend to maintain a strong connection with the oars and water. Cocked wrists and misalignment tend to break that connection, affecting the transmission of power and speed. Boat direction often changes as a result.
- The athlete's grip on the oars should be light, always. Thick calluses and blisters on the hands indicate the athlete may be holding the oars too tightly. A lighter touch allows the oars to perform their design function, particularly in bad weather where a lightly held oar will naturally square at the catch and release cleanly.

Feathering, squaring and the finger roll

A well-executed finger roll is crucial to the dynamic technique because the front-end transition is quick. The recommended approach is to square at the pre-catch in one smooth motion, timing the blade entry perfectly with the reversal in direction. More about this later, but without a well-developed finger roll, the catch will always be uncertain.

The best way to develop a finger roll is outside of the boat in a concerted effort to acquire what is a fairly challenging skill. Using a spare handle or a similarly sized tube, the wrists remain flat and in line with the forearms and the fingers move in and out. The spare handle is nestled lightly in the curled fingers, as it should be when sculling. The articulation is through the knuckles on the hand. The thumb helps maintain a gentle outwards pressure and assists with the roll. Thus, the thumb is not placed over the centre of the oar handle but, rather, slightly down from it on the perimeter and contributes actively to the rolling process. Success comes when the athlete can roll the spare handle in and out fluidly, with the palm and oar handle facing downward and with a light finger/thumb grip.

Transferring the above skill to the boat requires only a few adjustments. The equipment is designed to assist with feathering because the mass of the oar requires a bit more energy to initiate the roll. However, the collar on the oar is rounded and flat so that once the feathering is initiated, the oar tends to roll naturally and stop when the flat collar meets the flat gate bottom. It is important to apply that energy only at the beginning so as not to tire out the hands and fingers that, with their small muscles, fatigue easily.

Feathering and the finger roll begin in two sequence positions: pre-catch and pre-release. At each of these positions the oars are in a different alignment with the fingers, hands,

Fig. 63 Position of the hand with oars feathered, hand and wrist flat, first finger joints up.

Fig. 64 Position of the hand after blade squaring, hand and wrists flat, knuckles up.

Fig. 65 Thumbs on perimeter to aid rolling and hands loose.

arms, wrists, upper arms and shoulders. It is important to practise finger rolls at both the extended arm position (at the catch) and retracted arm position (at the release). That is, practising what is actually going to happen (the Principle of Specificity, about which more in Chapter 8).

For athletes who have finger roll and feathering habits that they would like to change, this is an opportunity that will pay big dividends. It will take time. Start as above with the spare handle at home. But also in the boat, do small work. The athlete sits in the boat and rolls just one oar while looking at their hand to ensure the desired result. Alternate with the other hand. Practise at the release. Practise at the catch. All athletes should build finger rolling exercises into their workout, frequently but in small amounts, as the old habit is replaced with the new one. The change in connectedness and stability, and reduction in blisters and hand/forearm cramps, will provide an excellent incentive for change.

THE BIOMECHANICS OF THE DYNAMIC TECHNIQUE

The best way to explain the advantages of the dynamic technique is two simple exercises: the stand-up and the jump.

The stand-up exercise involves an athlete bending over at the waist, extending the arms as they would going to the catch and slowly compressing the body and legs until the hands reach the floor. The athlete then reverses this process. Next, the athlete does the stand-up several times, fluidly.

The important things to notice are:

- The leg muscles engage throughout. They are never totally disengaged. However, different leg muscles engage at different times. The muscles at the front of the leg, including the quadriceps, are working closer to the ground, transitioning to the muscles in the back of the legs (hamstrings, calf and glutes) as the athlete completes the 'stand-up'.
- The core muscles engage when the leg muscles engage.
- Standing up is a very natural action with the legs pushing first, the torso unfolding and the hips coming forward.
- The process of bending down and standing up are smooth.
- The arms and hands play only a tiny role.
- Weight is continuously through the feet.

Properly executed, the dynamic technique mirrors the stand-up exercise in terms of the sequencing and muscle use. That is, execution of the stroke will feel like standing up.

The jump exercise explores the biomechanical advantages of elasticity. The athlete does the stand-up exercise but stops when fully bent over. The athlete then jumps as high as possible. It is helpful to do this next to a wall with a piece of chalk. Next, the athlete goes through the whole stand-up sequence fluidly, not stopping at the bottom but jumping smoothly. The added elasticity of the muscles will add extra height.

Properly executed, the dynamic technique capitalizes on this natural muscle and joint elasticity to add power to the stroke. That is, the front-end transition is like a bounce or a jump.

SEQUENCING

The components of the dynamic technique are divided into sequence positions and steps. These are best learned one by one, then strung together in short combinations. While these sequence movements are natural if the athlete is standing up, they become less natural when sitting on a seat. For example, core muscles must be engaged when an athlete does the stand-up exercise to ensure stability of the torso. An athlete sitting on a seat does not need to engage core muscles, as they should do when using their legs because the weight of the torso on the seat will provide that stability. Thus, additional awareness is required to ensure that what muscles should be engaged are engaged.

The equipment will 'talk' to the athlete in this regard. If a required muscle group is not activated, the boat will wobble. When the required muscles are engaged, the system will be stable. The athlete is connected. When the connection breaks, it is usually because of specific muscle disengagement that can be explained more appropriately step by step.

Step by step means the initial stages of learning the dynamic technique can be awkward. Doing two sequence steps individually to a high degree of competence before linking them is recommended. The recommended starting point is the release because the system is more stable. It is important that athletes play, explore and experiment understanding that the objective in these early stages is connectedness, and thus stability, for the entire stroke. To that end, much of the exploration is in the boat sitting still or moving very slowly, when disconnectedness will be easier to identify and correct.

The individual sequence steps follow. The table accompanying each sequence step includes experiments for the sculler to try. They are intended to be performed at a standstill, which may be a challenge for those new to stability and connectedness. The athlete should feel free to leave oars on the water while they explore and play. As connectedness and stability improve, the athlete can work towards undertaking the experiments with oars off the water.

Also, as the reader goes through the below sequence steps, try mimicking them first on dry land. Most of the sequence steps can be executed sitting in a chair, on the floor or on an ergo. The dry land advantage is being able to use a finger to poke into various muscles as the skill is executed, learning which muscles engage and which do not. If a mirror is available, even better.

THE PRE-DRIVE SEQUENCE

The purpose of the pre-drive is to achieve acceleration of the boat. This acceleration is achieved in two ways. First, the body flips over energetically, launching the hands forward, with the resulting reaction a small but measurable forward movement in the boat. Second, the legs quickly gather the boat, pulling it in towards the body using the quadriceps. This achieves significant acceleration and forward movement of the boat. Well executed, the boat's fastest velocity is achieved at the pre-catch position, putting the athlete in a position to preserve that velocity through a fluid, dynamic drive.

The pre-drive sequence steps are:

- Release
- Body flip
- Hand launch
- Pre-drive transition
- Boat gathering
- Pre-catch

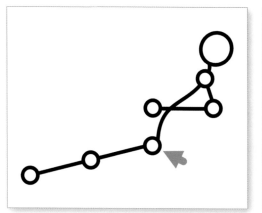 

Fig. 66 Release position showing pelvic weight to the back.

Release

The sculler is stationary and connected through feet (heels down, toes up), seat (core engaged) and light hands (thumbs pushing out slightly). The pelvic weight is back. The boat is running. During that run, the boat starts to decelerate. If the sculler does nothing, the boat eventually stops. The objective for the sculler is to facilitate that boat run by remaining connected and stable.

The release allows the sculler to recover physiologically. The timing at the release, and when the sculler transitions to the body flip and pre-drive sequence, also determines whether the system achieves maximum boat run.

Sequence highlights	The sculler is connected primarily at the feet and seat.
Timing	The time in the back end is determined by the stroke rate. The lower the stroke rate, the longer in the back end, allowing the boat to run.
Outcomes	Maximize boat run.
Considerations	If the sculler disconnects, the system may wobble and if so, speed will be affected.
Experiment 1	Stationary at the release, disrupt the connection at the feet by relaxing the feet and legs. Observe if this affects the stability of the boat. Take a stroke, repeat and see if a disrupted connection affects the length of the boat run.
Experiment 2	Stationary at the release, disrupt the connection at the core by relaxing the core. Observe if this affects the hands and oars. Then, as above, take a stroke and see how a relaxed or engaged core affects boat run.

Table 15 Key elements of the release.

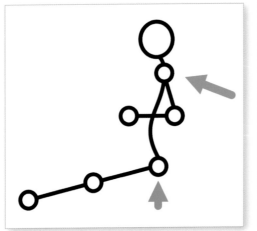 

Fig. 67 Body flip position showing torso swinging quickly forward from the hips with pelvic weight shifting forward.

Body flip

Prior to boat deceleration, and as late as possible, the sculler initiates the pre-drive sequence. The first step is the body flip. The hands remain close to the chest. Depending on where the athlete carries their hands at the release, the hands may need to be offset during this motion. The body flip is initiated by the lower abdomen core muscles and involves pivoting the body around the hip joints. The spine and head alignment remain the same, preserving the natural curve of the spine. The pelvis rolls to midpoint.

Sequence highlights	The sculler remains connected at the feet, seat and hands. The torso rotates around the hip joint while retaining the spinal alignment. Hands remain at the chest. The torso rotates quickly and strongly.
Timing	The movement begins just prior to the boat decelerating.
Outcomes	Hands are set up for launch. Small forward movement in boat due to shift in sculler's mass.
Considerations	The feet, legs and core must remain connected or no forward movement will be observed.
Experiment 1	Perform the body flip with oars off the water from a standstill. Observe whether a small wake is created.
Experiment 2	Disconnect the feet and/or legs (relax the muscles) and perform the body flip. Observe what happens to stability. Do the same, relaxing and engaging the core.

Table 16 Key elements of the body flip.

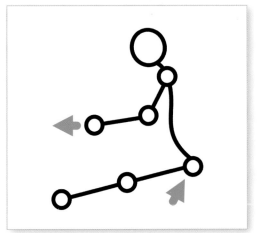 

Fig. 68 Hand launch position showing hands and arms being extended and pelvic weight continuing to shift forward. The hands are moving very quickly forward.

Hand launch

The body continues energetically forward from its approximately -25 degree position towards a forward +25 degree position. The pelvis is rolling continuously forward. At the height of the body flip, the hands are launched forward. The speed of the hands is now quicker than that of the body, necessary because the hands need to travel the furthest. The hands remain light on the handles, thumbs pressing slightly out. The oars gain significant momentum that will assist with the finger roll prior to the catch. This momentum helps the oars remain level.

Sequence highlights	Heels down, toes up. Core engaged. Hands with flat wrists and relaxed arms launch the oars forward while retaining shoulder blades on the torso. The body flip continues around the pelvis with head and spine in alignment.
Timing	Hands launched approximately at the height of the body flip.
Outcomes	Body flip continues with hands accelerating out quicker than the speed of the body flip so that they quickly reach extension.
Considerations	Because two things are happening at once (hands launched and body flip continuing), a focus on retaining the feet, legs and core connection is required.
Experiment 1	Launch the hands prior to the body flip. Then launch the hands after initiating the body flip. Observe the difference in stability. Observe the difference in the wake.
Experiment 2	At the start of the hand launch, disconnect the feet, legs or core. Observe the difference in stability.

Table 17 Key elements of the hand launch.

Fig. 69 Sequence of hands through the pre-drive sequence.

Hand position from release to body flip through hand launch

The sculler will need to try different hand crossover configurations. This sculler in Fig. 69 separates hands at the body flip and then stacks during the hand launch for the brief crossover. This keeps her shoulders and body aligned perpendicular to the boat but has a tendency to roll the boat, which can be compensated for by the feet. The method chosen should be the one most comfortable for the sculler and which allows a quick, smooth movement of the hands all the way from release to pre-catch.

Pre-drive transition

This sequence step describes the body position at the end of body flip and hand launch. The pelvis has rolled to its front. The body should be forward approximately 25 degrees. The hands have moved forward and the arms are fully extended. At the transition point, the hamstrings should feel tight and, if they are not, the athlete's body may have slumped. The feeling should be one of height in the body and tension in the lower thighs.

This position is problematic for athletes who have restricted flexibility. These athletes may tend to compensate for that inflexibility by collapsing and rounding the lower back, releasing the shoulder blades from the torso and bending knees. Athletes should endeavour to improve flexibility but, in the meantime, the body flip may not reach 25 degrees. It should reach the point where the hamstrings are felt but no further than is comfortable.

The important aspects of this transition point are hands moving forward at a high speed with arms straight, shoulder blades on the torso, natural head and spine alignment retained, legs straight and heels down. If the body remains more upright (not 25 degrees) for the moment, there is an adjustment in the next sequence step that is not ideal, but will compensate while the flexibility is attended to.

The feeling at this transition should be one of the hands moving forward quickly with the need for the body to follow. Thus, at this transition point, a lot is going on. The body flip completes. The hands are shooting forward. The hamstrings are being stretched, encouraging the sculler to bend the knees. The potential for disconnectedness is high. It's recommended to practise this series just sitting in the boat (slow work): body flip, hand launch and stop at the pre-drive transition, checking to ensure that the body is still connected and the boat is stable. The engagement of the lower core at this time and from this point forward is crucial.

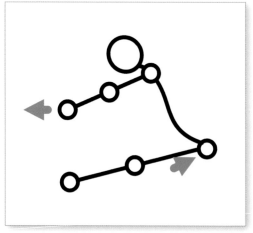 

Fig. 70 Pre-drive transition showing arms extended and continuing to move forward while pelvic weight is now at its most forward position. The athlete is beginning to gather the boat.

Sequence highlights	Heels down, legs connected, core engaged. The body should be fully over at the time the arms reach their fully extended position.
Timing	The sequence steps up to this point should be energetic, smooth and fluid.
Outcomes	Small forward boat movement and body positioned to further accelerate the boat.
Considerations	Connection at the feet, legs and core is crucial to stability.
Experiment 1	Execute the body flip and hand launch from release, but instead of stopping rock back and forth. Observe the pelvis roll from back to front as well as how the hamstrings feel at the pre-drive transition position.
Experiment 2	Execute the same rocking motion, approximately -/+25 degrees. Observe the head alignment and spinal alignment.

Table 18 Key elements of the pre-drive transition.

Boat gathering

When the body has rocked to its forward position, the hands leading at a greater rate of speed, the sculler pulls their thighs to the chest and feet towards their seat. The pelvic weight is forward. The boat is pulled in towards the sculler quickly (after the skill is learned). This accelerates the boat forward and, done properly, the speed of the boat will be at its highest point at any time in the stroke.

The feeling in the legs is the same as in the stand-up exercise above during the time

the athlete lowers themselves towards the ground. The quadriceps and anterior tibialis (front of the leg) will be engaged. The gastrocnemius and hamstrings (back of the leg) less so. Using a finger to push against each muscle will demonstrate the differences in its engagement. Or sitting in a chair, pull the thigh towards the torso and heel towards the seat. The muscle engagement will be as described.

The way to determine if the boat gathering has been successful is to look at the wake. Even starting at a standstill, there will be a distinctive wake. Under way, the wake will be even more pronounced. From a standstill, boat gathering can move the boat half a metre forward.

Disconnectedness during boat gathering occurs in two ways. First, the enthusiastic sculler forgets to retain an engaged core. The boat will wobble and, since the sculler is headed to the pre-catch position and the front of the boat, the ride can be very exciting. Thus, athletes new to this skill are encouraged to try quarter slide, half slide, three-quarter slide, then full slide increments, only proceeding to the next increment when the stability and connectedness are retained from the prior one. Oars on the water are fine.

Second, disconnectedness creeps in through the legs. The legs should be very engaged through this boat gathering process with the muscles on the top of the leg (quadriceps and tibialis anterior) engaged throughout. (The hamstrings and gastrocnemius, muscles at the bottom of the leg, are not engaged.) Some athletes have leg dominance differences that can contribute to this disconnectedness. An exercise to address this, and one for any sculler, is to do shorter pull-ins, alternating legs to become aware of the difference and then pulling together.

Another way disconnectedness creeps in through the legs is the leg wobble around the centreline of the boat. The legs need to pull in evenly with muscles engaged throughout, preferably with knees out. The 'knees out' position provides a pontoon-like effect around the centreline. As oftentimes happens particularly for female athletes whose splay is too narrow, knees clash and create less forgiveness in the system's tendency to roll. To the degree it is comfortable and feels normal, scullers should be encouraged to keep their knees apart during the boat gathering. If this is a problem, athletes should consider whether changing the splay might help. A helpful proprioceptive cue, if it works for the individual athlete, is for the knees to touch the inside of the upper arms at the pre-catch.

The feeling from the pre-drive transition position is one, almost, of chasing the hands up to the pre-catch position. Thus, the speed of the hands remains the same (quite fast) and the boat gathering needs to be dynamic enough to keep up with them. The feeling should be one of smooth connectedness, not jerky and uneven.

Athletes who have flexibility challenges mentioned in the pre-drive transition sequence will need to continue to rotate on the pelvis during the boat gathering step. This is not ideal. It increases the chances for instability. However, it will achieve the objective of the athlete's thighs on chest at the end of the pre-drive sequence with approximately a 25-degree rotation. The preferred solution is to increase flexibility.

The athlete should be attentive to wobbles. A wobble indicates the athlete is disconnected.

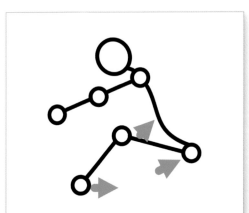

Fig. 71 Boat gathering with thighs to chest, heels to seat, while pelvic weight remains in its forward position.

The best way to address a wobble is to back up a sequence step or two to the place where the athlete was well connected and the skill was executed correctly. Then, proceed slowly through the next sequence steps, checking all the connectedness points in order: feet, legs, pelvis, core, torso and head, shoulders, arms, hands.

Athletes who experience wobbles and instability should know these are normal in the skills development process. They are the boat 'talking' to the athlete about what needs to happen to improve the sculling system. All wobbles can be fixed by going slow, being attentive and achieving small successes.

Pre-catch

At the pre-catch position the feet should be engaged, preferably with the heels no more than 1cm off the footstretcher, shins perpendicular, torso on thighs, pelvic weight forward, the natural alignment of the spine and head maintained, shoulder blades on the torso, arms straight, oars squared but above the water (arms are articulated up).

Experiment: Accelerating the boat during pre-drive

At the shore, the assistant stands at the end of the boat in front of the sculler with the boat touching the assistant. The sculler executes the body flip and hand launch. Observe whether the boat moves away from the assistant and, if so, how far.

Next and with the assistant and boat in the original position, the sculler goes to the pre-drive transition position and energetically pulls the thighs to chest and feet to seat. Observe whether the boat moves away from the assistant and, if so, how far. Also observe the level of connectedness and stability.

Finally, put it all together. Starting from the release, execute the entire sequence through to pre-catch. With oars off the water and properly executed, the boat will move forward approximately half a metre. Even with the oars on the water, the boat will move forward.

Sequence highlights	All connections retained. Then thighs to chest, knees to seat, strongly, evenly and smoothly.
Timing	Boat gathering starts as soon as the arms are fully extended and proceeds quickly enough to keep up with the hand speed.
Outcomes	The boat accelerates.
Considerations	Connectedness is crucial, from feet all the way through to hands. Any wobbles in the boat are a function of disconnectedness. Key locations are core and muscles on the top of legs. Knees out if possible.
Experiment 1	From the pre-drive transition position, relax the core, raise the thighs to chest and pull feet to seat. Repeat but engaging the core first. Observe the differences in stability at quarter, half, three-quarter and full slide.
Experiment 2	From the pre-drive transition position, engage all appropriate muscles but slide slowly up the slide using the hamstrings and gastrocnemius, not the quadriceps and tibialis anterior. Now use the quadriceps and tibialis anterior. Observe the differences at quarter, half, three-quarter and full slide.

Table 19 Key elements of the boat gathering.

One aspect of the pre-catch is that the oars are rolled from the feathered to squared position. The momentum of the hands through boat gathering will assist with the squaring. The less time the blade is square, the less time waves and wind have to act on the blade face. Thus, the preferred skill is for a continuous, smooth blade squaring, through light hands, just at the time the sculler arrives at the pre-catch position. This will lead quickly and smoothly to the catch.

Ways to experiment with this blade squaring include leaving blades flat on the water (as well as blades off the water later as the skill is acquired). Execute the body flip, hand launch, pre-drive transition and body gathering sequence but, in the first instance, only to the extent that the arms are straight. Then, square the blades smoothly. For this to work well, the connectedness must be preserved and the hand rolling must be light. When successful, keep progressing further along the slide until the skill can be executed at the pre-catch position without wobbles.

The athlete needs to be confidently stable at the pre-catch position. This ensures that when the catch and drive are initiated, these are consistently executed with competence. Ensuring the finger roll and squaring is a light, smooth action helps maintain that stability.

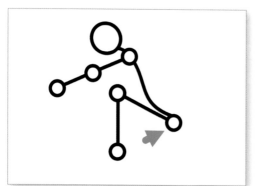 

Fig. 72 Pre-catch with arms extended, shoulder blades on torso, spine and head aligned, pelvic weight on front and shins perpendicular.

Sequence highlights	Strong, connected position, particularly through feet, legs and core. Stability at the pre-catch position. Weight is on the front of pelvis, blades squared.
Timing	Hands and body arrive at the position simultaneously.
Outcomes	Stable preparation for the drive.
Considerations	Blade squaring occurs smoothly, with light hands. Connectedness and stability crucial.
Experiment 1	At the pre-catch position, blades flat on the water, take one hand off an oar handle for one second. Or start at quarter slide and work forward incrementally until successful. Observe what muscles need to be engaged to retain stability. Work up to five seconds.
Experiment 2	At the pre-catch position, blades square but in the water, open hands using only gentle thumb pressure outward. Observe what muscles need to be engaged to retain stability.

Table 20 Key elements of the pre-catch.

Summary: pre-drive sequence

The entire pre-drive sequence is done energetically, with purpose and smoothly. The objective is to reduce the time the sculler is at the front end. Referring to Figs 61 and 62, as the sculler approaches the front end of the boat, the pitch of the boat changes. This is not a problem when the boat is sitting still. When the boat is in motion, it is a problem. Drag is created and the boat slows. A sculler in the front end is applying virtual brakes to the sculling system in this front end position, which is one reason why boat gathering and accelerating the boat at this time is so important.

A sculler using the dynamic technique will, at the pre-catch, see a continuous wake that

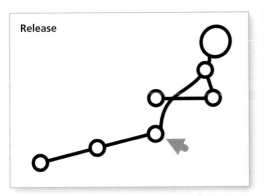

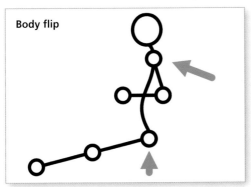

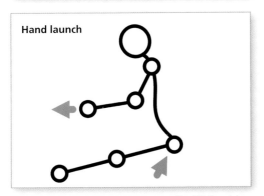

Fig. 73 Pre-drive sequence summary.

Fig. 73 Pre-drive sequence summary (cont'd).

may well be larger than when they initiate the drive sequence. This is because the boat gathering increases boat speed, usually to its highest speed at any time in the stroke.

Sequence highlights	The pre-drive sequence is smooth, quick and accelerates the boat.
Timing	The pre-drive sequence is initiated after allowing the boat its maximum run and differs at different stroke rates and levels of effort.
Outcomes	Boat accelerates to its fastest speed. Sculler stable and prepared to begin the drive sequence.
Considerations	The front-end transition occurs as a continuous reversal of direction and begins at the end of the pre-drive sequence.
Experiment 1	From the release and with blades on the water, execute each pre-drive sequence step, adding a step at a time through quarter, half, three-quarter and full slide. Eliminate wobbles by backing up a sequence step or two when they occur.
Experiment 2	From the release with blades off the water, execute the entire pre-drive sequence (sometimes referred to as a roll-up). Observe where the boat wobbles and which muscles may need to be recruited to execute the perfect pre-drive sequence.

Table 21 Summary elements of the pre-drive sequence.

FRONT-END TRANSITION

The front-end transition describes the change in direction. The front-end transition sequence steps are:

- Boat gathering
- Pre-catch
- Catch
- Initiate leg drive

Since the latter two have not yet been discussed, it's a bit premature to focus on the front-end transition at this moment. However, unless we do, the perception may be that the sculler arrives at the pre-catch position and stops. This could not be further from the truth.

The front-end transition is executed much like the jump excercise above. The continuity between these four sequence steps is fluid. The sculler arrives at the pre-catch position then immediately reverses direction, initiating the leg drive. The blades enter the water (the catch) exactly at the moment of that reversal (difficult to execute) or very, very slightly

thereafter. Thus, practically, the catch is frequently executed after the leg drive begins, as measured in microseconds, about which more in the catch section below.

The boat is gathered quickly. The entire front-end transition is executed at the same speed. The feeling at the front-end transition is a dynamic one, as in a jump or a bounce. The quality of that jump or bounce is controlled. The objective of the movement is to recruit the elasticity of the leg muscles and increase power by so doing. Thus, there is no slowing, stopping or pausing at the front-end transition. The resulting motion needs to be horizontal.

For many athletes, this transition sequence has historically been inconsistent with no two front-end transitions alike. This is usually due to rushing through an uncontrolled transition in the hopes of getting it over with faster. This rush is often accompanied by tensing of the hands, arms and shoulders, decreasing stability. Stroke consistency at this critical front-end transition is crucial to an efficient stroke. Rushing and muscle tensing interfere with consistency.

Sequence highlights	A smooth reversal of direction that retains connectedness and stability. The body is at 25 degrees for the entire time.
Timing	No stop, pauses or slowing down. The entire transition should occur at a uniform quick speed.
Outcomes	The sculling system is stable throughout such that the initial leg drive launches the boat optimally.
Considerations	Unevenness in timing; excessive force at the leg drive initiation; and disconnection from the oars all lead to instability.
Experiment 1	Blades flat on the water, execute the entire pre-drive sequence but add the front-end transition. Ensure the change in direction is smooth. Observe disconnectedness and determine which muscles need to remain engaged.
Experiment 2	Perform the continuous pre-drive and front-end transition sequence with oars off the water while the boat is at a standstill. If instability occurs, go back a step or two to the last sequence steps performed well and proceed incrementally until successful.

Table 22 The key elements of the front-end transition.

The antidote is: go slow when learning this skill. Build incrementally, sequence step by sequence step, until the athlete can confidently sit at the catch holding only one oar, for one second (one Mississippi – the whole word). After which, more transition speed can be explored.

Summary: front-end transition

Understanding that the reader needs first to complete the sections on Catch and Initiate Leg Drive below, the summary of the front-end transition follows. The front-end transition is a smooth continuation of the pre-drive sequence. During the entire front-end transition sequence, the torso and arms are aligned in exactly the same way. The only minor difference is to the arms, which articulate around the shoulder, allowing the blades to enter the water.

The front-end transition is as smooth, energetic, purposeful and quick as the pre-drive sequence. It will feel like a jump. The maximum power will be achieved as a function of catch timing. If the catch is timed too early, the boat will check. A higher level of slip will occur because the maximum form drag of the blades has not occurred. The wake will break and, in extreme cases, a clear puddle will form.

If the blade placement is timed at, or microscopically after, the athlete's front-end transition, the form drag on the blades will result in minimal slip. The wake will be continuous. The entire fluid action is similar to the jump exercise directed horizontally. With heels driving the boat forward, the athlete will lift off the seat.

6 | DYNAMIC TECHNIQUE: DRIVE SEQUENCE

The drive sequence is where major propulsion occurs. The boat is gathered quickly and then the athlete reverses in a continuous jumping motion. The oars, squared at the pre-catch, enter the water as the arms articulate around the shoulders. Engagement of the strong leg muscles lift the athlete off the seat and provide the initial horizontal propulsion that will continue throughout the entire drive sequence, ending at the back-end transition.

This chapter begins at the point of directional reversal during the front-end transition.

THE DRIVE SEQUENCE

The drive sequence includes six steps:

- Catch
- Initiate leg drive
- Initiate body
- Early mid-drive
- Mid-drive transition
- Pre-release

The first two steps, catch and initiate leg drive, are part of the front-end transition. The last drive sequence step, pre-release, is part of the back-end transition. In order to get maximum speed for minimum effort, the six drive sequence steps need to flow smoothly, continuously and with an application of power that respects hydrodynamic considerations. Then, the back-end transition needs to be executed with a keen awareness of timing.

Catch

During the pre-catch, the oar handles will be moving quickly forward. That momentum will assist with squaring the blade. The athlete executes the finger roll at the very end of the pre-drive sequence and right before lifting the hands. The catch then places the blade in the water in one continuing motion. There is no delay between the finger roll and blade placement. Properly executed, the momentum of the pre-drive sequence will help square the blade and facilitate the oar/gate connection at the catch. Capitalizing on this momentum reduces the effort required from the fingers and hands to square the blades. In addition, the fluidity of this squaring approach improves stability and, secondarily, minimizes the time the blade is exposed to wave and wind action.

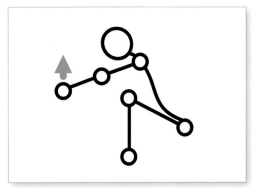 

Fig. 74 The body position is the same as at pre-catch, only the arms rotate around the shoulder.

The catch establishes the sculling system's connection with the water. The boat is moving. The finger roll completes. Straight arms articulate. Hands move slightly upwards. The blades lower into the water. The blade placement results from an upper arm pivot at the shoulder joint, shoulder blades remaining on the torso. The arms remain straight, wrists flat, the hands curled over the handle grips but still light. The objective is to have a loose enough grip on the oars that the blades can find their design level in the water, squaring naturally.

One experiment is lowering the oars with open palms, the fingers uncurled, using only the thumb's slight outward pressure to maintain connection. This experiment can be done at quarter, half, three-quarter and full slide, building confidence that boat stability can be maintained with a very light grip on the oars.

Because at high speeds the force of gravity will be insufficient for the blades to enter the water quickly enough, it is helpful to speed their journey with a gentle uplift from the thumb. The fingers remain light. This thumb engagement is a good skill to acquire because it serves to keep the collar and gates connected throughout the early portion of the catch. The objective is to ensure that the blades reach their design depth at initiation of the leg drive. Experimenting with blade placement, with very light hands lifting the oars slightly with the thumb, helps establish habits where blades are not driven too deeply into the water.

The placement of the oars into the water needs to be achieved at a time that facilitates the boat speed. The options for establishing the system's connection with the water include: (1) slowing the boat, (2) not affecting the boat speed or (3) facilitating boat speed. The way to determine which is happening is to look at the wake. If the catch has slowed the boat, the wake will show a break or, in the worst cases, a clear smooth puddle. A clear smooth puddle indicates the boat is not moving. Ideally, the wake of a boat during the catch will be continuous. When the boat speed is facilitated, the continuous wake will show an increase in height because force has been added efficiently.

Another way to assess catch timing is to look at the splash of the oars entering the water. A splash that goes backwards indicates an early catch and that the boat is being slowed. No splash or a slight splash that is perpendicular indicate the desired catch timing. A splash that goes forward indicates a late catch. While not ideal, a late catch will slow the boat less than an early catch.

Observing splashes real time, particularly from the front end, is challenging. Sitting still in the boat and working at quarter and half slide will allow the athlete to look at the

Sequence highlights	Body same position as pre-catch. Hands lifted through a pivot at shoulders. Arms and wrists straight. Hands are flat with a loose grip.
Timing	Timing of the blade entry should facilitate the boat speed.
Outcomes	When coordinated with the leg drive, increases boat speed and minimizes slip.
Considerations	Allow blades to seek their design level and position; lift with thumb at higher speeds.
Experiment 1	At quarter, half, three-quarter and pre-catch positions and standstill, square the blades in a continuous motion, observing instability and resolving if needed. If significant instability results, square only one oar at a time. When squared, explore the difference between an early square and continuous square. Explore the difference between dropping the blade into the water and using the thumb to lift.
Experiment 2	Same as Experiment 1 in motion. Observe the articulation (pivot) at the shoulder. Ensure the rest of the arm, wrist and hand remain flat, particularly with a loose hand grip. Disconnect at the arm or bend the wrist and observe what happens to the blade and boat stability when the blade enters the water.

Table 23 Key elements of the catch.

blade and observe. One-handed blade placement experiments at a standstill are good, too. Splashes that are in the wrong direction at a standstill will more than likely be in the wrong direction in motion, with the skill much easier to correct sitting still, one oar at a time.

Becoming familiar with the wake is highly recommended. The wake indicates boat speed. It indicates direction. For example, a catch that is uneven will cause a fishtail in the wake. One objective for the catch is not to interfere with the strong, continuous, straight wake established during the pre-drive sequence.

Initiate leg drive

The initiation of the leg drive is less a specific action than a continuation of the jump motion that began with boat gathering, followed by the front end reversal of direction. The leg drive timing needs to be synchronized with the catch. Ideally the 'no splash' blade entry, the front-end transition, the initial application of leg effort and the realization of boat speed

will occur almost simultaneously. This skill is one of the eternal quests that makes sculling a challenge for life.

Initiating the leg drive involves driving the boat, primarily through the heels. A small amount of heel lift, no more than 1cm, is preferred by some athletes since it accentuates the pull, push and jumping motion that characterizes the entire front-end transition. However, heel lift adds instability and requires recruitment of small muscles that fatigue more easily. Other athletes will find that flatfoot, with no heel lift, achieves more connection and stability. Either way, the toes should be up. Toes up in the shoes force the heels down. Then when leg pressure is applied, that pressure can be articulated around the heel (talus) such that the drive results in a horizontal movement of the boat.

This articulation is important because many Masters will have a rake that is flatter than before. The flatter rake and initial leg drive will have a tendency to move the athlete off the seat and vertically. The athlete will need to compensate for this by adjusting how the leg force is transmitted through the foot, usually

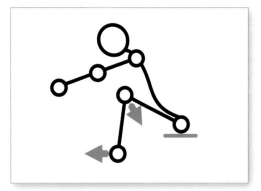 

Fig. 75 Initiating the leg drive moves the boat forward horizontally as the knees lower and the seat rises.

the heel, as well as how the legs are engaged. At the end of initiating leg drive, the athlete should be off the seat, but only very lightly or as much as a piece of paper, and ensure that the energy of the drive is directed to horizontal, not vertical, movement.

At the beginning of initiating leg drive, the muscles used are the same as used for boat gathering. Perform the stand-up exercise to feel how there is continuity of the muscles engaged at the front-end transition. However, soon after the initial leg drive the other leg muscles are recruited, including the calf, hamstrings and glutes. At this stage, these oppositional muscles work well together to articulate the knee downward. However, when oppositional muscles are engaged, they eventually tend to counteract each other's effect and restrict extension. This becomes another transitional period where leg and pelvic muscle

Experimenting with initiating leg drive and 'off the seat'

One way to learn how to initiate the leg drive is to place the blades square in the water. Start at half slide and, as the skill is mastered, progress to three-quarter and full slide. The torso remains in the same catch position throughout, on the thighs. The arms are in the same straight position, too, wrists flat. The shoulder blades are on the trunk.

Pull the boat in approximately half slide, as in boat gathering. Proceed through the front-end transition steps with a very light, smooth, jump. Do this slowly to become comfortable with the blade resistance, ensuring stability. Initiate the leg drive evenly, at the same speed and intensity as the boat was gathered. Continue with a slow pulsing push-pull motion, back and forth. Gradually increase the speed and intensity of the boat gathering and front-end transition, maintaining a strong, stable position.

When the speed and intensity maximize form drag on the blade, the blade will not move in the water and the athlete will come off the seat. This is at the point where the oars act as Class 2 levers and the blades are now relatively fixed. Check that the body position has not changed and that the arms remain straight throughout. In the early stages, more enthusiastic athletes may come well off the seat or lose their seat entirely, which means they are mastering the skill. Experimentation and play will develop the athlete's ability to execute a strong, horizontal initial leg drive while achieving lightness in the seat. This experiment will help increase stability through the entire front-end transition.

Sequence highlights	Body in same position as pre-catch and catch. Pelvis rolling back but still forward. Arms straight. Horizontal drive articulated through heels and lifting off seat.
Timing	Continuous, smooth flow throughout entire front-end transition.
Outcomes	Increased system propulsion.
Considerations	Minimizing yaw and achieving even application of power.
Experiment 1	Execute the front-end transition including initiate leg drive at varying speeds and intensity. Observe what happens to the wake. This can be done progressively from quarter, half, three-quarter and full slide.
Experiment 2	During the dry land warm-up, practise the jump exercise. See what jump technique results in the greatest height. Do the jump exercise with eyes closed. On the water, close eyes and execute the front-end transition using the various jump results. Observe what front-end transition sequence results in the best feelings of stability, connectedness and power.

Table 24 Key elements of initiate leg drive.

engagement changes. When the lower leg and upper thigh are approximately at 90 degrees, it is time for the next sequence step.

Initiate body

When the lower legs and thighs are at 90 degrees, initiate the body movement. Initiating the body involves both Group 1 and the pelvic girdle. First, the legs continue their drive, the heels pushing horizontally on the footstretcher. The knees continue their articulation downward. As the motion

progresses, the hamstrings take over from the quads. Arms remain straight, shoulder blades on the torso. The quads should then be released since their continued engagement is oppositional.

The second motion involves the pelvic girdle and the glutes. The athlete is already off or light on the seat. This continues. The body pivots backwards on the pelvis around the hip joints. Group 2 remains aligned with core engaged. Then, the strong, powerful glutes engage, or they don't.

Gluteal inhibition is a recognized phenomenon, known popularly as 'gluteal amnesia'

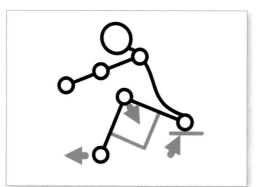

Fig. 76 The body begins to rock backwards when the lower legs and thighs are approximately at 90 degrees.

or 'dead butt syndrome'. Due in large part to the amount of time involved sitting in chairs, glutes are notoriously lazy. If they can avoid engaging, they won't. Unfortunately, sitting on a boat seat mimics sitting in a chair. The result is no differential cueing for the glutes to indicate that an athletic endeavour is under way. Because the glutes are the largest muscles in the body, it is important to recruit them into the sequence at this time. Activated glutes assist with a strong, continuous leg drive and propulsion. Without glute support, Group 2 and the lower back are at risk.[1]

The athlete needs to provide the cuing necessary to activate the glutes. To feel how the glutes should engage, refer back to the stand-up exercise. The point of flexion where the body begins to rise and the hips move forward requires the glutes to engage in order to perform the motion as well as stabilize the rest of the torso against the force of gravity. Putting a finger into the glutes will demonstrate what happens. The athlete can sit in the boat, using one oar for stability, and repeat the inquiry, or an assistant

can hold the boat. Initially the glutes are likely to be flaccid. Engaging and disengaging them at a standstill will help inform how these muscles should feel under way.

During this sequence step, the indicator that glutes are not engaged is that, relying only on Group 1 and weak back muscles, the athlete will come down onto the seat. One activation strategy is to consciously engage the glutes at the beginning of this sequence. Some athletes use a very small 'kick' through the heels that cues the glute activation. Another strategy is to visualize standing up, which will result in the hips being lifted, Group 2 stabilized and additional force being delivered to the footstretcher. Doing the stand-up exercise with eyes closed as part of the warm-up, then taking that feeling into the boat, will help. The verification of success comes from the feeling of being off the seat throughout this and subsequent sequence steps.

Sequence highlights	Pelvis has begun to roll backwards around hip joints but is still forward. Off or light on the seat. Transition to hamstrings, releasing quads. Beginning of glute engagement.
Timing	Begin approximately when upper legs and lower legs form a 90-degree angle.
Outcomes	Continued propulsion.
Considerations	Fluid reversal and continuation from pre-drive sequence.
Experiment 1	Starting at hand launch, complete the front-end transition sequence steps at quarter, half, three-quarter, then full slide, raising the blades just after initiating the leg drive (sometimes called pic or Russian pic drill). Ensure the body is lifted off the seat. Verify that the arms remained straight and the body over, remaining on the front of the pelvis. Observe stability/connectedness and resolve.
Experiment 2	Same as Experiment 1 but complete a continuous series of five. Vary between no cueing of the glutes and the various strategies for glute cueing. Determine which works best for the athlete.

Table 25 Key elements of initiate body.

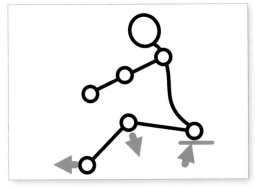

Fig. 77 Early mid-drive capitalizes on the glutes with a more pronounced body opening.

Early mid-drive

Early mid-drive is a continuation of initiating the leg drive. The glutes are now fully engaged. With activated glutes, Group 2 remains aligned with the lower back supported as the body rotates backward around the hip joints.

As the body rotates back with Group 2 retaining its constant alignment, the elevation of the shoulder girdle rises. This shoulder rise begins at mid-drive and can cause performance problems if the hands are allowed to rise simultaneously. Fig. 78 depicts the catch, mid-drive transition and pre-release sequence steps. The

Fig. 78 As the body naturally opens through the drive sequence a tendency for the hands to rise occurs.

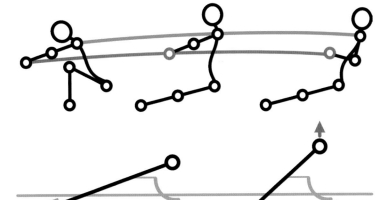

Fig. 79 The rising of hands lowers the blade in the water, lifting the boat and reducing speed.

Fig. 80 A level hand position can be achieved during the drive sequence by articulating the arms at the shoulders.

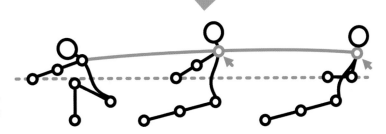

Sequence highlights	Continued glute engagement as the body opens, driving through the heels. Seat off or light.
Timing	Smooth and continuous follow-on from the front-end transition speed.
Outcomes	Continued propulsion.
Considerations	Natural rise in shoulders needs to be compensated for by articulation at shoulder, keeping hands level.
Experiment 1	Execute the front-end transition plus mid-drive, slowly such that the athlete does not come off the seat. With two fingers and arms straight, observe the natural blade path and depth in the water.
Experiment 2	Execute the front-end transition plus mid-drive, slowly such that the athlete does not come off the seat. Articulate the arms around the shoulders to obtain the natural blade path and depth as observed in Experiment 1. Increase intensity and propulsion through the sequence, ensuring Group 3 articulates at the shoulder throughout the stroke.

Table 26 Key elements of the early mid-drive.

green line shows the normal arcing of the shoulders that should occur. This arcing indicates the Group 2 alignment has been preserved and the athlete is not slumping. However, if the arms are retained in the same alignment throughout the drive sequence, the hands will follow the red line. Consequently, the oar handles will arc.

This hand arcing will direct the oar blade deeper into the water (Fig. 79). The oars provide optimal propulsion when they are horizontal. When deep in the water, the athlete's propulsive force will tend to drive the boat up, reducing the forward horizontal propulsive force. Speed drops off. The secondary effect is that the hands and forearms become misaligned as they hang on to the too high handles, with biomechanical and performance implications.

The solution is to articulate the straight arms at the shoulders throughout the drive (Fig. 80). If the shoulder blades are not engaged where they should be – on the torso – this endeavour will be very unstable. If the shoulder blades are engaged, the arms can pivot up and down freely while simultaneously remaining straight and well connected to the oar.

Mid-drive transition

The mid-drive transition occurs when the legs are fully extended. However, because of the glute engagement and position of Group 2, the connection through the feet is retained. The athlete is still off or light on the seat. The continued body action backwards, pivoting around the hip joints, includes an articulation at the pelvic girdle, which now lifts to allow for the energy from the continued body rock to be transmitted through the feet. Through an accumulation of lesser muscular engagement, the athlete continues to achieve propulsion.

The timing between the body opening and the legs fully extending is important here. If the body opens too early, the athlete will come down into the seat. If the pelvis is involved too late, the athlete will also come down into the seat.

The entire motion is a continued feeling of standing up. Much like the pre-drive transition where the body was flipped first, then the boat was gathered, these drive steps need to be smoothly sequential. The rocking motion from catch to mid-drive is continuous and fluid. The hips cantilever up in a stand-up feeling initially with the body remaining over. As the

Sequence highlights	Legs fully extended. Arms straight. Pelvic roll at midpoint. Continued glute engagement as the body continues to open, driving through the heels. Seat off or light.
Timing	Smooth and continuous follow-on from the front-end transition speed.
Outcomes	Continued propulsion.
Considerations	Smooth transition between sequence steps. Retain Group 2 alignment through glute engagement.
Experiment 1	Blades flat on the water, rock back and forth from catch position to slightly behind mid-drive position. Then, engage blades at catch, lift off seat and retain seat lift until slightly behind mid-drive. Notice glutes engagement and pelvic lift through the transition from forward to backward pelvis roll.
Experiment 2	Perform Experiment 1, driving through the heels, but vary the degree of pelvic lift to determine when it is sufficient to stay light off the seat and when it is insufficient and the seat comes down. Ensure arms are straight throughout.

Table 27 Key elements of the mid-drive transition.

legs reach their full extension, the cantilevered pelvic girdle and trunk combine to add power. A good way to observe this is the force curve on an ergometer. The force curve should be smooth and continuous with no dips or bumps.

It is crucial that the glutes remain engaged since they are supporting the pelvic girdle as well as stabilizing Group 2. Lack of glute engagement or destabilized Group 2, to which slumping contributes, can result in force being transmitted through the lower spine leading to injury. This injury risk is heightened through fatigue.

Pre-release

The rocking motion continues to pre-release where the body begins to exhaust the contribution it can make to propulsion. It is during this step that the arms act as shock absorbers, hanging on the handles as the body continues to rock backwards, the glutes continue to engage and the connection from oar blade to feet is retained. The elbows articulate outwards, 'chicken wing' as opposed to 'praying mantis'. The shoulders follow backwards with the front of the chest pushing outward, lifting

Fig. 81 The mid-drive transition occurs when the legs are fully extended. The athlete is light or off the seat.

Sequence highlights	Begins with athlete off or light on the seat and ends with athlete on the seat. Hands and forearms articulate. Core engaged.
Timing	Ends when the blades release.
Outcomes	Obtain optimal propulsion. Minimize wash.
Considerations	Light hands and allowing the oar blades to exhaust their design capabilities.
Experiment 1	Repeat the blade release exercise above but while executing the drive sequence and 'hanging on the handles'. The speed and effort should be low. Identify at what body position the release occurs: seat comes down, blades, release, connection with feet and propulsion ends.
Experiment 2	Explore the latter part of the drive sequence from early mid-drive to pre-release. To do this, use the same 'push – pull' technique used for leg drive initiation to come off the seat. Then retain this seat lightness through a continuous unfolding until the blades release and the seat comes down into the seat.

Table 28 Key elements of the pre-release.

and expanding the chest cavity. Propulsion results. However, the power contributed to the stroke is decreasing. There is a logical end.

The logical end is when the blades of the oars can no longer retain a connection with the water. If the blades are not connected, they cannot contribute to propulsion and their continued immersion will slow the boat. When is this point of disconnection? It is not necessarily when the athlete is at -25 degrees or 40 degrees release. Those numbers are nominal starting points. The disconnection point is: when the blades release and the athlete is no longer able to propel the system forward.

The longer an effective stroke arc, the more efficient the transmission of the athlete's power to the sculling system. This longer transmission of power results in speed. All other things being equal, a longer effective stroke arc will generate more speed than a shorter one. In the dynamic technique, the objective is to squeeze every watt of efficiency from the sculling system through an optimal effective stroke arc. One way to achieve this is to let the oars work as long as possible.

When the oars stop working during the drive sequence is, oddly enough, obvious when one knows what to look for. The larger oar blades will actually pop out of the water because of the change in hydrodynamics. To experiment with this, use extremely light hands. Two-fingered sculling works well to start with since this is not a 'hang on the handle' exercise. With some speed, leave the blades in the water and continue leaning back, employing a very light grip. The athlete continues to lean back bringing the hands closer to the chest. At a certain point, the blades will release. Unless impeded by tight hands or gate, the blades will usually roll flat onto the water. Notice the blades do not release straight up and down but, rather, roll backwards.

The point at which the oars release is the point of interest; the body position of the athlete at this point of release is, too. Athletes often find themselves well back of where they normally would be, approximately at the 25-degree position but sometimes a bit more or less, depending on how they are rigged. For many this feels very odd.

There are two issues here. The first is achieving the longest effective stroke arc. The second is what happens if the blades are extracted too early? An early extraction involves forcing the handles down while the blades (and athlete) are still connected with

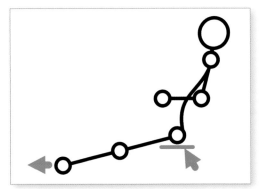 

Fig. 82 The pre-release continues the hip pivot backwards while remaining light on the seat.

the water. Early extraction causes the blade face to interact with the water in a different way because it changes from a Class 2 lever, fixed in the water, to a Class 1 lever, moving in the water. This interaction slows the boat. The early extraction requires the athlete to use Group 3 (shoulders, arms, hands), the weakest group, to perform a delicate, precise movement in disconnecting the boat and athlete from the water at a time in the stroke when Group 3 is most fatigued. Stability issues occur, as does wash. The effective stroke arc is truncated.

Thus, instead of wrestling the blades out of the water prematurely, the technique here is to let the blades inform the system as to when their job is completed, odd though that may feel. The athlete can facilitate this by learning at what backwards body angle that release is most likely to occur and incorporating that position into their pre-release. The body angle is determined not only by when the oars release but by when the athlete can no longer provide propulsion through the feet. A good indicator is that the athlete comes down into the seat. This seat release, blade release and end of propulsion should ideally occur simultaneously.

The other way the athlete can facilitate this pre-release sequence is light hands. The oars will behave as designed and release themselves. At that point, the athlete need only articulate the hands and forearms, in their 'chicken wing' position, slightly downward to raise the blades away from the water, to complete the sequence step.

The above properly executed will determine the release angle. Again, that is nominally around 40 degrees but can vary +/- five degrees. If there is extra release angle beyond 40 degrees, the athlete might consider moving that to the front end by moving the footstretcher forward. This is frequently a rigging adjustment athletes make after determining where the blades release because they find their body position much further back than before. Moving the footstretcher forward increases the catch angle and has positive performance implications.

Summary: drive sequence

The drive sequence is where propulsion is delivered by the athlete and speed is achieved. The drive sequence is less about strength than it is about the intelligent, fluid, coordinated use of the sculling system. Over-powering, jerky and uneven power application yields less propulsive effort than a smooth, even, purposeful one. Because of the human body's design, the initial part of the stroke is necessarily stronger with the body's largest muscles engaged. However, the continued ability to achieve propulsion throughout the entire drive sequence will significantly affect the boat's final speed.

Fig. 83 Drive sequence summary.

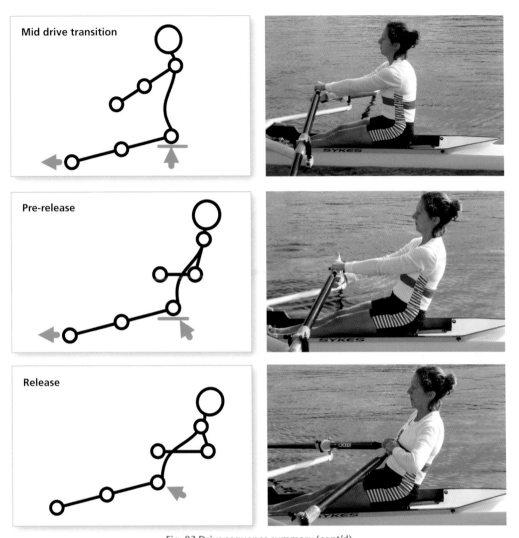

Fig. 83 Drive sequence summary (cont'd).

The athlete's position on the seat is the key indicator of how effort is being applied. Regardless of their anthropomorphic size or strength, all athletes can and should be light or off the seat. Maintaining that seat lightness as long as possible throughout the drive sequence will allow the oar blades to remain fixed as long as possible and achieve the athlete's maximum effective stroke arc.

Sequence highlights	A steady, smooth, application of effort through the legs, pelvis and body where the hands hang on the handles at the end.
Timing	Follows on smoothly and uniformly from speed of the front-end transition. Ends when the oars release.
Outcomes	Propulsion and optimal effective stroke arc, minimizing slip and wash.
Considerations	The smooth transition between sequence steps. Back health through glute engagement and fatigue management.
Experiment 1	Perform the entire series of sequence steps, pre-drive and drive, with blades on the water. Next, with blades off the water and executing the catch through the pre-release. Execute the entire series while slowly under way. Identify points of instability and disconnectedness. Stop, back up in the sequence and resolve when they occur.
Experiment 2	Perform the entire series of sequence steps, pre-drive and drive, with blades on the water. Next, with blades off the water. At a standstill. Identify points of instability and disconnectedness. Stop, back up in the sequence and resolve when they occur.

Table 29 Summary elements of the drive sequence.

THE BACK-END TRANSITION

There are two ways to approach stroke timing. One is to vary the timing for the infinite number of speeds available. In that case, adjust the pre-drive and drive sequence steps to achieve a particular speed. For faster speeds, the sequence steps would occur faster. For slower speeds, they would occur slower.

The end objective of the sculling stroke is optimal speed for the least effort. The infinite timing approach would require the athlete to acquire an infinite number of timing skills and habits in order to achieve this end objective. This infinite variability is burdensome and likely to delay the acquisition of competence. There is a simpler way: vary only one timing aspect of the stroke.

Sequence highlights	Establishes timing for the entire stroke.
Timing	Varies depending on the rating and speed.
Outcomes	Propulsion and optimal effective stroke arc, minimizing slip and wash.
Considerations	Accentuates asynchronicity of the stroke at lower speeds.
Experiment 1	Execute the entire drive sequence but add in the back-end transition. Ensure the change in direction is smooth and that stability and connectedness are maintained during boat run. Observe which muscles need to be engaged and which do not.
Experiment 2	Perform the continuous drive sequence with oars off the water while the boat is at a standstill. If instability occurs, go back a step or two to the last sequence step performed well and proceed incrementally until successful.

Table 30 The key elements of the back end transition.

The dynamic technique varies only one timing aspect: the back-end transition. The back-end transition steps are:

- Pre-release
- Release
- Body flip

The timing for the entire stroke evolves during the back-end transition. Ideally, the timing for the rest of the sequence steps remains the same, regardless of rating or speed. Thus, the athlete needs to acquire only one front-end transition, not an infinite number. The front-end transition is executed consistently and quickly, the same speed every time, be it at 18spm or 34spm. The other sequence steps are, too.

The added benefit to this differential timing approach is that the time in the front end with its increased drag factor is reduced. The time

Timing – 1–2–3

This is a fun experiment to explore the back-end transition timing. Ideally a measuring device such as a Nielsen-Kellerman SpeedCoach is available. CrewNerd is an affordable mobile application that will also suit. For those without a measuring device, the other option is to identify two points certain on the water, to be discussed below as a variation on the experiment.

Row a consistent 16–18spm using current technique for a determined length, say 200m. Check the average speed or average stroke distance. Next repeat that length at the same 16–18spm rating and effort level. In the back end count to '1' before continuing the stroke. Counting '1' – without the Mississippi – will have the effect of speeding up all the other sequence steps. Unless the athlete speeds these other sequence steps along, the rating will drop. Once the athlete can do the 200m with a consistent stroke counting '1', check the average speed or average distance per stroke for that piece.

Repeat the experiment but this time count '1–2'. Again, all the other sequence steps need to happen more quickly to retain the rating. Ensure stroke consistency is achieved before measuring the result. Check speed and distance per stroke again. Finally, count '1–2–3'. The remaining sequence steps will need to be quite quick, about as quick as they will need to be at 30–32spm, which is a competitive rating, to be discussed later in the book. Check the results.

As the athlete counts '1–2–3' while sitting in the back end, the boat still continues its run. The athlete has time to recover physiologically. The front-end transition, no matter what the technique, is now quicker than for the count of '1'. An athlete who is not well connected may be challenged, which is an indication that opportunities are to be had in the connectedness and stability areas. Thus, if '1–2–3' is not going well, the '1–2' should be able to provide an indication.

Observe what happens to average speed and average distance per stroke over the four pieces: normal and three experiments.

For those without a measuring device, and those who would like a slightly different challenge, pick a certain distance on the water, preferably not a particularly long one, say from a jetty to another jetty. Do the same experiment above but count the number of strokes needed to complete the distance. For example, scull one piece while counting '1' in the back end before proceeding. Replicate, at the same rating, this time counting for the other '1–2–3' breakdowns.

Observe the data again. Those with excellent connectedness will be able to wave at passers-by, with both hands, while counting '1–2–3'.

in the back end is increased, capitalizing on boat run and free speed. To the uninitiated, the differential timing may make the stroke look unusual at low ratings.

Summary: back-end transition

The back-end transition is where the stroke ends and begins again. It is punctuated at the release sequence step by a timing event, delay or pause, as determined by the desired rating and speed. That delay provides the athlete with recovery time and, most importantly, allows the boat to run. At slow speeds this looks very different from traditional sculling. The athlete is encouraged to play with various ratings and timing to verify what optimizes the distance per stroke or speed for them.

OTHER TOPICS

Back preservation strategies

The dynamic technique's focus on retaining the alignment of Group 2 helps protect the athlete from back injury, provided that alignment is retained. Achieving this Group 2 alignment throughout the stroke is a critical skill. When learning the technique, it is important to go slow, break the technique into its sequence steps and execute correctly each sequence step at a standstill before beginning to string sequence steps together. Especially when working through the drive sequence steps, where the back is at particular risk, the athlete should check head/shoulder/pelvis vertical alignment regularly.

During the initial learning process, power should be at a minimum for both injury prevention and skills acquisition purposes. Power tends to embed skills. If power is applied too early in the process, the suboptimal skills embed. Patiently applying power to one or two perfectly correct sequence steps

is, in the initial learning stages, preferred before moving on to consecutive and sequential power application.

The next contributor to back injuries is the inhibited glutes discussed in the *Initiate body* sequence step. Not all athletes have inhibited glutes, but many do. Activating the glutes during the drive should be a key skill acquisition for all sculling and rowing athletes. When checking Group 2 alignment, the athlete should check glute status and correct if the glutes should have been involved and weren't.

The final and biggest contributor to back injuries is fatigue. When fatigue sets in, the glutes go walkabout, leaving other minor muscles to maintain Group 2 alignment during the stroke, which they cannot do. In addition, fatigue in other muscle groups causes a misalignment and ineffective connection amongst these groups. When learning this technique, or any new skill, stop before fatigue sets in. There is always plenty of small and slow work to do that is less demanding and will yield benefits without sacrificing the back.

Steering

The athlete has initiated the leg drive and is now off the seat. The arms are straight and will remain so for most for the drive sequence. How is steering accomplished? Quite simply: through the feet. Of course, boats can be steered using oars. To do so, the oars act as Class 1 levers, which is problematic during a race. The more efficient mode of steering is using the Class 2 lever, the athlete as the connector between the oars and the hull, and putting uneven pressure on the feet. The hull will yaw, which introduces drag. Thus, the preferred steering is subtle and small to minimize the effects of yaw, which will make itself known by the fishtail in the wake.

A good steering exercise is to first turn the scull 360 degrees using only the oars. Next, turn the scull 360 degrees by going up and down the slide, creating enough movement to maximize form drag on the blade and initiating the drive with only one foot. Observe the rotation speed or count how many strokes it takes to come full circle.

Another steering exercise is to row well and at a moderate speed, changing only the pressure on the feet, five to ten strokes in a scull with left foot pressure. Then, five to ten with the right. The objective is to execute a serpentine movement while retaining a consistent stroke with minimum speed reduction.

The effort throughout the drive sequence

The load on the oar is a function of effort or force. It is rarely the same for one part of the stroke to the next. Biomechanically, the large leg muscles are able to apply more force than the weak arm muscles. Thus, it makes sense to use those large leg muscles optimally. This occurs at the beginning of the stroke. Later in the stroke the torso rotates backwards, generating another force that is significant but less than that obtained from the large leg muscles. Finally, the athlete hangs on the handles, driving with the feet to the release, with the load dropping off then ending.

Load is a function of technique and how the athlete manipulates the application of the force. An athlete can 'load up' as early as possible in the stroke and generate a large force curve that then diminishes throughout the rest of the stroke. This results in a large load as well as a high physiological demand. Or, the athlete can endeavour to spread the load throughout the stroke. One way to determine how the athlete is applying his or her effort and spreading the load is whether their seat is off or light for the entire stroke.

There are two reasons for exploring spreading the effort throughout the drive sequence. This is not to suggest that the total effort is diminished in any way; rather, that it is applied more smoothly. The first reason for

so doing is the drag factor on the boat. Large, uneven applications of force create changes in drag. Constant velocity is the objective to gain optimal performance of the boat. Oars, too, respond to large uneven applications of effort with slip and wash, performing optimally with an even application of effort.

The limitation to achieving constant velocity is that the muscle groups of the human body produce uneven force. One strategy for modulating this is to ensure that segues between sequence steps and groups (as discussed in Chapter 3) are smooth. Instead of thinking of driving with the legs, then opening the body, then driving through the handles, the motion should be fluid and as continuous as possible. A good way to look at an athlete's execution of these segues is on the force screen of an ergometer.

The human body tends to operate along the same principles as the boat: increased effort places an exponential, not linear, demand on the athlete's physiology. The more even the application of effort, the more physiologically efficient. Thus, uneven demands on the cardiovascular system, particularly when the largest demand is at the beginning, will undermine the athlete's ability to perform. Unfortunately with sculling, the initial drive action is necessarily demanding. However, the clever athlete can learn to 'spread' their total effort. One strategy is ensuring that muscles are engaged in the sequence needed and relaxed when they are not. Or, instead of focusing on peak power during a stroke, the athlete can focus on total power over the entire stroke, with the goal of optimizing both their physiology and the performance of the equipment.

Boat run and free speed

The athlete, using the oars, propels the boat. Next, the boat, using that propulsive force, goes forward. It is a partnership. The better the propulsion and the quieter the athlete in a boat, the longer the boat will run. It is not unusual for the distance per stroke to be, say, 7m. Most of that 7m is boat run, not the athlete propelling. Thus, preserving this boat run is a crucial part of sculling efficiently, as is timing out of the back end and quickness at the front end.

Free speed describes tactics and strategies for making the boat go faster with the same effort. Its polar opposite is: work harder. The '1–2–3' experiment is one opportunity to explore how doing things differently, with the same effort, can yield free speed. The dynamic technique is continually on the hunt for free speed, which will present itself differently from one athlete to the next. While Chapters 5 and 6 provide an introduction, each athlete is encouraged to explore, experiment and play to make discoveries of their own.

How the dynamic technique feels in action

For those who have tried the '1–2–3' experiment, the feeling is probably very different. At low speeds, the differentiation in timing is accentuated. This provides more time in the back end to recover and, also, to think about what went well and what needs to change in the next stroke. At 16–18spm, the athlete should expect to count '1–2–3' at the back end. At 24–26spm, '1–2'. At 30–32spm, '1'. Higher, some fraction thereof. Speed or distance per stroke should verify the optimal timing at a given rating.

Later, as the sequencing comes together and the athlete can scull at consistently higher ratings, the feeling changes. The pre-drive and drive sequences smooth out. The timing becomes natural. The feeling becomes one of continual connectedness and fluidity. To the outside observer, the stroke looks effortless. To the athlete, it takes on an almost metronomic quality.

SUMMARY: DYNAMIC TECHNIQUE

To this point, topics have focused on the sculling system with the athlete as a component of that unified system. In reality, the equipment does not change much. However, the variability amongst athletes is considerable. It is the athlete's capacity to provide propulsion that ultimately determines speed.

The next chapters will focus on the athlete. Chapter 7 provides a comprehensive assessment to determine the individual athlete's current capacity and opportunities. The following chapters provide methods and practices for building on that capacity and capitalizing on those opportunities.

Endnote

1 Freeman, S., Mascia, A., McGill, S., 'Arthrogenic neuromusculature inhibition: a foundational investigation of existence in the hip joint', *Clin Biomech* (Bristol, Avon). 2013 Feb; 28(2): pp.171–177. doi: 10.1016/j.clinbiomech.2012.11.014. Epub 2012 Dec 20. PubMed PMID: 23261019.

7 | ATHLETE ASSESSMENT

The scull and oars are exquisitely designed to perform their engineered task – make the boat go fast. The previous chapters described the biomechanical and propulsive implications when the athlete joins the sculling system. With the sculling system complete (boat + oars + athlete), the quest is to optimize that system's stability and speed. The boat will not change much. Indeed, single scull design has not changed substantively in decades. The oars will not change much, although there are different types to explore (smoothie, Fat2, soft shaft, grip size, etc.). The athlete is another consideration. The athlete can change, improving both their biomechanical relationship to the scull and propulsive force. In order to determine what the future holds for an individual's sculling system, obtaining baseline data about the athlete is crucial.

This baseline data will assess the athlete on four dimensions: technique, fitness, FMB (flexibility, mobility, balance) and support activities. Later chapters will use this data to create a training programme and guide decisions about training priorities and goals. The base-

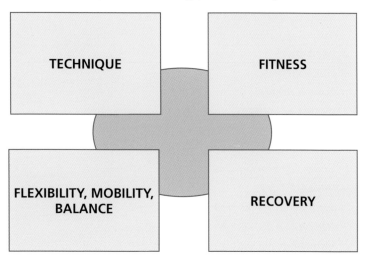

Fig. 84 Four assessment dimensions.

INDIVIDUAL TRAINING PROGRAMME BASELINE DATA

Name	Date
1. ORTHOSTATIC HEART RATE	
Resting Heart Rate (RHR)	
Orthostatic (standing) Heart Rate (OHR)	
Orthostatic Heart Rate difference	
2. MAXIMUM HEART RATE	
Resting Heart Rate (RHR)	
Maximum Heart Rate (MHR)	
Heart Rate Reserve (HRR = MRR-RHR)	
3. BODY MASS INDEX (BMI)	
Weight (kg)	
Height (m)	
Body mass index (W/H2)	
4. O'NEILL TEST	
Distance in metres (4 min)	
O'Neill Ranking (very good, good, etc.)	
5. ON WATER TEST	
1,000m on water time @ 18spm	
FISA age grade (D, E, F, G, etc.)	
Total time average (upwind/downwind)	
MPS (metres per stroke)	
SPM (strokes per minute)	
HR (heart rate for the piece at end)	
6. FLEXIBILITY, MOBILITY, BALANCE ASSESSMENT	
Flexibility opportunities	
Mobility opportunities	
Balance opportunities	
7. POWER TEST	
Peak watts (PW)	
Power/weight ratio (PW/weight (kg))	
8. SUPPORT ACTIVITIES	
Sleep	
Number of hours a night	
Quality (1 = poor, 5 = excellent)	
9. AVAILABLE TIME	
Top training days per week last year	
Training days per week available this year	
Top number of hours per week last year	
Training hours per week available this year	

Table 31 Baseline data worksheet with information that guides the creation of an individual training programme.

line data will be used to evaluate an athlete's progress during the training season as well as their competitive performance.

Gathering baseline data involves the athlete completing a task and/or taking a measure. The tasks are designed to be completed individually or in a group. Each task has a protocol to be followed for the initial data gathering as well as subsequent retests. Some tasks have normative standards. For other tasks, a follow-on calculation is required and described. One example is heart rate measures. The athlete will establish their resting heart rate (RHR) and maximum heart rate (MHR). Next, the athlete calculates heart rate reserve (HRR) and their individual training ranges (T1–T5). These training ranges will be used to create the athlete's training programme (Chapter 9), determine how the athlete can train most efficiently and measure performance (Chapter 12), and develop competition strategies (Chapters 13 and 14).

Every athlete is unique. Each athlete will have individual strengths and opportunities in the four different dimensions. Thus, the following chapters will guide the athlete to use that information to train efficiently and optimally for them.

ASSESSMENT TASK INTRODUCTION

Table 31 provides a sample baseline data worksheet. It is helpful to create a spreadsheet with additional columns for retesting results. The tasks, with a short description of each measure, are:

1. Orthostatic Heart Rate – resting and orthostatic
2. Maximum Heart Rate and Heart Rate Reserve – resting and maximum
3. Body Mass Index – weight and height
4. O'Neill Test – four-minute ergometer
5. On water 1,000m at 18spm
6. FMB (flexibility, mobility and balance) assessment
7. Peak Power Test
8. Support activity questions
9. Available time

Prior to completing the tasks, the athlete's training load and stress should be low. Pre-season or start of the training season is a good time. The tasks that involve aerobic effort should be spread out over time. Three to four weeks is reasonable. Completing the assessment tasks in a group is fun and athletes discover how truly unique they are. This acceptance of

Training Range	%HRR	Bottom of Range Calculation	Top of Range Calculation (%HRR)	Bottom of Training Range (bpm)	Top of Training Range (bpm)
T1	<60	OHR	RHR + 60% × HRR		
T2	60–75	T1 Top	RHR + 75% × HRR		
T3	75–85	T2 Top	RHR + 85% × HRR		
T4	85–95	T3 Top	RHR + 95% × HRR		
T5	95–100	T4 Top	RHR + 100% × HRR		

Table 32 Training range calculation worksheet to create individual training ranges.

individual differences is important in fostering the understanding that an efficient training programme is not a 'one size fits all' programme. The more that individual differences can be factored into a training programme, the lower the athlete's injury risk profile and the better their chance of improvement.

In addition to the baseline data, the athlete will calculate individual training ranges in *Task 2. Calculating Training Ranges*. Table 32 is for the athlete's use. An example in the *Task 2. Maximum heart rate (MHR)* section will guide the reader through the required calculations. The training ranges are the foundation of aerobic and anaerobic training. Their use allows for efficient training that yields optimal performance results.

TASK 1. ORTHOSTATIC HEART RATE (OHR)

This task involves taking two types of heart rate measurement and calculating the difference. The Orthostatic Heart Rate difference provides a baseline for future comparison during the training season as well as identifying potential pre-training issues.

Task 1. Protocol

Resting Heart Rate (RHR). Take a resting heart rate (RHR) upon awakening naturally in the morning, preferably during a normal week and over several days. If awakening to an alarm clock, wait several minutes. The measure is taken while lying down. Multiple measurements averaged over three to five sequential days are preferred. The result should be in beats per minute (bpm). For retests, ensure the methodology used is consistent over time (finger on pulse, heart rate belt, same duration of measurement, etc.).

RHRs vary significantly amongst individuals and low RHRs may or may not be indicators of fitness or pathology. The objective is to establish the baseline RHR under best circumstances so that the RHR number provides a useful comparison during the training cycle. During the training season, the RHR should be checked at least monthly to identify unexplained shifts. To ensure a valid comparison, these monthly checks should use the same method.

Orthostatic Heart Rate (OHR). After taking the RHR, stand up for three minutes. If the measure is taken before three minutes, the athlete may observe falsely high results. Take the orthostatic heart rate (OHR) using the same method for RHR. The OHR will be higher than the RHR.

Task 1. Calculation and normative standard

OHR Difference. The calculation is OHR minus RHR. Five to ten is in the expected difference range. The OHR difference is a good measure to watch during the training season. Significant variations should be questioned, particularly when the variations are consistently below five or over ten. While this difference is not always an indicator of fatigue, overreaching or overtraining, for some athletes it is. If an athlete experiences an unexpected variation, a simple test is to take a day or two off training. The variation will usually resolve

Taking a heart rate

Place index and third fingers next to the windpipe just below the chin. Or, at the wrist, place fingers between the bone and tendon over the radial artery on the inside of the wrist below the thumb. Count fifteen seconds and multiply by four.

Another option is using a device with a heart rate belt. Ensure the sensors are wet and a good connection made. Observe the heart rate on the device, which is usually beats per minute (bpm).

itself with rest. If after five days off from training the variation has not resolved itself, further investigation is advised to determine whether this is (a) normal for the athlete or (b) an indicator of illness or training-related systemic stress. A number of phone apps are available to make the task of taking and interpreting the OHR difference easier.

By example, an athlete with an RHR (70) and an OHR (78) would have an OHR Difference of eight, which is in the expected range of five to ten (Table 33).

Orthostatic Heart Rate (OHR)	78
Resting Heart Rate (RHR)	70
OHR Difference	8

Table 33 Example of the calculation OHR difference for athlete OHR (78), RHR (70) and OHR Difference (8).

TASK 2. MAXIMUM HEART RATE (MHR)

This task determines the athlete's Maximum Heart Rate (MHR). Under exertion heart rates usually plateau at a certain point for each individual, but not always. This certain point usually declines with age, however not always. The range of heart rate behaviours in athletes is huge. For example, in athletes over sixty years of age, the maximum heart rate can range from 200bpm to 105bpm.[1]

Maximum heart rate formulae do not work; the standard normal distribution is the reason why. For a large standard population, like human beings, the population is distributed in such a way that many people may have a similar characteristic but others fall further from average. A way of representing this diversity is the standard normal curve (Fig. 85). This bell-shaped curve of normalcy includes a large percentage, say 68 per cent, of the population that falls within the 'normal' range. In this

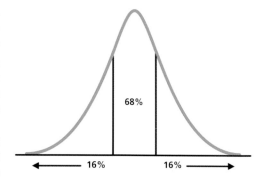

Fig. 85 Sample distribution of population Maximum Heart Rates (MHRs).

case, the remaining 32 per cent of individuals lie some distance from 'normal', as defined by one standard deviation. Using one popular formula of (220 − [minus] age), the result would be generally accurate for individuals within one standard deviation of the population, or 68 per cent. For the remaining 32 per cent, the formula would provide an invalid number. A training programme developed for these 32 per cent using a formula will cause undertraining or overtraining. A more detailed example of how this can go wrong is provided in *Task 2. Calculating training ranges* below.

Precision is important, especially with achieving training efficiency. This means determining each athlete's individual MHR, which involves athletic effort and observing what that maximum is. The *best* MHR is one observed doing the sport. Thus, a MHR observed during an all-out effort during an on water race is ideal. Use this if known, provided the timeframe is within six months. If unknown, then a Maximum Heart Rate Test will provide a baseline MHR. If a higher MHR is observed during the sport, this higher MHR should replace the baseline MHR.

Task 2. Protocol

Do not undertake this protocol if the athlete is not fit and healthy. If unsure of fitness levels, seek physician advice before proceeding. The athlete will have had no alcohol in the last twenty-four hours and no caffeine in the past four hours.

The test is simpler with an ergometer-compatible heart rate belt. Other heart rate belt options will work, e.g. NK SpeedCoach or bicycle computer mounted on the ergometer monitor (turn off auto shut down before starting). Taking a manual pulse is acceptable but is a less precise approach. Recording heart rates at each stage will illuminate when the athlete's heart rate plateaus. The test finishes when the heart rate stays the same between sequential stages or the athlete abandons the test.

Warm up on the ergometer at a drag of 110–120. Put the ergometer screen on watts. The following times are incremental, not duration at the stage. That is, Stage 1 is two minutes long, Stage 2 is two minutes long (total of four), Stage 3 is one minute long (total of five) and all subsequent stages are one minute. Continue to exhaustion or until two to three sequential stages yield the same heart rate (HR).

Stage	Workload	Time (min)	Heart Rate (HR)
1	75W	2	
2	125W	4	
3	150W	5	
4	175W	6	
5	200W	7	
6	225W	8	
7	250W	9	
8	275W	10	
9	300W	11	
10	325W	12	
11	350W	13	
12	375W	14	

Table 34 Stages of Maximum Heart Rate Test with watts and sequential times.

Clever athletes will figure out ways to combine this test with the O'Neill because the objective is not necessarily following the MHR protocol, it is obtaining a maximum heart rate. If that objective is achieved with, say, an all-out sprint at the end of the O'Neill, that saves doing two tests. As mentioned, the ideal MHR is obtained when performing the sport, so that is an option as well.

Task 2. Normative standard

There are no normative standards. The Maximum Heart Rate is the *individual athlete's* Maximum Heart Rate. It is a unique physiological marker. Comparisons with other athletes are meaningless. Comparisons within the athlete are highly useful. For example, if the MHR unexpectedly or significantly exceeds the baseline value during training (or the MHR Test), stop. Reassess whether the source of the original MHR was valid. False indicators include a deficient initial MHR test and loose HR belt. Accurate indicators are training-related stress and a cardiac event. If the heart rate belt is working and erratic changes are observed, say from twenty or more beats per minutes in a few strokes at similar effort, the athlete may be fatigued, overreaching or overtrained. If the heart rate jumps precipitously without explanation, stop and consult a doctor.

Another way in which MHR variations manifest themselves in athletes is during emerging illness, from small infections to life threatening. Consider whether potential illness or pathology may be the cause of an unexpectedly high heart rate. Again, medical advice is important to help determine whether the observed heart rate data is simply a function of the athlete's uniqueness or if it is a function of pathology. Thus, being aware of an individual MHR is helpful in planning training and monitoring health.

Task 2. Calculating training ranges

This book uses heart rate training ranges as the basis for achieving efficient and effective adaptive changes in the athlete. These changes lead to improved aerobic fitness. For the more advanced athlete, the training programme may work towards achieving a higher aerobic threshold and improved anaerobic fitness. To obtain precise, individually accurate training ranges involves laboratory testing. The training ranges below are simple to calculate and simple to use. Chapter 9 will discuss the nuances of working with these training ranges as well as some of their limitations and how the athlete can accommodate them.

Heart Rate Reserve (HRR) is the heart rate range between the athlete's resting heart rate (RHR) and maximum heart rate (MHR). HRR will be later apportioned into training ranges. The formula is Maximum Heart Rate (MHR) – Resting Heart Rate (RHR) = Heart Rate Reserve (HRR). An example is a forty-five-year-old athlete with MHR (159) and RHR (70). The HRR is 159 – 70 = 89.

Maximum Heart Rate (MHR)	159
Resting Heart Rate (RHR)	70
Heart Rate Reserve (HRR)	89

Table 35 Sample calculation of HRR for an athlete with MHR (159) and RHR (70).

Training ranges are subsets of the range of an individual's heart rate. Each range targets a specific physiological adaptation. For example, T2 in which 80+ per cent of the athlete's training will occur, achieves an increase in muscle and capillary growth. That is, improved aerobic capacity. Thus, if an O'Neill Test (Task 4 below) indicates that the athlete has a significant opportunity to improve aerobic fitness, the training programme would focus on T2 training since this results in improved aerobic fitness. Alternatively, T5 does not result in improved aerobic fitness but, rather, an increase in the aerobic threshold. This is useful in, say, training for end of race sprints and understanding the athlete's ability to increase the length of their ability to function anaerobically. However, T5 does little to increase aerobic capacity and is physiologically demanding. Thus, these training ranges become very important in creating an efficient training programme and targeting optimal adaptive changes for each individual athlete.

Using the athlete example above (who has an OHR of 78), the calculation for T1 would be 78 (the OHR) for the Bottom of the T1 training range. The top of T1 would be the Resting Heart Rate (RHR) + 60% × Heart Rate Reserve (HRH) = 70 + .6 × 89 = 123. The bottom range of Training Range T2 is the same as the top of training range T1. Similarly, the calculation for the top range of Training Range T2 would be: RHR + .75 × HRR = 70 + .75 × 89 = 137. Completing these

Training Range	%HRR	Bottom of Range Calculation	Top of Range Calculation (%HRR)	Bottom of Training Range (bpm)	Top of Training Range (bpm)
T1	<60	OHR	RHR + 60% × HRR	OHR	123
T2	60–75	T1 Top	RHR + 75% × HRR	123	137
T3	75–85	T2 Top	RHR + 85% × HRR	137	146
T4	85–95	T3 Top	RHR + 95% × HRR	146	155
T5	95–100	T4 Top	RHR + 100% × HRR	155	159

Table 36 Sample calculation of training ranges (T1–T5) for athlete with MHR (159), RHR (70) and HRR (89).

calculations for each category yield training ranges for T1 to T5 (see Table 36).

Because the individual athlete's training ranges will be used extensively throughout this book, and because they may change based on alterations to the MHR or RHR over time, a spreadsheet is helpful. Such a spreadsheet can be shared amongst a group and, again, reinforce the uniqueness of each athlete's training considerations. Table 32 should now be completed for the individual athlete.

Now back to the example of the sixty-one-year-old athletes with MHRs of 220 and 105. From the calculation below you can see what would be the result if an individual MHR is not obtained but a formula is used, demonstrating why each athlete needs to determine his or her own individual MHR.

Our first example athlete has a true MHR of 200 and an RHR of 70. This athlete's heart rate reserve (HRR) is 200 − 70 = 130. Calculating this athlete's individual, accurate T2 training range yields: 148–168bpm. Using the training range that results from the formula 220 − age, yields: 123–137bpm. Thus if the formula is used, the athlete's training ranges will be too low. That athlete will not train at an efficient nor optimal physiological adaptive level.

For the athlete with a 105 MHR, the T2 training range should be 91–96bpm. Using the 220 − age formula will yield training levels that are too high for this athlete. Fatigue, overreaching and overtraining are almost assured.

Many other formulae have been developed and are available. They have exactly the same problems when developing a precise, efficient, individual training programme. No generic formula is recommended.

TASK 3. BODY MASS INDEX (BMI)

When developing a training programme, it is helpful to understand how lean an athlete is or, conversely, how much deadweight the athlete is carrying. BMI is not an ideal measurement of body mass, however, it is simple and inexpensive.

Task 3. Protocol

The protocol is: supply weight (kg) and height (m).

Task 3. Calculation and normative standard

The formula is weight (kg) ÷ height (m) squared. The simpler approach is a BMI calculator on the internet. The sample below is for an athlete of 75kg and 172cm (1.72m). The calculation is weight (75kg) divided by height (1.72) × height (1.72), or 75 ÷ (1.72 × 1.72) = 75 ÷ 2.96 = 25.35.

Weight (kg)	75
Height (cm)	172
Height (m)	1.72
Height (m) squared	2.96
Calculation	75
	÷ 2.96
Body Mass Index (BMI)	25.35

Table 37 Example of a Body Mass Index (BMI) calculation for a 75kg 1.72m tall athlete.

The international normative standards are shown in Table 38.

	BMI
Underweight	<18.5
Healthy weight range	18.5–24.9
Overweight	25–29.9
Obese	30 and over

Table 38 Body Mass Index (BMI) normative standards.

This athlete is slightly overweight. This is where heated protestations about 'big-boned' begin.

Men	Excellent	Good	Above Average	Average	Below Average
19–29 Lwt	1243	1203	1122	1042	962
30–39 Lwt	1227	1187	1107	1026	946
40–49 Lwt	1208	1168	1087	1007	927
50–59 Lwt	1172	1132	1051	971	891
60–69 Lwt	1131	1091	1011	931	850
70–79 Lwt	1052	1012	931	851	771
80–89 Lwt	953	912	832	752	672
19–29 Hwt	1281	1241	1161	1080	1000
30–39 Hwt	1237	1197	1117	1037	957
40–49 Hwt	1219	1178	1098	1018	938
50–59 Hwt	1182	1142	1062	982	901
60–69 Hwt	1141	1101	1021	940	860
70–79 Hwt	1061	1020	940	860	780
80–89 Hwt	993	953	872	792	712

Table 39 O'Neill Test normative standard for men.

The athlete may not be overweight or obese, but they probably are. Even in sports-mad Australia the most recent figures (2014–15)[2] show an adult population 63 per cent overweight or obese, with the figure reaching 80 per cent for men aged forty-five to seventy-four. Women were only slightly less overweight and obese, at 68 per cent for the same age bracket. While participation in sport yields positive benefits, there are no guarantees that healthy weight is a given.

Here's how to validate the BMI: the Two Fist Test. Put hands slightly below the navel and grasp as much flesh as possible. If the fists can grip flesh, and even if the athlete's BMI is in the healthy weight range, there is opportunity here. The 'Mirror Test' provides helpful information. Stand in front of a mirror, preferably naked. Weight tends to gravitate to the middle as the athlete ages. A large abdomen requires the sculler to use shorter inboards, making their stroke ineffective or, if the oar gearing is not adjusted, setting the athlete up for injury. Losing weight will also improve performance because the cardiovascular system is less taxed than supplying oxygen to dead weight.

TASK 4. O'NEILL TEST

The O'Neill test was created many years ago by Terry O'Neill, ex-Great Britain coach and international coaching consultant. It is a fundamental approach used across many sports to provide a simple and reliable test of aerobic fitness.

Women	Excellent	Good	Above Average	Average	Below Average
19–29 Lwt	1078	1038	958	878	798
30–39 Lwt	1050	1010	929	849	769
40–49 Lwt	1030	990	909	829	749
50–59 Lwt	1011	971	891	811	730
60–69 Lwt	992	951	871	791	711
70–79 Lwt	973	933	852	772	692
19–29 Hwt	1105	1065	985	905	824
30–39 Hwt	1057	1017	936	856	776
40–49 Hwt	1044	1004	923	843	763
50–59 Hwt	1037	997	917	836	756
60–69 Hwt	1023	983	903	823	743
70–79 Hwt	944	904	823	743	663

Table 40 O'Neill Test normative standard for women.

Task 4. Protocol

Set up the Concept2 ergometer monitor for four minutes. (The normative standards are for a Concept2 ergometer only and may not be accurate for other types of ergometer or rowing machine.) Row for four minutes – best effort. Record the metres rowed.

Task 4. Normative standards

Check the total metres rowed against Table 39 (Men) and Table 40 (Women). Lightweight (Lwt) for women is 61.5kg (135.6lb) or less. Lightweight (Lwt) for men is 75kg (165.3lb) or less.

Our slightly overweight example is sixty-one years old and weighs 75kg. He rows 1,011m in four minutes. As a lightweight (75kg and below), his aerobic fitness is 'Above Average'. Adding a kilogram or two to his weight would require the heavyweight tables and an O'Neill ranking of 'Average'.

TASK 5. ON WATER TEST

The previous tasks have obtained dry land athlete data. Task 5 is sport-specific. The data will provide a considerable amount of information about the athlete's sculling performance baseline. This data will assist in determining their training programme priorities. Coincidentally, Task 5 provides a brief introduction into the training approach of this book.

First determine the athlete's FISA World Rowing Masters age grade. Age is determined by the athlete's age during the calendar year. Thus, an athlete with their fiftieth birthday on 30 November, is considered D grade as of 1 January, eleven months prior. The sport is fortunate in that FISA regularly reviews improving the competitiveness at the Masters levels, most recently implementing of new or modified grades J–M for the 80+ age group. Our example athlete at sixty-one is F grade.

FISA Grade	Age Range
A	27–35
B	36–42
C	43–49
D	50–54
E	55–59
F	60–64
G	65–69
H	70–74
I	75–79
J	80–82
K	83–85
L	86–88
M	89+

Table 41 FISA (World Rowing) Masters age groups (2018).

Task 5. Protocol

The objective of the 1,000m @ 18spm on water test is to determine the athlete's technical competence. A still day with no wind, tide or current is preferred. The athlete sculls 1,000m at 18spm from a standing start. A measuring device, such as a SpeedCoach, is necessary to capture the data. Heart rate data is very beneficial, specifically the athlete's heart rate at the end of the 1,000m. The baseline data are: total time, metres per stroke (if available on the measuring device), strokes per minute for the entire 1,000m piece and heart rate at the end of the piece. If there is wind, tide or current, the athlete needs to perform two (2) tests, one in the more favourable and one in the less favourable direction. The data are then averaged.

Task 5. Normative standard

See Table 42 for the normative standard. The table contains, by FISA age grade, the metres per second and times for 18spm, calculated as 76 per cent of the M1X and W1X winning prognostic times developed by the Rowing Australia Masters Commission, Handicap Sub-Committee in its *November 2013 Report and Recommendation*[3] as already discussed in Chapter 1.

For example, the D grade men's comparable 18spm prognostic is 3.521 metres per stroke (mps) or 4:44. The D grade women's comparable 18spm prognostic is 3.123 metres

MEN		A	B	C	D	E	F	G	H	I	J	K
M1X	1,000m mps	4.830	4.808	4.729	4.633	4.523	4.400	4.261	4.092	3.857	3.522	3.105
18spm	76% mps	3.671	3.654	3.594	3.521	3.437	3.344	3.238	3.110	2.931	2.677	2.360
Time			4:32	4:34	4:38	4:44	4:51	4:59	5:09	5:22	5:41	6:14	7:04

WOMEN		A	B	C	D	E	F	G	H	I	J	K
W1X	1,000m mps	4.284	4.265	4.195	4.109	4.011	3.899	3.767	3.595	3.335	2.928	2.339
18spm	76% mps	3.256	3.241	3.188	3.123	3.048	2.963	2.863	2.732	2.535	2.225	1.778
Time			5:07	5:09	5:14	5:20	5:28	5:37	5:49	6:06	6:35	7:29	9:23

Table 42 1X age grade prognostics for 18 strokes per minute (spm).

per stroke (mps) or 5:20. Few athletes will achieve these times because, amongst other things, this is a pre-season or early season test. These normative standards represent where the athlete is headed in the years ahead with a thoughtful, efficient training programme.

Our example F grade male athlete sculled a time of 5:15, at 3.17 metres per stroke (mps) and 18 strokes per minutes (spm). Table 42 indicates a performance between G and H grade. If our athlete were a woman, her performance would be very close to C grade (5:14).

Task 5. Calculations

Fig. 86 Flexibility test 1: Knee to wall. Heel on ground. The measurement is from the toe to the wall.

Fig. 87 Flexibility test 2: Apley scratch. This athlete's fingers are not touching, indicating an opportunity to improve shoulder girdle flexibility.

This book uses metres per second (mps) instead of times as the core measurement for training and performance. The reason is that analysing and manipulating time data is awkward. To average 4:01.03 and 4:30.49 is a far more challenging task than averaging 3.82mps and 4.01mps. For that reason, normative standards for ratings as well as training strategies use metres per second (mps). Times have been provided in Table 42 for convenience.

To convert times to metres per second (mps) is a straightforward calculation: distance (m) ÷ time (sec) = metres per second (mps). For a time of 5:00:00 the total seconds are 5 minutes × 60 seconds = 5 × 60 = 300 seconds. The distance is 1,000m. To calculate mps: 1,000 ÷ 300 = 3.333.

TASK 6. FLEXIBILITY, MOBILITY, BALANCE (FMB) ASSESSMENT

This assessment is the single most important. Its purpose is to identify injury risks. Sculling puts specific demands on the athlete. Common injury sites are the back, knee, hip and shoulder. Masters athletes with their age and life diversity have generally experienced past injuries. The problem arises when rehabilitation does not bring the athlete back to full function and balance. Additional guarding behaviours may contribute to imbalance, both musculoskeletal and proprioceptive, putting the athlete at further risk.

The following FMB Assessment is a simple tool. Developed with funding from the Western Australian Department of Sport and Recreation along with Masters Rowing Western Australian Incorporated, its target population is Masters scullers and rowers. The FMB Assessment is suitable for groups and team building as well. Tables 43, 44 and 45 provide descriptions of each test, the acceptable ranges (normative standards) and space for data entry. Each table is followed by photographs showing the testing position to help clarify how to conduct the assessment.

The added value of the FMB Assessment is that, to remediate most observed limitations, the athlete need only do more of that item as part of a remedial strategy. For example, if the Knee to Wall test (Item 1) needs attention, a remediation strategy is to assume the testing position a bit further from the wall and do gentle bounces as a way of improving flexibility in the ankle joint. The athlete does more of the gentle bounces on the less flexible ankle. Thus, both flexibility and musculoskeletal balance are improved. In another example, the way to improve Planks (Item 12), is to do Planks. The same is true of the proprioceptive tests. Ideally significant imbalances and performance issues will be referred to a competent professional for a remedial programme that, as the FMB issues are resolved, will lead into to a strength and conditioning programme. The FMB Assessment should be conducted at the beginning of each season.

Our example athlete meets the acceptable range in all categories except the following items: flexibility (4 and 5), mobility (7, 8 and 10) and balance (14). The baseline data worksheet shows 2, 3 and 1 to reflect the number of items needing remediation.

Fig. 89 Flexibility test 4: Sit and reach. Arms straight and not overreaching.

Fig. 90 Flexibility test 5: Straight leg lift. Leg straight.

Fig. 91 Flexibility test 6: Femur to chest. Hands on floor.

Fig. 88 Flexibility test 3: Dynamic flexibility torso. Face forward.

121

	Flexibility Tests	Tests	Acceptable Range and Notes	L or All	L or ALL Accep Range (Y/N)	R	R Accep Range (Y/N)
1	KNEE TO WALL (cm)	Ankle	**10–12cm**: kneeling, heel not off ground. Left = left leg being measured				
2	APLEY SCRATCH TEST (cm), hands behind back touching	Shoulder	**Fingers not touching but less than 5cm apart**: middle fingers cross over, left = left arm on top				
3	DYNAMIC FLEXIBILITY TORSO (deg), seated rotation of upper body	Thoracic	**45+ degrees from straight ahead:** hands together, arms out level with shoulders, even fingers. Left = fingers pointed left				
4	SIT AND REACH (cm), fingers over toes	Lumbar and hamstring	**6+cm beyond toes**: fingers on top of each other, toes straight up, 3 attempts allowed				
5	STRAIGHT LEG LIFT, from floor	Hamstring	**80+ degrees – floor to mid-thigh leg**: back flat, knees not bent, if back pain experienced stop immediately (referral)				
6	FEMUR TO CHEST (deg), knee to chest	Hip	**110+ degrees – floor to mid-thigh leg**: passive, hands not pulling leg in				

Table 43 Flexibility tests.

Fig. 92 Mobility test 7: Broomstick overhead squat. The heels remain down, shoulders, hips and ankles in vertical alignment. At the bottom of the movement, the thighs should be parallel to the ground.

Fig. 93 Mobility test 8: Sit to stand, both legs. Movement is controlled, pushing through the feet.

Fig. 94 Mobility test 9: Sit to stand, one leg. Movement is controlled, pushing through the foot.

Fig. 96 Mobility test 11: Push ups. Body is in a straight line.

Fig. 95 Mobility test 10: Calf raise individual. Knee is locked and leg straight.

Fig. 97 Mobility test 12: Plank. Body is in a straight line.

	Mobility/ Stability Tests	Tests	Acceptable Range	L or All	L or ALL Accep Range (Y/N)	R	R Accep Range (Y/N)
7	BROOMSTICK O/H SQUAT, heels down, stick remains O/H	Hip/Knee/ Ankle sequence	**10 times:** back vertical, heels down, 90 degree angle. A few warm-ups are allowed				
8	SIT TO STAND, both legs	Leg	**5 times:** arms crossed on chest, controlled				
9	SIT TO STAND, individual leg	Leg	**5 times each leg:** arms crossed on chest, controlled				
10	CALF RAISES, individual	Calf	**10 times each leg:** lock out knee, raise all the way up, look for hip out or hamstring assist				
11	PUSH UPS, on toes or knees	Upper body	**10 times:** nose to floor. Start with toes. Go to knees if unable to do 10 on toes. Count all				
12	PLANK	Core	**1 min:** body straight, buttocks not raised or lowered				

Table 44 Mobility tests.

	Mobility/ Stability Tests	Tests	Acceptable Range	L or All	L or ALL Accep Range (Y/N)	R	R Accep Range (Y/N)
13	STANDING EYES OPEN (Thigh 90 deg)	Balance	**30+ seconds with no touchdowns:** touchdown = foot to floor or hand to wall/other person. Angle of passive leg is not crucial				
14	STANDING EYES SHUT	Balance	**30+ seconds with no touchdowns:** touchdown = foot to floor or hand to wall/other person. Angle of passive leg is not crucial				

Table 45 Balance tests.

TASK 7. POWER TEST

The power test captures the comparative power of the athlete. The test is completed on an ergometer with the objective being to obtain the maximum watts. This score is then normalized for weight. The following protocol limits the first test of the season to no more than 120 drag factor to reduce injury risk (approximately the '4' setting on a Concept2 ergometer). Thus, the results cannot be compared to other Power Tests that may recommend beginning with a higher drag factor. The athlete will row full slide at full effort for ten seconds.

Task 7. Protocol

The athlete will need an assistant. This is a wonderful test to do as a group.

- Set the ergo monitor to display 'watts'. Ensure the assistant can read the monitor from where they are standing.

- Set the drag at between 100 and 120. Larger more fit athletes will use the higher drag.
- Warm up for five to ten minutes or until light sweating starts.
- Stop and coordinate with the assistant. The assistant's job is to time the ten second test and identify the highest 'watts' number on the monitor.
- Start. Row full slide for ten seconds with the objective being to generate the highest watts.
- Record the highest number of 'watts' observed.
- Retest. The athlete may retest but with fatigue comes injury risk. A better strategy is to complete the test monthly to observe progress.
- Cool down completely. This is a demanding test and continuing to row afterwards ensures that muscles lengthen and waste products are metabolized.
- Stretch, rehydrate and refuel.

Task 7. Normative standards and calculations

The calculation provides a power/weight ratio (peak watts per kilogram). Unlike maximum heart rate, the power/weight ratio is comparable amongst athletes. A sample calculation would be for a 78kg athlete whose peak watts were 412. Peak watts (412) ÷ weight (78kg) = 5.28 power/weight ratio. A smaller athlete (55kg) with the same peak watts would have a 412 ÷ 55 = 7.49 power/weight ratio. The higher the number the better the ratio.

For single scullers, the best application of this measure is to assess progress over time. First, additional fitness should improve the total watts produced. Second, as the athlete becomes fitter, the drag can be increased. The test may be a good measure of physiological capacity but no Masters research has been undertaken to determine how Masters' results compare to elite male results, for which some research does exist.

Our example athlete achieved 480 watts. Weighing 75kg, the power/weight ratio = 480 ÷ 75 = 7.4.

TASK 8. SUPPORT ACTIVITIES

Performance in sport is not solely a function of the athlete's aerobic fitness and technical sculling abilities. It is so much more than that: sleep, nutrition, hydration, psychology, family, work and an entire non-sport-related world. An athlete with a well-managed life who attends to the support activities that improve training efficiency, for example recovery management, is an athlete that will thrive. An athlete whose life is in disarray and who, rushed for time, eats fast food, gets insufficient sleep and is stressed, is at risk of overreaching and illness. This task captures one of the most important parameters: amount and quality of sleep.

Task 8. Protocol

Record the number of nightly hours *available* for sleep, on the average over the past week. Going to bed at 10pm and arising to row at 5am yields seven hours. Add to this time that includes pre-sleep strategies of no more than an hour's duration, for example a cup of warm milk and reading in bed. Next, record the average quality of that sleep on a scale of one to five for the same period (1 = poor, 5 = excellent).

Task 8. Normative standards

Sleep is only one of many support activities, but the effect of a lack of quality sleep on athletic performance and health is profound. For example, an athlete who is sleeping fewer than six hours a night on average is not going to retain new skills learned earlier in the day and may eliminate skills learned in preceding days. That athlete increases his or her risk of long-term health problems including non-genetic Alzheimer's, diabetes and cardiovascular disease. Tables 46 and 47 provide normative standards for sleep.

Our example athlete makes nine hours a night available for sleep. However, he wakes during the night on occasion for a toilet break or a partner's restlessness but wakes without the aid of an alarm clock feeling refreshed. Thus, the assessment is '9' (Acceptable/Preferred) and '4' (Acceptable).

	Number of Hours Available for Sleep
Fewer than 6.0	Needs immediate attention
6.0–7.0	Needs attention
7.0–8.0	Low acceptable
8.0–9.0	Acceptable
9.0+	Preferred

Table 46 Quantity of available hours for sleep assessment.

	Quality of Sleep
1 (Poor)	Needs immediate attention
2 (Below Average)	Needs attention
3 (Average)	Low acceptable
4 (Above Average)	Acceptable
5 (Excellent)	Preferred

Table 47 Quality of sleep assessment.

TASK 9. AVAILABLE TIME

Masters scullers are rarely full-time athletes. Sculling is an important component of their lives but may range from recreational to elite levels of commitment. Problems arise when aspirations are inconsistent with available time. It is unlikely that any athlete who has only three hours a week to commit to their sculling is going to be competitive at the national level. But they don't need to be. Three hours a week is sufficient time to progress on many dimensions and with the long career runway Masters have, incremental progress can achieve significant results over time. This task helps the athlete develop realistic expectations as to the training time available, since the individual training programme will be designed using available time.

Task 9. Protocol

The first question to answer is what happened last year? If an athlete was training last year, the number of training days and the number of hours per week they actually completed provide a fairly realistic predictor of what will be available this year. Thus, the first two questions ask: during the top training week last year (peak week), (a) how many days did the athlete train and (b) for how many hours? The next question is what are the number of days and hours available this year?

Because this chapter leads into how to create a training programme, this is a good point in time to explore why identifying a realistic amount of training time is crucial. Sculling is a very inefficient sport from a training time perspective. Time needed to drive to the boatshed, put the scull on the water, take the scull off the water and drive home are amongst the activities that make the sport more inefficient from a time use perspective than, say, running where the athlete can run right from their home. A normal training session in a scull is usually one+ hour training and one hour of ancillary activities. An athlete who plans to scull three times a week needs more than three hours of available time. In fact, six is not enough for many due to the travel considerations.

Thus, the first assessment is the days/hours of training last year. The second is, how happy was the athlete about how that worked? If the answer is 'not happy', the days/hours need to be reassessed.

Next, what are the days/hours planned for this year? Do those days/hours deviate significantly from last year? If yes, where is the time coming from and is this realistic? 'I retired' is a fair answer. 'I am going to get less sleep' may not be.

For newer athletes when the last year question yields 'I did not train at all last year', the exploration is what their new training commitment will be. This commitment should be realistic, achievable and satisfying. The same maxim is true for experienced athletes.

Task 9. Calculations

Table 48 helps refine expectations. The goal is to create a successful training programme that achieves performance improvements, but over time. Not in one year. And hopefully over a very long time, too. This task helps the athlete achieve the 'long' view and to set expectations that are realistic and achievable.

Enter into Table 48 all the athlete's weekly time commitments. Do not enter sculling time at this point. Items to include are:

1. Nine hours available for sleep, including getting ready for sleep and pre-sleep and waking routine
2. Family time
3. Work time
4. Other regular commitments including meals, shopping for meals and social activities.

What remains after subtracting 'Commitments' from 'Subtotal Available' are the hours available for training.

For an athlete with fewer commitments, the available time increases. Our example athlete has recently retired and has time to train every day. Athletes with jobs, families and other commitments are going to be, to some degree, challenged. The frustration that accompanies overestimating available training time and the consequent inability to execute a training programme make for an unhappy athlete. Thus, identifying the time available for a sculling commitment is an important exercise. Here conservative and accurate are better.

SUMMARY: ATHLETE SELF-ASSESSMENT

The baseline data gathered in this chapter will be used for two purposes. First, the athlete can track their progress by retesting. Second, the data will be used in Chapter 9 to create an individual training programme. Thus, the quality of the data is important to ensure that the resulting training programme assists the athlete with achieving the best possible results.

Our example athlete has not only completed the Training Range Calculation Worksheet but has also completed the Baseline Data Worksheet and is now ready to plan how to go faster!

Description	Mon	Tues	Wed	Thu	Fri	Sat	Sun
Total Hours	24	24	24	24	24	24	24
Available for Sleep	-9	-9	-9	-9	-9	-9	-9
Sub-total Available	15	15	15	15	15	15	15

	Commitments (Hours)						
Family							
Work							
Other							
Sub-total Commitments							
Sub-total Available for Training (Available – Commitments)							

Table 48 Available training hours calculation worksheet.

Endnotes

1 World Rowing. FISA Medical Commission. Hannafin, J.A., 'Common Rowing Injuries: Prevention and Treatment', *World Rowing. FISA Medical Commission* www.worldrowing.com/uploads/files/Prevention_of_Rowing_Injury_2011.pdf.

2 Australian Government, *Australian Institute of Health and Welfare. Overweight & Obesity.* www.aihw.gov.au/reports-data/behaviours-risk-factors/overweight-obesity/overview.

3 Mussared, M., *October 2013. Rowing Australia Masters Commission Handicap Sub-Committee November 2013 Report and Recommendation.* Rowing Australia: Canberra.

INDICATOR TRAINING PROGRAMME BASELINE DATA

Name EXAMPLE ATHLETTE	**Date:** Today

1. ORTHOSTATIC HEART RATE	
Resting Heart Rate (RHR)	70
Orthostatic (standing) Heart Rate (OHR)	78
Orthostatic Heart Rate difference	8

2. MAXIMUM HEART RATE	
Resting Heart Rate (RHR)	159
Maximum Heart Rate (MHR)	70
Heart Rate Reserve (HRR = MRR-RHR)	89

3. BODY MASS INDEX (BMI)	
Weight (kg)	75
Height (m)	1.72
Body mass index (W/H2)	25.35

4. O'NEILL TEST	
Distance in metres (4 min)	1,011
O'Neill Ranking (very good, good, etc.)	Above Average

5. ON WATER TEST	
1,000m on water time @ 18spm	
FISA age grade (D, E, F, G, etc.)	F
Total time average (upwind/downwind)	5:15
MPS (metres per stroke)	3,.17
SPM (strokes per minute)	18
HR (heart rate for the piece at end)	148

6. FLEXIBILITY, MOBILITY, BALANCE ASSESSMENT	
Flexibility opportunities	2
Mobility opportunities	3
Balance opportunities	1

7. POWER TEST	
Peak watts (PW)	480
Power/weight ratio (PW/weight (kg))	6.4

8. SUPPORT ACTIVITIES	Sleep
Number of hours a night	9
Quality (1 = poor, 5 = excellent)	4

9. AVAILABLE TIME	
Top training days per week last year	5
Training days per week available this year	5
Top number of hours per week last year	10
Training hours per week available this year	10

Table 49 Example athlete's completed baseline data worksheet.

8 | ASSESSMENT REVIEW AND INTRODUCTION TO TRAINING

Each athlete has different aspirations: get fitter, improve sculling skills or go faster. The previous chapter measured the athlete's skills and capacities. Adding to these the training time available and the possibilities begin to emerge. The training programme incorporates aspirations, training history and available time while embracing basic training principles. It shapes the possibilities into probabilities.

Creating the first year's programme is a challenge, usually because athletes new to using a structured training programme overestimate (a) the amount of time available or (b) a realistic annual improvement. The results from Chapter 7, to be reviewed here, will put these in perspective. Masters do not need to rush. More important are staying engaged with training, the quality of it and remaining injury free.

REVIEW OF THE ATHLETE'S ASSESSMENT RESULTS

This is a review of 'what is', not a value review. An athlete's assessment results are not 'good' or 'bad'. The reference point is not how one's

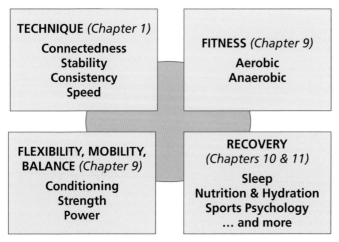

TECHNIQUE *(Chapter 1)*
Connectedness
Stability
Consistency
Speed

FITNESS *(Chapter 9)*
Aerobic
Anaerobic

FLEXIBILITY, MOBILITY, BALANCE *(Chapter 9)*
Conditioning
Strength
Power

RECOVERY *(Chapters 10 & 11)*
Sleep
Nutrition & Hydration
Sports Psychology
… and more

Fig. 98 Four assessment dimensions expanded to include chapter references.

friends did. The reference point is whether the athlete completed the assessment tasks to the best of their abilities so that the baseline data is accurate. The baseline data provide the foundation information for the individual athlete's training programme. The example athlete's results will be discussed, while the individual athlete follows along, assessing their own results in tandem.

The starting point is the four assessment dimensions, but other parameters will unfold. The following chapters will cover all of these dimensions and more.

Aspirations

What are the athlete's long- and short-term aspirations? For example, a new athlete may aspire to improve fitness and sculling skills. That athlete may want to enter their first competition in their first year and, in five years, be competitive at a regatta. An experienced athlete may aspire to achieve progressive improvement in their 1,000m time with a five-year objective being to meet their grade's international prognostic. Having these aspirations in mind provides perspective while reviewing the athlete's assessment results.

Next, are the athlete's aspirations realistic? For example, the plans in the above paragraph provide both long- and short-term objectives. The broader timeframe provides ample opportunity to achieve improved fitness, skills and to adjust a training programme. Trying to achieve the same objectives in only one year is a recipe for frustration. Staging the gains over multiple years allows for flexibility, the unexpected and success.

The athlete's training programme, with baseline data, will allow that athlete to measure their improvement over time. An athlete with a solid training programme will know well before their target regatta what their expected time and/or competitive position is likely to be. With realistic aspirations in hand, the next step is to review the self-assessment.

Orthostatic Heart Rate (OHR) (Baseline data 1)

The athlete should start the season with an OHR of less than ten. Over ten, and the athlete should skip to the recovery chapters and ensure that enough recovery is happening in their daily life. While the OHR is not a definitive measure of systemic fatigue, it is a good starting point. It is important for athletes to become familiar with it as a tool in assessing fatigue throughout the training season, understanding that the best indicator of fatigue is how the athlete feels.

Referring to our example athlete's baseline data at the end of Chapter 7, we see an OHR of eight. Our athlete also feels ready to train – all good.

Maximum Heart Rate (MHR) (Baseline data 2)

The athlete has calculated their MHR as well as their training zones. There are many models of training zones. For any model that uses calculations, not laboratory testing, the athlete must be aware that the boundary zones are not precise. That includes the training zones used here. For instance, our example athlete had a T2 range of 123–137bpm and a T3 range of 137–146bpm. The boundary appears to be 137bpm. This is a soft interface. In reality it may be 134 or 143. Precise laboratory testing will establish that interface, on the day of testing. It may change next month. Thus, the athlete's calculated training zones are guidelines.

As guidelines the training zones do provide an 'alert' to the athlete to develop self-awareness as to when physiological changes occur. For many athletes these transition indicators are distinct, say a skin prickling. This happens most commonly in the transition from T4 (aerobic) to T5 (anaerobic) because the physiological changes from one energy system to another are significant. The transition sensa-

Training Zone	%HRR	Conversational Ability	Perceived Effort
T1	<60	Full conversation	Very light
T2	60–75	Full conversation	Comfortable
T3	75–85	One to two sentences	Somewhat hard
T4	85–95	Short phrases	Hard
T5	95–100	Words or noises	Very hard

Table 50 Alternative training zone indicators.

tion is driven by changes in lactic acid build-up as well. However, learning to recognize these changes is helpful.

This book uses heart rate zones because training to heart rate is an efficient approach. The athlete will need access to a heart rate measuring device. For those who do not have access or prefer not to use a heart rate monitor, there are alternative indicators (Table 50).

Different adaptations occur at different training zones. A sustained T2 effort indicates to the body that it needs to develop the capacity to function efficiently at a new level of steady exertion. The short-term options for the body are: (a) the heart pumps harder to deliver oxygen to progressively taxed muscles or (b) the body starts developing new muscles and oxygen delivery system so that the heart can pump less, muscles can work less and the body can operate at a new normal.

'Sustained' is the operative word,

Training Zone	%HRR	Exercise Type
T1	<60	Aerobic
T2	60–75	Aerobic
T3	75–85	Aerobic
T4	85–95	Aerobic
T5	>95	Anaerobic

Table 51 Aerobic and anaerobic exercise by training zone.

meaning months. With sustained, long-term T2 training, the body develops capillaries, muscles and the supporting neural network, as well as many other adaptations. The body improves its ability to oxygenate. For the same effort as before, the athlete's heart rate will decrease. Performance rises. With sustained effort and properly managed with recovery, this progressive adaptation can continue for years. For athletes for whom aerobic fitness is a priority, the training focus will be at T2.

For athletes whose aerobic fitness is excellent, as measured by the O'Neill, the majority (80%+) of their training programme will still be at T2. However, these athletes may want to improve their aerobic threshold – the place at which the body transitions from aerobic to anaerobic. Increasing that threshold provides the athlete with more aerobic runway. To achieve this involves working at T4 and, eventually, cycling back between T4 and T5. This physiological change at T4 and T5 is *not* building capillaries, muscles and neural networks. It is creating a change in oxygen utilization, a completely different physiological process.

Training programmes need to reflect the appropriate training heart rate to achieve the desired goal. An athlete who wants to improve aerobic fitness will train efficiently and achieve that goal at T2. Spending time at T4, for this athlete, is counterproductive. Working 'hard' at levels that the athlete can only speak in 'short phrases' (see Table 50) may raise that lower fitness athlete's anaerobic threshold. However, with that athlete's already low aerobic base, their overall performance improvements will be negligible because he or she does not yet have the needed capillaries, muscles and neural networks.

Conversely, an athlete with an 'excellent' O'Neill who wants to improve their aerobic/anaerobic threshold will do some work in T4 (and T5). That athlete has an excellent aerobic base. But even for that fit athlete, most of their training will be at T2 to sustain, retain and improve their aerobic base.

Our example athlete has the training zones calculated and is eager to proceed (after surreptitiously comparing training zones and maximum heart rate to everyone else's).

Body Mass Index (BMI) (Baseline data 3)

BMI indicates whether the athlete has opportunities to change their body composition. The caution here is that for larger individuals whose leg muscles have adapted to carrying that weight, weight loss programmes should be supplemented by resistance training to retain that capacity. Because of the potential for introducing additional training stress, targeting weight loss is a good activity for off season.

Our example athlete's BMI of 25.35 is slightly 'overweight', which our athlete expects to change with improved nutrition during the upcoming training season. He maintains that he is 'big-boned' and not really overweight anyway.

Fitness as measured by the O'Neill test (Baseline data 4)

Fitness is defined here narrowly as aerobic fitness, measured by the O'Neill Test. An athlete scoring 'above average' to 'below average' has an opportunity to improve aerobically. That athlete's training programme will focus primarily on aerobic development, meaning the T2 heart rate range, which is conversational. Athletes scoring 'good' or 'excellent' will continue their aerobic development but have opportunities to explore their aerobic thresholds, including experimentation with some different types of training.

Aerobic fitness improvement takes time. Expect at least two years of sustained T2 training to move from one O'Neill category to the next. This assumes an appropriate six-month training season with off season as described below. During this time the body will construct new parts: building new capillaries, new muscles and new neural networks and all the supporting systems. The older the athlete, the longer these changes will take and the quicker the gains will dissipate if the T2 effort is not sustained.

There is no quick fix to increasing aerobic fitness. This includes high-intensity training (HIT). While research on sedentary adults indicates that high-intensity training (T4+) may kick-start their aerobic fitness development, there is no research on trained adult athletes supporting that such training is beneficial towards improving the athlete's aerobic base over the long term. Both the physiological systems targeted by HIT (anaerobic) and the additional training stress argue against it as a predominant training mode.

Be aware that aerobic fitness improvements will be masked by fatigue during the training season. For example, the athlete may find that monthly O'Neill tests do not improve. This is a good reason for not doing these tests monthly because aerobic fitness gains will be better observed annually or semi-annually. A well thought out and executed training programme, and confidence in it, will produce the desired result.

Our example athlete is an F grade heavyweight man with a distance of 1,011m, an 'above average' O'Neill. He would like to achieve a 5 per cent improvement to 1,061m.

Technique as measured by the on water test (Baseline data 5)

The on water test has two components: speed and heart rate. An athlete performing at or below grade (E grade athlete performing at B grade) and completing the 18spm piece at T4 is an aerobically different athlete than one producing the same results at T2. The latter is fitter and probably better technically. Thus, the training programme that evolves for these two athletes will be different.

5. ON WATER TEST	
1,000m On Water Time @ 18spm	
FISA Age Grade (D, E, F, G, etc.)	F
Total Time Average (upwind/downwind)	5:15
MPS (Metres per Stroke)	3.17
SPM (Strokes per Minute)	18
HR (Heart Rate for the piece at end)	148

Table 52 Technical results (on water test) for example athlete in Chapter 7.

Training Zones	Bottom	Top
T1	OHR	123
T2	123	137
T3	137	146
T4	146	155
T5	155	159

Table 53 Training heart rate zones for the example athlete in Chapter 7.

		F	G	H
M1X	1000m 100% mps	4.400	4.261	4.092
18spm	76% mps	3.344	3.238	3.110
Time			4:59	5:09	5:22

Table 54 Extract from 1X men's age grade prognostic table (Table 41).

Our example athlete has performed as in Table 52 with training zones in Table 53.

Referring to the Table 54 excerpt in the men's prognostic table, at 3.17mps, this F grade athlete falls between G and H grades. The question is: what are the different contributions of technique and fatigue? The athlete's heart rate was 148, which is at T4. That athlete was working hard to achieve the result. In order to be competitive at grade, an athlete needs to complete this 18spm at prognostic and at T2.

Thus, two factors are operating. One is that the athlete fatigued, as evidenced by a heart rate of 148bpm. This is expected given the athlete's O'Neill was 'above average'. Second, there is technical opportunity because even with that greater effort, the athlete performed between one and two grades higher (G/H to their actual F grade).

Our athlete now has two training programme objectives. First, improve aerobic fitness, which will result in a reduced heart rate. If the athlete cannot perform low rating pieces at low heart rates, that athlete will have limited capacity to perform higher rating pieces. The second training objective is technical. If our athlete cannot perform at their prognostic grade at 18spm, they will not perform at their prognostic grade no matter how high they rate. All of this can be improved upon through appropriate training.

Our example athlete would like to go faster and achieve 3.238mps at 18spm in T2: a speed improvement of 2 per cent, a fitness objective moving from T4 to T2 – and the next prognostic grade!

Flexibility, mobility and balance (FMB) (Baseline data 6)

Adult athletes are hotbeds of pathologies. That sprained ankle twenty years ago resulted in an imperceivable limp that, long term, created an unobservable muscular imbalance. Years of not rolling around on the floor, doing cartwheels or jumping have reduced mobility and flexibility. Visual dependence now dominates proprioceptive balance. All are natural, normal trends with most completely reversible.

Good FMB has performance implications, too. A flexible athlete will have a greater effective stroke arc than their inflexible selves. 'Stiff' athletes who need to make sequence position adjustments on the fly, such as completing their body flip during the boat gathering because of tight hamstrings, will compromise connectedness and stability. A specific measure of interest is the athlete's result on the plank. This is a measure of core strength. Athletes need to meet this one-minute minimum before they can achieve sustained connection. Capitalizing on FMB opportunities should be the athlete's highest priority.

Whatever the athlete's ranking on the individual FMB tests, the objective is to be able to do all of them to standard. The tests have been designed so that just doing them repeatedly will help remediate deficiencies; for example, for the Apley scratch test, using a broomstick to walk hands closer to each other and back again. Ideally, those substandard test results should be repeated three times a week and complemented by daily stretching to retain the successful FMB results.

Our example athlete has a number of FMB opportunities: flexibility (2), mobility (3) and balance (1). Core strength is a focus item.

Power test (Baseline data 7)

While this is an important item, no research-based normative standards are available for Masters. Thus, until such time as those are available the athlete should test for improvement but set this item as a lower priority.

Our example athlete's power test was 480 peak watts with a 6.4 power to weight ratio (watts/kg).

Support activities (Baseline data 8)

The importance of adequate sleep cannot be overemphasized. Sleep is not the absence of activity; it is a separate biological state where many unique, fundamental processes occur. Chapter 10 will explore the effects of shortened or poor-quality sleep, including the increased risks of: hypertension, type 2 diabetes, obesity, cardiovascular disease, non-genetic Alzheimer's and mortality, to name but a few.[1] The impacts of shortened sleep are cumulative and can have effects decades later, with many pathologies including non-genetic Alzheimer's beginning in the forties and fifties.

Aside from the general health aspects of adequate sleep is the effect of insufficient sleep on new skills acquisition. That is, athletic training. During the late stages of a night's sleep, new motor skills shift from short-term storage to long-term memory. If the last hours of sleep do not occur, transfer of the day's motor learning is impeded (or does not occur at all).

The appropriate questions to be answered here are: (a) are nine+ hours of time for sleep available each night and (b) is the quality of sleep acceptable? If the answer is no to either, this item needs to move to the top of the training programme priority list with, perhaps, a reduction in training time so as to achieve more sleep hours.

Our example athlete has nine hours for sleep and reports the quality as acceptable.

Available time (Baseline data 9)

The increase between last year and this year's training should be no more than 10 per cent. If it is, the three most common reasons for an increase in training hours are: (a) a new athlete who has trained little in the previous year, (b) a change in life circumstances and (c) overenthusiastic assessment. The tactics for programme creation for these three groups vary.

New athlete

The training objective for the new athlete is to create a programme that provides for structure. That is, the primary goal of a new athlete's first-year training programme should just be showing up at training, preferably on time. The magnitude of personal habit change that is required to form new scheduling habits is considerable, as is acquiring the habits associated with sculling. Thus, the training schedule for the new athlete needs to achieve a high level of compliance. Compliance is achieved through small successes and fun. The goal is for the new athlete to be retained in the sport.

Change in life circumstances

Cutting back work hours, the children going off to university and retirement provide new opportunities for sport, including too much of it too fast. The body adapts incrementally. However, new available time can be put to good use at lower levels of exertion, including T1 and T2. Sitting in a boat acquiring skills is a very good use of time, and not likely to lead to overreaching or overtraining. Increasing last year's aerobic and anaerobic workload by 50 per cent will have a detrimental effect. This athlete needs to use as a basis for their training programme the actual training hours and days from the previous year with a training increase in the order of 10 per cent.

Accuracy of time assessment

A realistic estimate of available time is needed so that the training programme will be realistic. Otherwise the athlete will find themselves not meeting training objectives, feeling disappointed and stressed. The training programme will then need to be revised. Thus, being conservative in available time calculations will result in a programme that is achievable without later recriminations and rework. The same rule applies: an aerobic/anaerobic training increase of no more than 10 per cent from last year.

Our example athlete retired three years ago but is very excited about improving his performance, originally indicating that his actual hours per week and available training days are increasing by 100 per cent. He is now going to plan for 5.5 hours and 5.5 days of aerobic and anaerobic training (10 per cent over last year). Any extra time will be used for small work at T1, FMB and stretching.

Prioritization

There are three key items: flexibility, mobility and balance (FMB); fitness; and technique. The athlete has a limited amount of time, so training priorities need to use that time efficiently.

The first priority is FMB, particularly developing core strength. Without FMB, the athlete will be unbalanced both muscularly skeletally and proprioceptively. The next priority is aerobic fitness because it contributes to general health as well as performance. The last is technique. No amount of technical prowess will overcome deficiencies in FMB and aerobic fitness. The next step is to explore how that training programme will achieve performance results.

Summary of the example athlete

Our example athlete has selected the following priorities:

Primary priorities (recommend three)

P1. Address FMB opportunities. Can do this at home.

P2. Improve aerobic fitness. Raise O'Neill from 1,011 to 1,061, a 5 per cent improvement.

P3. Improve technique. Achieve a 3.238mps at 18spm at T2: a speed improvement of 2 per cent but at T2 (also a fitness improvement).

Secondary priority

S1. Achieve a healthy weight range

Our example athlete now has all the information needed to craft a thoughtful training programme. But what is training and what is it meant to accomplish? How is the training programme structured? And, how does one create a specific training programme for that very individual athlete?

PRINCIPLES OF TRAINING

There is no research to indicate that a Masters sculling athlete needs to reduce their training volume, intensity and frequency over their lifetime. That does not mean creating a high volume, intense, training programme is in the athlete's best interests. It does not mean that 'more' and 'harder' achieve better performance results. The 'less' and 'targeted' approach is preferred because injury risk is reduced, recovery needs are lower and adaptation progresses at a comparatively faster rate.

The objective in training is to be clever and determine the most efficient training approach for an athlete. Efficiency achieves the desired training outcome with the least physiological stress. An efficient training programme minimizes fatigue and injury/illness risk. It speeds recovery and adaptation.

The basic training principles include seven categories (Table 55). The reader will already recognize most of them as being thematic in the book.

Individuality

Every athlete is unique. To be efficient, their training needs to reflect that uniqueness. A one size fits all training programme, which will achieve optimal results for all athletes, does not exist. This is particularly true of Masters, whose ages range over decades. Similarly, a training programme used for high school athletes is ill advised. Generalist approaches will result in suboptimal performance. It takes time and effort to create an efficient, individual training plan. The first year, particularly, is a challenge. It is time well spent.

Progression

Progress takes time. The body evolves incrementally, and training needs to reflect that. The training included here includes an annual training plan (training programme + off season) with an eye to successive years. The training programme contains incremental increases in training stress, its own sub-progression. Masters have decades to discover,

Training	Description
Individuality	Each athlete is unique and their training programme needs to reflect this
Progression	Progress is made over time and involves different training aspects
Reversibility	The cessation of training results in the training gains regressing
Specificity	Training should reflect the athlete's aspirations and target event
Overload	Training needs to stress the system in order to achieve improvements
Recovery	Adaptation cannot occur without recovery
Adaptation	The body will become more efficient, producing more for less effort

Table 55 Principles of training.

improve and enjoy methodical, injury free progress. A five-year plan is encouraged.

Reversibility

The body seeks the lowest level of complexity to sustain itself. This regression is efficient from an evolutionary perspective. Thus, while training progresses, the body continues to wage its regressive war. When training stops, regression wins. Adaptation goes backwards. The older one is, the more quickly that reversal will proceed. There are buffers, though, such as the body has a tendency to maintain fitness for several weeks while determining whether the cessation in training is permanent. How the athlete approaches off season has a large effect on how reversibility plays out.

Specificity

The principle of training specificity holds that the closer the training routine is to the training objective, the better the outcome will be.

For the athlete competing at Masters regattas, training pieces at high rating and speed should be done at 1,000m (or some organized subset of same), the better to mirror the target race. Not 1,500m or another random length. When training stress is applied to a set of muscles or systems disassociated from the training objective, adaptation will occur for those disassociated muscles and systems. That training will be inefficient. Efficient training targets the physiology, through appropriate activities, in relationship to the training objective.[2]

Overload (stress), recovery and adaptation: the training equation

Overload (stress), recovery and adaptation are the interdependent training principles that underpin the training programme. Training stress (overload) comes in a range of forms. It can be aerobic stress, which taxes the cardiovascular and pulmonary systems. Learning new technical skills, mastering them, and embedding them as habits

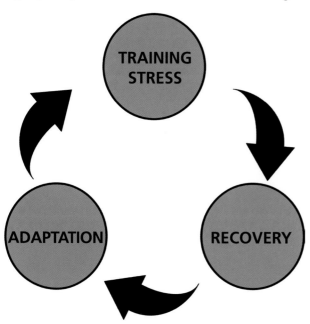

Fig. 99 The training equation with balanced training, recovery and adaptation.

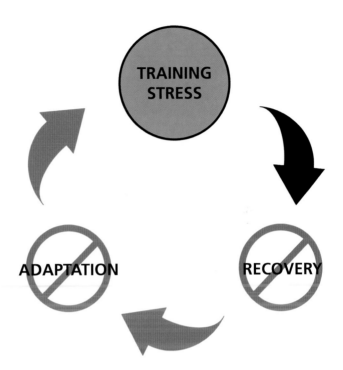

Fig. 100 The unbalanced training equation where recovery does not occur, nor does adaptation.

create motor and cognitive stress. To these can be added life's stressors, too, from the physical of too much gardening to the emotional stress when a child, partner or parent becomes seriously ill.

All of these physiological stressors combined (training, competition and life) create total stress. Sometimes the results of these stresses are obvious. Symptoms of muscular stress are soreness, swelling and limited motion. When the brain overloads learning new skills, athletes experience the 'fried brain' syndrome. Psychologically, athletes (and their coaches) get cranky. The athlete feels fatigued.

Then a new day dawns. Post-workout nutrition and hydration, coffee, massage and a good night's sleep resolve the previous day's total stress. Post-workout nutrition and hydration provide the carbohydrates that muscles need to restore glycogen and protein for muscle repair. Muscle soreness is reduced or eliminated. Coffee provides hydration (as well as performance-enhancing caffeine) and the psychosocial context for dealing with the

crankiness. A massage helps move wastes into the appropriate physiological system, relaxing and lengthening muscles that will now be more capable of executing skills. Sleep provides an extensive range of general health and sports-specific benefits, as well as facilitating the acquisition and embedding of the new skills. These restorative processes are cumulatively called recovery.

Recovery can be informal and involve a break from the stressor. Or, it can be more targeted and managed, benefitting from evidence-based strategies that will accelerate and comprehensively resolve training stress. When recovery is rapid and complete, stress resolves. Adaptation can occur. If recovery does not occur, adaptation does not, either.

Adaptation describes the torn muscles that, properly fuelled with protein, repair and grow. After cardiovascular stress and when the athlete rests, adaptation describes the new capillaries that are constructed. Blood flow increases. Adaptation describes how the athlete learns to cope psychologically, developing self-awareness and intervention strategies. In its totality, adaptation describes the athlete's goal: more propulsion for less effort. Or, going faster. Or, having more fun because they don't fatigue as quickly. Whatever that adaptive goal, stress needs to be resolved through recovery. Thus, the training equation: stress + recovery = adaptation.

But what role does ageing have in the process? The athlete's physiological processes slow down and become more inefficient with age. How this progresses for adult athletes as a cohort is not well understood. How this progresses for an individual athlete will be our next experiment as the athlete's training programme emerges.

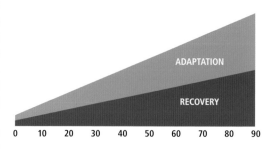

Fig. 101 A conceptual view that adaptation and recovery times increase with age.

Recovery

Recovery changes with age. Physiological systems slow down. They are less efficient. The recovery that took a short time in the thirties takes a considerably longer time in the sixties. Thus, what needs to change with age is the incorporation of and attention to recovery tactics. The wisdom of age will come in handy here, as will an awareness of fatigue, which is an accurate overall indicator of whether recovery has taken place.

Recovery is the foundation of success for an adult athlete. Two whole chapters in this book are devoted to recovery. As an adult athlete ages, recovery, not training, arguably becomes the most important consideration in their ability to achieve continued fitness and performance improvements.

Adaptation

Adaptation takes longer with age, too. Just as it takes a skin cut longer to heal, so it takes muscles longer to regenerate and new capillaries longer to form. With proper recovery, adapt they do.

One instance where adaptation does not occur is when the athlete does not introduce enough training stress. The Australian Government's Department of Health recommends, preferably, daily activity accumulating between 150–300 minutes of moderate intensity physical activity, 75 to 150 minutes of vigorous intensity physical activity, or a combination of the two. Muscle strengthening activities at least two days a week are recommended.[3] For those sixty-five and older, the emphasis is on daily activity. Other countries have similar guidelines.

These volumes and intensities may, or may not, be sufficient to induce adaptation for an individual athlete. For the uninitiated and new athletes, they provide some entry level guidelines to temper expectations. That is, training at 300 minutes at moderate intensity, or five hours a week, is terrific for general health. If the athlete's objective is winning national competitions, the training plan will need to reflect an increase in volume, intensity and/ or frequency. Or, even better, a multi-year approach to success.

Adaptation will not occur if the stress has been insufficient to trigger an adaptive response. The athlete who does the same workout, every time, at the same intensity, volume and frequency for months and years on end is an example. This is true even if the training loads are relatively high. The human body relentlessly seeks ways to minimize physiological stress. Thus, a training programme that provides no variability results in the initial levels of adaptation and then, thereafter, none.

To counteract this tendency towards equilibrium, training programmes need to be periodized within the day, week, month and year. Periodized means doing more on some days (or weeks or months), less on others. This keeps the body guessing and efficiently achieves adaptation. Periodization provides for regular recovery during the day, week, month and year as well. For the athlete who manages a periodized programme well, the fitness gains provide a foundation for future annual gains.

Limits of adaptation

The body does not have an infinite capacity to adapt. Whatever the original adaptive capacity, it changes with age. As the body's recovery processes become more inefficient, so do adaptive processes. Thus, the older athlete can gain benefits from being self-aware and training with that change in mind. There are many clever ways to continue a high level of training while accommodating these age-related changes. With physical activity, excellent training management and high-quality recovery, the older athlete's performance capabilities are a complete frontier.

THE PHASES OF TRAINING

Creating an individual training programme is a hierarchical process that starts with a five-year plan tied to aspirations. That five-year plan can

TRAINING YEAR	
Off Season	**Active Training**
Systemic recovery	Stress, recovery and adaptation

Table 56 Overview of the training year.

be as simple as: have fun and get better. Or, it can be: exceed the international prognostic time for my grade. Five-year plans are aspirational. They change. It helps to have a larger view, though, so that the annual plan has perspective. If things don't go as well as expected, it's nice to have a larger five-year context, and the next year, to fall back on. If training does go well, it's exciting to see in advance what can happen in the years ahead.

The annual plan is also aspirational, but with the athlete's assessment and priorities providing a quantified foundation. For the competitive athlete, a key timing determinant will be: when is the athlete's target event? Then, iterative steps proceed backwards. The year is broken into four logical phases: annual, month, week and day. The training programme that results from planning each of these provides a personal map and itinerary for the annual journey ahead.

Off season and active training

The first breakdown is: off season versus active training. Off season is the time for systemic recovery. For our purposes, active training will cover twenty-six weeks, or half the year, and off season the other half. A longer active train-

Fig. 102 Year-to-year training gains with off season.

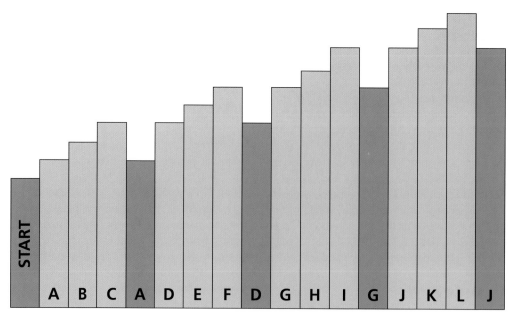

Fig. 103 Sample portion of a 3 and 1 periodized programme with programme start and recovery weeks (green).

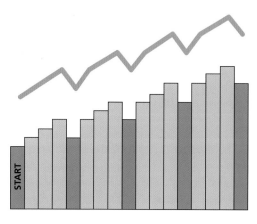

Fig. 104 Sample portion of 3 and 1 periodized programme showing 7.5 per cent progression.

significantly increases the risk of systemic failure such as overtraining.

During the training year, the athlete has achieved gains in aerobic, anaerobic, strength, speed and other improvements. The purpose of off season is to preserve the previous season's gains while simultaneously allowing the body to recover from the sustained stress of training. There is an inherent tension in training; the athlete progressively pushes limits. The body will adapt, but this takes evolutionary energy, since the body is pre-programmed to seek the lowest level. This tension can create systemic overload. Managing this tension and making progress for six months is the hallmark of good training.

The body needs a break from this progressive limit pushing. It is time to consolidate. There will be some regression. Reversibility will not be complete, i.e. back to the start of the previous season's levels, unless the athlete does absolutely nothing during off season. If the athlete remains athletically engaged, the retained gains will be slightly less than at

ing period can be set by the athlete with a concurrently shorter off season. However, the off season needs to be an appropriate length to achieve full systemic recovery. Athletes should not actively train twelve months a year, since this achieves limited or no adaptation and

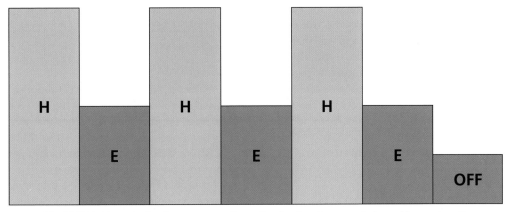

Fig. 105 Weekly periodized programme alternating hard and easy work days with one day off.

season's end, providing a new, higher starting point for the next training season (Fig. 102).

From an aerobic perspective, three days a week of aerobic activity will sustain some of these gains. The guidelines for maintaining general health are the minimum, preferably, daily activity accumulating between 150–300 minutes of moderate intensity physical activity, 75 to 150 minutes of vigorous intensity physical activity, or a combination of the two. Ideally, these activities will be different and diverse to assist with developing better skeletal-muscular balance.

Flexibility, mobility and balance can be improved during the off season. Strength and conditioning programmes are well suited for emphasis during off season. For athletes who have water access, off season is ideal for exploring stability and connectedness through small and slow work. Weight loss is another project that lends itself well to off season.

The first week of the active training programme will be at the off season training level. It is important to come back to training with a restored body, an eagerness to train and with a preservation of last year's hard won gains.

Active training and periodization

Adaptation is achieved through stress + recovery. From a timing perspective, the most efficient gains are achieved through periodization. Periodization reflects a steady increase in volume and/or intensity of training to achieve adaptation. This process is accelerated when regular reductions in training load occur. The timing of these training load increases and reductions can be on a variety of schedules and is usually expressed in terms of 'weeks on' and 'weeks off'. Fig. 103 is an example of a three weeks on and one week off programme, or '3 and 1'.

The programme can be periodized in other ways but three weeks on and one week off approximates one month and is a very conventional periodization timing. It's a misnomer because the 'off' week is not truly 'off' but, rather, a backtracking to provide some recovery relief. The backtracking serves to keep the body guessing as to what is happening so that systemic adaptation continues.

The rate of increase, usually measured in volume as opposed to intensity, can alter as well. The increase should never be more than a 10 per cent rate of increase over the entire programme. Even 10 per cent is the outer limit

143

of what will achieve adaptation for Masters athletes without heightening the risk of systemic problems. Aggressive and well managed recovery strategies can reduce this risk, but high load increases are a dance with the devil. Because there is ample time, the recommendation is to start with a 7.5 per cent increase, and for newer athletes, less is fine. As competition or the end of the training season get closer, undercooked is better than overcooked.

Weekly periodization

The days within a week are periodized but in a different way. It is during the week that stress is truly introduced by varying the training load more dramatically. The convention is to refer to these as 'hard' and 'easy' days, or 'H' and 'E' for short. The contrast between these two days should be significant, particularly so during speed work with a 50 per cent variation. A simple example would be sculling 4km one day at the T2 training heart rate (easy conversational) on an easy day, followed by a day of 8km at T2. During speed work, another example would be to do the same 4km but with increased intensity and speed. The goal is to keep the body guessing and in adaptation mode. This hard and easy variation allows for recovery. Every week should have a full day off from all workload, including gardening and other physical endeavours that interfere with recovery. This rest day is as important to achieving adaptation as the training itself.

SUMMARY OF ASSESSMENT REVIEW AND INTRODUCTION TO TRAINING

The athlete now should have their self-assessment reviewed and prioritizations identified. This assessment review defines where the athlete is, at the moment. It defines that athlete's aspirations, i.e. where they would like to go. Future chapters include methodologies and information to help the athlete make successful progress from where they are to their chosen destination.

Endnotes

1 Hillman, D.R., Lack, L.C., 'Public health implications of sleep loss: the community burden', Med J Aust. 2013 Oct 21; 199(8): pp.S7–10. PubMed PMID: 24138358.

2 Hawley, J.A., 'Specificity of training adaptation: time for a rethink?', J. Physiol. 2008 Jan 1; 586(1): pp.1–2. doi: 10.1113/jphysiol.2007.147397. PubMed PMID: 18167367; PubMed Central PMCID: PMC2375570.

3 Australian Government, Department of Health. Fact Sheet: Adults (18–64 years): Background information regarding Australia's Physical Activity and Sedentary Behaviour Guidelines for Adults (18–64 years). 7 Feb 2014. www.health.gov.au/internet/main/publishing.nsf/Content/fs-18-64years.

9 CREATING THE INDIVIDUAL TRAINING PROGRAMME

In this chapter the athlete will prepare their individual training programme. The programme will create a progression. The major steps start with assessing the athlete's available hours, referencing aspirations and last year's actual training workload. Next comes spreading the available hours progressively throughout the season. A discussion of volume and intensity will guide the athlete in allocating training time, as well as understanding how the progression increases in volume, intensity and frequency.

The primary purpose of the training programme will be to create a plan for aerobic development. FMB, strength, conditioning and power will be reviewed briefly with recommendations for improving in those dimensions. Chapter 12 discusses technique development. The final outcome of this chapter will be a training programme and an understanding of how it was developed.

VOLUME, INTENSITY AND FREQUENCY

The first question most athletes ask about their training programme is: how much volume? Unfortunately, no evidence-based answer is available, even for high-performance younger sculling athletes. As we have seen, Masters can accumulate increased performance improvements for years through thoughtful annual training and off seasons (Fig. 102). Thus, the pressure to achieve quick gains is not there. From the perspective of volume, the approach here is to start with what can be achieved comfortably, first reflecting on what was achieved last year.

In some environments, too much emphasis is put on huge workloads without the supporting assessment tools to verify that the workload is achieving performance improvements. Athletes training at volumes, intensities and frequencies that are too high for them are unduly stressing their physiological systems and setting themselves up for injury or, worse, overtraining. Excessive stress requires additional recovery time. It slows down adaptation. Performance times go down, not up, and athletes lose their enthusiasm for sport.

The balance amongst volume, intensity and frequency is highly individualized and based to some degree on training history. Even in endurance-based training, intensity and volume of training are trade-offs. As one goes up, the other goes down. This balances the physiological stress at the systemic level, which is our objective.

Intensity is defined as training heart rate: T0, T1, T2, T3, T4 and T5. T5 has the highest training intensity, T0 has none. A strong evidence base exists supporting that low-intensity workouts (T2) are the path to increased aerobic development, creating more capillaries, muscles and neural networks. While high-intensity (T4/T5) training methodologies may achieve quick changes at the cellular level, particularly in the sedentary subjects, there is less evidence to support that the cells being changed are ones related to increased aerobic capacity. That is not to dismiss high-intensity training but to indicate that it is early days in developing an entire sculler's training programme based only on high intensity. Approximately 80 per cent of the athlete's programme is at T2, with a 'comfortable' perceived effort and the ability to carry on a full conversation.

Last is frequency. How often to train? This is the one question that does have an answer: how much time does the adult athlete have available and want to invest in training? This may seem backwards to those familiar with Olympic training programmes for athletes whose entire existence is bound to their training effort. For adult athletes, one of the biggest stressors is creating a training programme that is unachievable and, as a result, introduces considerable psychological stress into training. Thus, the training programme to be created in this chapter will start with – time available.

ASPIRATIONS AND TIME AVAILABLE

Whatever the athlete's aspirations, those have a good chance of being realized if the training programme is long enough. New athletes with a five-year plan can achieve steady progress each year. Experienced athletes who try to accomplish huge performance jumps in one year will find that a multi-year programme has its benefits. There is one thought to keep in mind: adaptation = stress + recovery. Less, done efficiently and well, is more.

What are the athlete's specific aspirations this year, as defined by the main event? The main event then aligns with Week 25. Since the overall purpose of a training programme is improvement, an athlete does not need to compete to achieve it. For those who do not have a main event, a target end date for their training year will do.

Each athlete now has their well-considered training hours available per week. Write down the hours available. Next, those hours need to be spread over the training season so that incremental adaptation occurs. A training programme model provides the methodology, after which the athlete will start filling in their programme.

TRAINING PROGRAMME MODEL

Endurance training begins the season with a focus on building aerobic capacity. Over the training season, higher intensities, in terms of increased training heart rates, are introduced in small volumes. The training programme model described here does just that.

Fig. 106 shows an overview of the training programme model. There are twenty-six weeks covering the active training portion of the year. The remaining twenty-six weeks are for off season. The active training programme contains a progressive build-up in volumes, as shown by the vertical bars. Each week (1–26) is easy (E) or hard (H). A complementary increase in intensity will occur, with the volume to intensity balance discussed below.

The progression is 7.5 per cent. Weeks 1–18 involve steady increases in volume and intensity. At Week 19 there is a significant recovery week that experience has shown works well both for international elite teams of younger rowers as well as Masters. It provides a chance to recover before speed work starts. A taper is included at Week 24 and the athlete's main event is on Week 25, with the following week a recovery week.

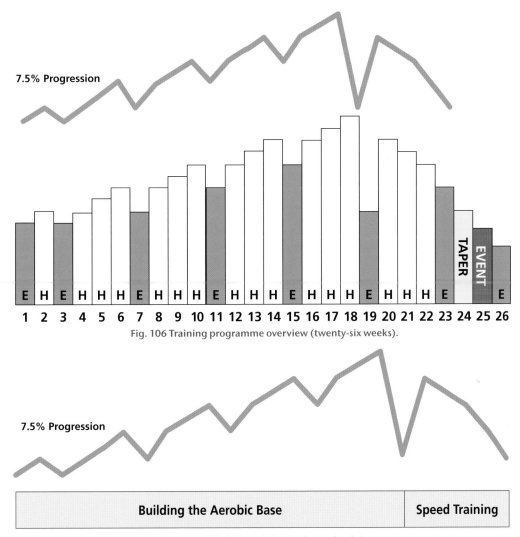

7.5% Progression

E	H	E	H	H	H	E	H	H	H	E	H	H	H	E	H	H	H	E	H	H	H	E	TAPER	EVENT	E
1	2	3	4	5	6	7	8	9	10	11	12	13	14	15	16	17	18	19	20	21	22	23	24	25	26

Fig. 106 Training programme overview (twenty-six weeks).

7.5% Progression

Building the Aerobic Base	Speed Training

Fig. 107 Aerobic base training and speed training.

Calculating training times by week

The first part of the season (Weeks 1–19) targets the development of aerobic fitness and building the aerobic base. The second part of the season (Weeks 20–25) is speed training. That is not to say that speed work occurs only at the latter part of the season. Speed work continues throughout. However, in the latter phase, training should match as closely as possible the target event, here 1,000m (Principle of Specificity). This increase in intensity (which has been occurring gradually throughout the season), is complemented by a reduced volume of work, improving recovery and preparing the athlete technically.

The progression for base training is shown in Fig. 108. This is a *percentage* of available training hours per week. Our new example athlete has ten hours available for training, which was the available hours she had last

Fig. 108 Progression percentage calculations for base training (Weeks 1–18).

Progression Percentages (%): Base																	
W1	W2	W3	W4	W5	W6	W7	W8	W9	W10	W11	W12	W13	W14	W15	W16	W17	W18
44	50	44	50	56	63	50	63	69	75	63	75	81	88	75	88	94	100

Week	WK1	WK6	WK10	WK14	WK18	WK22
E/H	E	H	H	H	H	H
Progression	44%	63%	75%	88%	100%	75%
Available Hours						
4	1.8	2.5	3.0	3.5	4.0	3.0
5	2.2	3.2	3.8	4.4	5.0	3.8
6	2.6	3.8	4.5	5.3	6.0	4.5
7	3.1	4.4	5.3	6.2	7.0	5.3
8	3.5	5.0	6.0	7.0	8.0	6.0
9	4.0	5.7	6.8	7.9	9.0	6.8
10	4.4	6.3	7.5	8.8	10.0	7.5
11	4.8	6.9	8.3	9.7	11.0	8.3
12	5.3	7.6	9.0	10.6	12.0	9.0
13	5.7	8.2	9.8	11.4	13.0	9.8
14	6.2	8.8	10.5	12.3	14.0	10.5
15	6.6	9.5	11.3	13.2	15.0	11.3
16	7.0	10.1	12.0	14.1	16.0	12.0
17	7.5	10.7	12.8	15.0	17.0	12.8
18	7.9	11.3	13.5	15.8	18.0	13.5
19	8.4	12.0	14.3	16.7	19.0	14.3
20	8.8	12.6	15.0	17.6	20.0	15.0

Table 57 Training times calculated from the total available time.

Fig. 109 Progression percentage calculations for speed training (Weeks 19–23).

Progression Percentages (%): Speed								
W19	W20	W21	W22	W23	W24	W25	W26	W27-52
50	88	81	75	63	Taper	Event	Post Event Recovery	Off Season

year, too. At Week 18, she will be training for all of them. In Week 7, 50 per cent or 5.0 hours. At the start (Week 1), 44 per cent or 4.4 hours.

This is one place in programme preparation that may need adjustment, in part because the instructions to date have been not as precise as they will now be. Week 18 is often known as 'Peak Week'. It is the week when the athlete spends the most training time during the year. It may be slightly disproportionately higher than the athlete's available training time on the average. Our example athlete is comfortable with ten hours a week, but she is willing to find a few extra hours in the later weeks of the

Week	1	2	3	4
E/H	E	H	E	H
Subphase	Load	Load	Load	Load
Periodization %	44	50	44	50
Available hours	10	10	10	10
Training Hours = Available Time x Periodization %	4.4	5	4.4	5
T2+ Activities Total Hrs.				
Sculling	3	3	3	2
Ergo				
Cycling	1	1	1	2
Swimming		1		
Walking	0.4		0.4	1
T0/T1 Activities Total No.				
FMB	3	3	3	3
Stretching	3	3	3	3
Technical	1	1	1	1

Table 58 Sample programme based on the example athlete's available time.

programme to accommodate a more diversified programme. As long as the additional time is spent in T2, low intensity, the injury risk is reasonable for this strategy. The approach has the benefit of starting the season at a slightly higher training workload that is still well within the available hours.

Thus, the athlete has some flexibility here. Table 57 provides a broader view of how the available time will play out. Designating the athlete's 'available hours' is an important decision. Too much is going to see the athlete possibly fatiguing early in the programme, unable to recover and adapt. Too little is going to see less adaptation but steady progress in that regard. The available hours is not a number that lends itself well to programme changes. An athlete whose decision was not well thought out will find themselves needing to go through all the programme creation steps again.

The objective is to create a programme that has a realistic chance of achieving compliance. If in doubt, be conservative and choose a lower 'available hours' target. Soon the athlete will spread these available hours precisely throughout all the weeks.

But first, speed training. From the perspective of available time, the volume of workload decreases steadily during speed training. The relative intensity is higher, but finding hours to train is less of a problem.

Week	1	2	3	4	5	6	7
Date							
E/H	E	H	E	H	H	H	E
Subphase	Load	Load	Load	Load	Load	Load	Load
Periodization %	44	50	44	50	56	63	50
Available hours							
Training Hours = Available Time x Periodization %/100							
T2+ Activities Total Hrs.							
Sculling							
Ergo							
T0/T1 Activities Total No.							
FMB							
Stretching							
Technical							

Table 59 Training programme template – Load subphase (Weeks 1–7).

Week	8	9	10	11	12	13	14	15
Date								
E/H	H	H	H	E	H	H	H	E
Subphase	High Load	High Load	High Load	High Load	Low Speed Trans	Low Speed Trans	Low Speed Trans	Low Speed Trans
Periodization %	63	69	75	63	75	81	88	75
Available hours								
Training Hours = Available Time x Periodization %/100								
T2+ Activities Total Hrs.								
Sculling								
Ergo								
T0/T1 Activities Total No.								
FMB								
Stretching								
Technical								

Table 60 Training programme template – High-load and low-speed transition subphases (Weeks 8–15).

Sample training programme based on hours

Table 58 presents a sample training programme, and only for the first four weeks. The athlete's completed training programme will be twenty-six weeks long. Some of the categories and concepts contained in this programme are now familiar, for example E/H (easy and hard), and T2+ as well as T0/T1 (training heart rates). The other new components, such as subphase, training hours and how they are spread, are covered below.

Available hours, training hours and dates

It is time to start filling in the first part of the athlete's individual training programme. Enter available hours (Tables 59–62). The number should be the *same* for every week because it will be multiplied by the above percentage (see Table 58 sample). To obtain training hours for each week, multiply the available time by the 'Periodization %', which will provide a large number. Divide by 100 to obtain training hours. Enter dates by counting back from the main event (Week 25), adjusting as needed to

Week	16	17	18	19	20	21	22	23
Date								
E/H	H	H	H	E	H	H	H	E
Subphase	Low Speed	Low Speed	Low Speed	Low Speed	High Speed	High Speed	High Speed	High Speed
Periodization %	88	94	100	50	88	81	75	63
Available hours								
Training Hours = Available Time x Periodization %/100								
T2+ Activities Total Hrs.								
Sculling								
Ergo								
T0/T1 Activities Total No.								
FMB								
Stretching								
Technical								

Table 61 Training programme template – Low-speed and high-speed subphases (Weeks 16–23).

accommodate absences or tapers longer than one week (see below sections for descriptions on how to do this).

Creating a spreadsheet at this stage is very helpful. Not only is it easier to manage in the first year, but if the programme is successful, the athlete can copy and paste to good effect next year.

Adjusting for vacations and other planned absences

Most adult athletes will have a disruption in their training programme in six months. Planned absences can be accommodated. Ideally these disruptions will involve alternate training activities; hiking instead of sculling, swimming instead of ergo. If the plan is to lie on the beach, here is how to proceed.

First, for absences up to two weeks. Try to plan the absence around the training programme such that those weeks fall on a hard (H) to easy (E) sequence. The absence then provides two weeks' recovery. The programme starts back as scheduled. So, the training programme continues as a twenty-six week programme, understanding that those two weeks are not going to happen.

For absences longer than two weeks when no activity is planned, a different strategy is needed because while fatigue will reduce, so will fitness. The programme will either need to be extended with some repetition of the prior weeks or the entire progression

Week	24	25	26
Date			
E/H	E	H	E
Subphase	High Speed	High Speed	High Speed
Periodization %	Taper	Event	Post
Available hours			
Training Hours = Available Time x Periodization %/100			
T2+ Activities Total Hrs.			
Sculling			
Ergo			
T0/T1 Activities Total No.			
FMB			
Stretching			
Technical			

Table 62 Training programme template – Taper, main event and post-competition recovery (Weeks 24–26).

will need to be shifted, resulting in Week 18 being less than 100 per cent. The objective is to ensure that the longer the non-training absence, the lower the re-entry requirements. Be conservative.

Taper, race and post-event recovery

The purpose of the taper is to ensure the athlete performs their best at the main event by reducing fatigue while retaining fitness. Thus, training volumes reduce significantly with a focus on retaining high-speed skills.

Aerobic adaptation is not the objective, recovery is. Fatigue is alleviated three times faster than fitness deteriorates. One taper week is included in the current programme. Two weeks for a multiday event, particularly for older athletes, has benefits. The plan is for the athlete to be rested, fit, enthusiastic and ready to do their best at the main event; this is known as 'peaking'. If the training programme is successful, including the taper, the athlete will perform at their season's peak during their main event. Chapter 14 further discusses tapers.

Based on what day(s) the main event occurs, it may require some schedule adjustments to ensure adequate taper. Also, post-recovery is an important part of the annual programme. One week is included in the programme, two weeks has additional benefits in shifting the athlete to off season regimes. Adjust the schedule accordingly.

SPREADING THE HOURS

There are two primary spreading approaches: hours or distance. This allocation can be done very simply, or a greater degree of precision can be built into how the available time is spread. The choice is a matter of personal preference and, most important, compliance. The training programme is a working document. It is used every week to evaluate the previous week, know what to do this week and plan for the next week. The athlete should create a training programme that suits their personal needs and that the athlete enjoys using. Start simply if this is the first year of using one.

The next differentiation is between activities that are T0/T1 and those that are T2+ (T2–T5) including cross training. Activities in both are important, with the athlete making choices about how their training time will be spent.

T0/T1 ACTIVITIES

The T0/T1 section of the training programme captures those activities that are very important to a well-rounded training plan but which don't contribute significantly to aerobic base development. They do contribute to injury risk prevention, learning new skills and recovery, thus they deserve specific consideration.

T0/T1 activities are planned, and accounted for, in number, not hours. Our example athlete's programme (Table 58) shows FMB at three times a week. This is the minimum recommended for all athletes. Each FMB session may take only twenty minutes. Stretching is recommended three times a week minimally, the ideal is daily. Stretching may take only fifteen minutes. The compliance concept is that if these activities are written down as objectives, they are more likely to happen than not.

The technical category is only slightly different. Much of acquiring new and refining old sculling technique can be done not only sitting in a boat but on the floor at home. Finger roils can be acquired. Sequencing can be practised. The athlete can define their own T0/T1 sessions, creating other categories as they see fit: tai chi, meditation, relaxation yoga, etc.

T2+ Activities and Cross Training

The T2+ activities use hours, not numbers. They can also use distance. The benefit to using distance on T2 activities is that it is easier to apportion a workout by intensity in the daily plan. The options are: complete one hour of training versus complete 8km. The other reason for using distance is that various activities are qualitatively different. An hour on the ergo is not the same as an hour on a bicycle, walking or sculling. Rationalizing this fact through the use of distance and weighting helps provide a more accurate assessment of the intensity of a given workout.

The value of cross training and using varied activities for aerobic training development are that:

- it makes training more interesting;
- different activities use different muscles, developing musculoskeletal robustness;
- in the event of injury, the athlete has other training modality options; and
- varied activities assist with a more fluid transition to off season.

The limitation of cross training is that it does not align as well with the principle of specificity. This will be partially compensated for by the training efficiency approach discussed in Chapter 12. Cross training is a trade-off. For long-term athlete development, it is highly recommended.

T2+ activities using hours

Using hours, the athlete splits their training time into the various activities. However, all activities are not alike. Walking for an hour at T2 does not have the same physiological effect as running at T2 for an hour. Table 63 provides some comparative estimates. It is the athlete's choice as to whether weighting is used in allocating their hours to various activities.

Activity	T2 Perceived Hourly Equivalent (Estimate)
Sculling	1
Circuit weights	1.25
Cycling	0.8
Ergo	1.35
Field sport	1.2
Running	1.4
Swimming	1.2
Walking	0.5

Table 63 T2 perceived hourly equivalent estimate sample.

Experiment: Calculating individual perceived T2 hourly equivalents

This experiment produces *perceived* T2 equivalents for activities. It requires a heart rate monitor.

1. Identify the activities for which equivalents are desired. Ideally these are activities the athlete either likes to do or in which a clear benefit is perceived, so as to aid compliance.
2. Complete the sculling first. Either a half hour or one hour is good. Its perceived effort is then given a value of 5.
3. Complete the same amount of time in the other activities at T2. All activities are completed at the same heart rate, such as either bottom of T2 or top of T2 range.

Activity	Athlete's Perceived Effort Raw Data	Athlete's Normalized Perceived Equivalents
Sculling	5	1
Circuit weights	8	1.6
Cycling	4	0.8
Ergo	7	1.4
Field sport	5	1
Running	9	1.8
Swimming	6	1.2
Walking	3	0.6

Table 64 Sample of raw data and calculation of athlete's perceived equivalents.

4. Rank the perceived effort you experienced in relationship to sculling (5) on a scale of 1–10, with 10 being very difficult.
5. Normalize the activities against the sculling T2 number. That is, divide every activity by 5. (See Table 64 where Rowing 5 ÷ 5 = 1, Walking 3 ÷ 5 = -0.6.)
6. The resulting table provides a rough estimate of the relative exertion of each activity for an individual athlete. Activities in the training programme can be weighted, but this is not necessary.

If the athlete chooses to weight his or her training programme using perceived equivalents, Table 65 provides an example using the estimates in Table 63. It not only recognizes the diversity in perceived exertion of various activities, it provides some assistance with achieving the weekly training programme hours.

T2+ activities using distance
A more precise approach is to use distances for aerobic programme planning and weighting. The reason is that perception is not required but measurement is. Some activities, such as weight training, do not lend themselves to this approach. In those instances, use hours or the athlete's perceived exertion equivalent.

For athletes new to training programmes, that athlete *may* use Tables 63 and 66 as a basis for spreading hours on their inaugural programme, understanding that the sample equivalents will not be accurate for them. However, starting the programme is more important than undertaking refinements that can take place as training progresses. For example, complete a one hour scull one day, complete a one hour cycle the next. With both at T2, that athlete can calculate equivalences and has started their experiment.

Benefits and limitations of the two methods: perceived hourly and distance
The major limitation of the perceived hour approach is that just because an athlete perceives an activity as being aerobically harder does not mean that it is. It does mean the athlete is probably less likely to do it. It is also difficult to compare year to year because perceptions change, sometimes dramatically. However, the hour approach

Activity	Perceived Equivalents Estimates	Option 1: Rowing Only (hrs)	Option 2: Cross Training (hrs)	Cross Training Weighted Hours
Sculling	1	6	3	3
Circuit weights	1.25			
Cycling	0.8			
Ergo	1.35		1	1.35
Field sport	1.2			
Running	1.4		0.5	0.7
Swimming	1.2		0.5	0.6
Walking	0.5		1	0.5
Total		6	6	6.15

Table 65 Using perceived equivalents from Table 63 to weight cross training activities.

Activity	Athlete's Distance Raw Data	Athlete's Normalized Distance Ratios
Sculling	8	1
Circuit weights	NA	NA
Cycling	24	3
Ergo	10.8	1.35
Field sport	NA	NA
Running	8	1
Swimming	2	0.25
Walking	4	0.5

Table 66 T2 distance by activity equivalent estimate sample.

is very simple to use: determine the available time, create the progression and spread the hours.

The benefits of using distances are two-fold. Distances, especially those the athlete develops for themselves, are more accurate. A mountain bike with low pressure in the tyres ridden through the forest will not result in the same cycling distance as a road bike on the flat. Distances are usually more manipulable when it comes to allocating times within a workout. But the real reason, and one that most will not admit, is that the distance version of the training programme produces a bigger number at the end of the week. For many athletes it is much more satisfying to complete 63.8km than six hours.

The athlete should choose a format that will encourage and reward them for their efforts. Modifications can be made during the training year, too, transitioning the athlete from hours to distance based on what they discover in the initial training months.

Mix and match activities

With this new activity flexibility, the athlete can identify training time efficiencies as well as retain a buffer for the unexpected. For example, if a sculling workout is scheduled with terrible weather forecast, a list of alternate options is at hand. The caution is that one of the objectives of the training programme is to build 'training programme habits'. Regularity in a training programme is helpful: Monday is sculling, Tuesday is cycling, Wednesday is swimming, etc. Regularity establishes training as a habit, facilitating compliance.

Subphase	Heart Rate	Week				
		1–7	8–11	12–15	16–19	20–23
		% Total by subphase				
Load	T2	100	95	90	85	80
High load	T2/T3		5	5	5	5
Low-speed transition	T2/T3/T4			5	5	5
Low speed	T4				5	5
High speed	T4					5

Table 69 Percentage of workload in each subphase.

Subphase	Rating (spm)	Training Zone	Sample Training Activity
Load	10–14 slow work; 16–22	T2	small work; slow work – 10/10, 11/11, 12/12, 13/13; 16–22 steady sculling to maintain T2
High load	14–18 slow work; 20–24;	T2/T3	small work; slow work up to 18spm with seat light or off; 20-24 steady sculling to maintain T2
Low-speed transition	20–24 up to 26, 28, 30, 32+ progressively	T2/T3	Up to race pace and back off; T2 steady sculling to maintain T2
Low-speed transition	22–32+	T2/T3/T4	Intervals of race subset (250m/500m) within 1000m total piece with T2 work in between
High speed	28–32+	T4/T2	1000m – with T2 in between

Table 70 Sample endurance training programme progression.

Load (100–80 per cent of total workload)

The purpose of the load subphase is to build aerobic capacity. One of the very particular ways to cycle within the load subphase is to do slow work such as 10/10 and higher. This describes sculling at 10spm achieving 10m stroke distance. The athlete can not accomplish this without good connection, stability and technique. In addition, slow work builds muscles, another objective of load. The efficiency gained is that both aerobic and technical development occur within one workout.

High load (5 per cent of total workload)

High load involves continued strength building as well as technique improvement. In the past, approaches such as bungies and cans tied to the boat were used. That is now discouraged because mechanical devices cause the boat to behave differently, including reducing boat run. The altered boat run interferes with the athlete's timing development and puts an artificially high demand on him or her.

There are two tactics to high load. First, is to extend the distance for 10/10+ (or whatever slow work level the athlete is proficient at). Five hundred metre pieces are appropriate and are aerobically, technically and muscularly very demanding. The second is to explore the athlete's 16–18spm rating work with the objective being to lower their time, remaining at T2. High load emphasizes the front end pickup, light or off the seat and a long continued stroke, counting 1–2–3 at the back end. It's challenging and a terrific way to build muscles and improve technique.

Low-speed transition (5 per cent of total workload)

Where load and high-load subphases targeted the athlete's improving of their 18spm prognostic, low-speed transition introduces verifying that speed improves with rating. The athlete starts at a rating where they can do the stroke technically well. Then, the rating rises to the point where speed does not improve. The athlete backs down to the level where previously successful, repeating the cycle. While the athlete may reach T4, the objective is to undertake most of the cycle in T2.

Another approach is speed play, then a recovery interval at low T2, then speed play again. This is called Fartlek. It is crucially important not to overdo it to the point where technique deteriorates. A low-speed transition session should end on the highest speed an athlete can do *well*.

Low speed (5 per cent of total workout)

This subphase begins to mimic racing. If the athlete's main event is a race, the progression should be: start at shorter intervals that are subsets of 1,000m. For example, 250m on/250m off/250m on/250 off. Back to T1. Repeat. The 250m 'on' is at a rating and effort that retains technique and speed. Thus, the ratings will increase over the weeks. The 250 'off' retains the *same technique* and can either reduce the effort down to T2, or reduce the

rating down to T2. The technique for the entire 1,000m should be excellent, with only the effort or rating changed. This is not easy to do. Low speed is the entry point for versatility work, described more fully in Chapter 12.

High speed (5 per cent of total workload)

If racing, high speed means 1,000m pieces adjusted for effort and rating to achieve the outcome desired for a training session. The more the session looks like the main event, the better. For example, long breaks between pieces to mimic heats, semis and finals, and the occasional Hard/Hard consecutive days to mimic successive races each day at the main event. Some T4/T5 cycling can be undertaken by experienced competitors.

RELATIVE TRAINING INTENSITIES

Just as weighting has been provided for hours and distances, this can be considered for training intensity. Again, it's not necessary but does provide for more precision in both the training programme and recording results. An athlete who is very performance focused will want to consider it.

All intensities are not alike. The systemic stress resulting from increased training intensities changes exponentially. This rate of change reflects the concept that certain training intensities result in particular physiological changes. From a training heart rate point of view, 1km at T4 is not the same as 1km at T2. What is important is that this rate of increased stress is so significant that the T4 category needed to be split to show the change to scale, with T4a and T4b added (Fig. 112 and Table 71).

These weighted intensity levels refine adjustments in training, particularly when adding subphases. The recommended workload per-

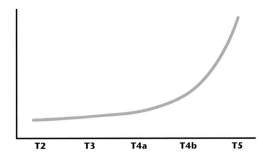

Fig. 112 Change in physiological demand as a function of training intensity.

Training Zone	%HRR	Weighted Intensity
T2	60–75	1
T3	75–85	1.35
T4a	85–90	2.1
T4b	90–95	5
T5	95–100	9

Table 71 Weighted intensity of various heart training zones.

centages by subphase in Table 69 are a good starting point. Athletes can then individualize it and may find benefits in so doing, particularly when managing workload in high training zones. For example, 1km at T5 is nine times more intense than 1km at T2. Conversely, 1km of T5 could be interpreted as the same systemic stress as 9km of T2. The physiologic system at T5 is anaerobic, while at T2 it is aerobic. They are doing different things. Higher intensities are useful for raising the aerobic threshold and practising race pace, lower intensities are good for aerobic capacity building.

Athletes may find adding an intensity dimension to their programme provides greater insight into the causality of fatigue. When excessive fatigue occurs, it is helpful to understand the implications of intensity. Because it is more systemically demanding, intensity increases fatigue more quickly than volumes alone might indicate. If training has progressed as planned

and recovery management is good, yet the athlete remains fatigued, workout intensity (and too much of it) may be the culprit.

DAILY WORKOUTS

The daily worksheets below have no magical properties. Any worksheet will do as long as it meets the athlete's needs and they record their results. Aside from providing insight as to whether the volumes planned are achievable, the daily workout sheet is a good place to capture fatigue. Even a simple scale of 1–10 will do. Athletes who are seriously fatigued often don't recognize it, but the build-up throughout the daily worksheets is observable. Table 72 is a sample of a completed daily workout sheet that is very typical for that time in the training progression. The important point is: writing down training plans for the week will improve the chance that the athlete will execute those plans.

PRIORITIES AND ASSESSMENT

Assessments are part of every performance athlete's programme. The assessment should be based on the priorities defined by the athlete in the previous chapter. Our example athlete's primary priorities were:

P1. Address FMB opportunities.
P2. Improve aerobic fitness. Raise O'Neill from 1,011 to 1,061, a 5 per cent improvement.
P3. Improve technique. Achieve a 3.238mps at 18spm at T2: a speed improvement of 2 per cent but at T2 (also a fitness improvement).

Assessments should be simple, easy to do and reflect the annual priorities and training objectives. They should show progress and, if not, the athlete's training programme, and execution of same, needs to be reviewed to identify ways to improve the training process. For most athletes, following the programme they created will yield excellent results. Here are some simple assessments for the example athlete's priorities:

P1 A. Retake the FMB test in three months for the items that did not achieve standard, or for the whole FMB test to ensure new issues have not developed.

P2 A. The fitness improvement is an annual goal. Doing O'Neill tests on a monthly basis are not recommended because systemic fatigue masks the magnitude of improvements. In other words, an athlete's result will usually under-report their actual fitness, which is demoralizing. An alternative measure that indicates progress in aerobic capacity is: time to recovery. That is, how long does it take for the athlete's heart rate to reduce from T4 to T1? This is best measured when sculling.

P3 A. Monthly performance tests over progressively longer distances.

MANAGING THE TRAINING PROGRAMME

The training programme is a tool, not a divine directive. The athlete has created it, the athlete can change it. There are some indicators that changes may be needed.

If an athlete misses a workout, that workout is gone forever. Workouts are not 'made up' when they are missed. Missing one workout is not a catastrophe and will have a trivial impact on the athlete's overall development. Missing 10 per cent+ on a regular basis means the programme needs to be scaled back. Determine what the *real* actual available hours are and recalculate the training programme to reflect those available hours.

If the athlete is fatigued and consistently so, the indication is that either sufficient recovery is not occurring or the workload is too high. A few days off are in order. Good recovery practices during this period will likely result in a renewed enthusiasm. If not, a few more days off are in order, up to a week. The impact on the athlete's development will be slightly more than trivial but much less than if they persist in training when fatigue is indicating that their system can't keep up. If a week is needed, this is another good time to reconsider the training programme. The mix of activities may be an issue, the athlete may not have calculated their own distances, or their system may just be less tolerant. Intensity may be an issue. A lower overall training load is indicated.

If the athlete is not fatigued and their aerobic fitness does not improve, it is likely that their workload, or intensity, is too low (T0/T1). The operative phrase in this scenario is the athlete is 'not fatigued'. That athlete may be recovering too much during activities, say executing a nice 500m piece to the top of T2 and then spending fifteen minutes on small work where the heart rate reduced to T0 for most of it. Shifting to activities that require more exertion is possible. Or if there is available time, adding additional workload may help. For a first-year athlete whose primary objective is to just 'show up', and they are enthusiastically fronting up on time, all good. There is next year for more emphasis on intensity and progress.

OFF SEASON PROGRAMME

The benefit of having a documented off season programme is that it is more likely to be executed. The off season programme is static, aimed at retaining gains. It does not progress in volumes and intensity. Its execution will influence the start of next year's programme.

FMB, STRENGTH, CONDITIONING AND POWER

Thus far, the focus has been technique, aerobics and FMB. Little information has been provided about strength, conditioning and power. Strength is the amount of force a muscle, or group of muscles, can exert against an external load. Power is defined as the ability to generate as much force as fast as possible. These are important, both for performance and general health. Both strength and power are an intrinsic part of the technical training described in Chapter 12, with slow work being one approach to same. This sport-specific approach is not enough. Every athlete should have a long-term, holistic resistance training programme.

Details on what that should be are not included here because the scope of how that will evolve for a particular athlete is unique. FMB needs to occur first. Strength, conditioning and power are a logical extension of that FMB rehabilitation process. All of this is highly individual, with few athletes scoring all 10s on their first FMB. Just as no rigging or training programme fits all, neither does a strength, conditioning, nor power programme.

The guideline for a strength, conditioning and power programme is: consult a professional. They should be accredited to advise on FMB rehabilitation as well as strength and conditioning, or be a combination of multiple providers. The athlete should have their FMB results in hand. A competent provider will use the FMB results as a basis, most likely undertaking further testing of their own. That provider will then develop FMB rehabilitation exercises specific to that athlete.

For those for whom strength and conditioning are desired or appropriate, that strength and conditioning programme should be broad based, not just sport-specific. It should focus on a full range of motion activities, as opposed to machines. The programme provided should be achievable and one with which the athlete complies. And, the sessions should be documented and tracked in the training programme.

ENDURANCE VERSUS ENDURANCE AND HIGH INTENSITY

This section will briefly explore the use of high intensity as a component of the training programme. It is presented here for experienced athletes (training years 3+), who compete, and who rate at a high level, say 30spm+. The reason for designating these athletes is that there is no real reason for using a high-intensity approach other than as described below.

The first question: did the athlete rate at 30+spm in competition last year? The second question: has that athlete retained that high rating skill, at a lower level of effort, through the off season? If the answer to both is yes, proceed. If not, the advice in this section will be unhelpful at this time. However, read on to see how this approach might apply in the future.

For the athlete who has retained that high rating skill in the off season, by doing short pieces, short ergos, or any combination of

Off Season Program							Season 2						
W27	W28	W29	W30	← →	W49	W50	W51	W52	W1	W2	W3	W4
3+	3+	3+	3+	Aerobic (hrs)	3+	3+	3+	3+	44	50	44	50
3+	3+	3+	3+	FMB/Stretching (each)	3+	3+	3+	3+	3+	3+	3+	3+

Fig. 113 Off season programme showing beginning of Season 2.

same, the opportunity exists to integrate some high-intensity work even in the early season workouts. Performing high ratings technically well is a specific skill. High rating skills deteriorate very quickly. The options are to relearn them every season, or to preserve as much as possible over off season and continue to cultivate this expertise during the early season and beyond.

The issue is that high ratings can lead to high heart rates, i.e. high intensity. This means that a training programme that includes early high-intensity work needs to cater for it in terms of adjusted volumes and recovery. If the athlete has protected this high rating skill during the off season, a good place to start the season is at that level, say no more than 5 per cent of the total on water workload with a reduction in total volume based on the intensity factors shown in the subphase section.

For example, an athlete has 24km of sculling in the first week of their programme. Five per cent of that is $24 \times 0.05 = 1.2$km. Intervals are a good approach and, for the skilled athlete, short interval work can be done at T2/T3. If the athlete is in T4, the total workload will need to be reduced by a factor of three to accommodate the additional stress. That is, $24 - 3 \times (1.2) = 20.4$ plus the 1.2 high intensity (T4). This percentage can be gradually raised to 10 per cent of total on water work by Week 12.

This high-intensity work will not improve aerobic fitness unless the athlete can perform the high ratings at T2, which then eliminates the need for any high-intensity considerations. And, which a technically proficient, fit athlete should be able to do for short distances. For those who find themselves at T4, different systems, including the anaerobic, create proportionately more systemic stress. The athlete will need to be more attentive about recovery and fatigue management when exploring this approach. The high rating work can be done on the ergo, although this is not preferred because of the biomechanical differences between sculling/ergo.

For those who did not answer yes to both questions but are reading this section, understanding how this works will provide an opportunity to incorporate the methodology into their next off season, providing a running start for the following year.

SUMMARY OF CREATING AN INDIVIDUAL TRAINING PROGRAMME

The athlete now has a training programme. It is a work in progress. The first few weeks of each training year are a settling in process. By the end of the load subphase, the athlete should be in a good rhythm with their training and able to identify what is working with their training programme and what is not. If a programme is not working, change it. Positive success is the desired environment within which the athlete will train.

The training methodology for each athlete needs to acknowledge two aspects of Masters training. First, that it is more important that the athlete train and continues his/her participation in the sport than reach their performance potential in one blazing year. A corollary of this is that having fun is important, as are small successes. Second, is that these small successes can be spread over decades, building incrementally from year to year. There is no indication of what the limits are for a well-trained, well-recovered and well-adapted adult sculler. From a performance perspective, the adult athlete's individual possibilities are a boundless unknown.

	PLAN	ACTUAL	NOTES
DATE			
WEEK	16		
PERIODIZATION	H		
SUBPHASE	Low speed transition		
PROGRESSION	88%		
FMB	3	3	
STRETCHING	3	4	
VOLUMES (km)			
ROW (8km = 1 hr)	24	22	
ERGO (9km = 1 hr)	9	3	
BIKE (20km = 1hr)	40	52	
TOTAL VOLUME	73	77	

Mon H			Slow work then intervals. Did 3 x 500m on and 500m off with recovery to T1. Felt really good and went on a 12km cycle ride. Forgot to do recovery nutrition and hydration – was in a rush.
FMB			
STRETCH	1	1	
SCULL	8	6.5	
ERGO	2	1	
BIKE		12	
Tue E			Not feeling very energetic. Did a little less on the bike.
FMB	1	1	
STRETCH		1	
SCULL			
ERGO			
BIKE	20	16	
Wed H			Tried doing the same workout as Monday and only managed two intervals. Paid attention to recovery nutrition and hydration afterwards.
FMB			
STRETCH	1		
SCULL	8	6.5	
ERGO		2	
BIKE			

Table 72 Sample of a daily worksheet completed.

	PLAN	ACTUAL	NOTES
Thur E			Got a good night's sleep. Took it easy on the bike. Just cruised.
FMB	1	1	
STRETCH			
SCULL			
ERGO			
BIKE	20	12	
Fri H			Feeling better. Did 250m on/offs for 3km. Went well with good speeds.
FMB	1	1	
STRETCH	1	1	
SCULL	8	8.5	
ERGO			
BIKE			
Sat E			Did a really easy T1/T2 bike ride early in the morning because it was so nice out. Will have effectively two days off and given this is week 16, feeling good.
FMB	1		
STRETCH		1	
SCULL			
ERGO			
BIKE		12	
Sunday rest			
Good week. Got into a little trouble early in the week but have managed it. Times for pieces are good. Technique is holding together at 30–32 and seeing speed increases in the early pieces. As fatigue sets in, need to drop down a rating to retain technique. Work on starts next week.			

Table 72 Sample of a daily worksheet completed (continued).

	PLAN	ACTUAL	NOTES
DATE			
WEEK			
PERIODIZATION			
SUBPHASE			
PROGRESSION			
FMB			
STRETCHING			
VOLUMES (km)			
ROW (8km = 1 hr)			
ERGO (9km = 1 hr)			
BIKE (20km = 1hr)			
TOTAL VOLUME			

Mon H			
FMB			
STRETCH			
SCULL			
ERGO			
BIKE			

Tue E			
FMB			
STRETCH			
SCULL			
ERGO			
BIKE			

Wed H			
FMB			
STRETCH			
SCULL			
ERGO			
BIKE			

Table 73 Blank daily worksheet.

	PLAN	ACTUAL	NOTES
Thur E			
FMB			
STRETCH			
SCULL			
ERGO			
BIKE			
Fri H			
FMB			
STRETCH			
SCULL			
ERGO			
BIKE			
Sat E			
FMB			
STRETCH			
SCULL			
ERGO			
BIKE			
Sunday rest			

Table 73 Blank daily worksheet (continued).

10 | RECOVERY STRATEGIES

Athletic training and performance cause physiological stress. There are restorative strategies that can accelerate the recovery process, increasing the likelihood and extent of adaptation. Athletes who complement their training programme with a comprehensive recovery programme will have an advantage. They will adapt more quickly and fully. They will have less soreness and fatigue, thus reducing injury and illness. Their mental health will be better. In competition, they will surpass comparable athletes who do not have a recovery programme.

The first challenge is understanding what evidence-based recovery strategies are available. The content below offers only glimpses into each of these important topics, highlighting the most relevant. Each of the sections in this chapter deserves a book of its own, and many have them. To that end, future reading references are provided. The limited research on recovery for adult athletes is beginning to be addressed, but the evidence base remains spotty. Thus, some of the information below is a necessary extrapolation of what is known for younger athletes.

The second challenge is changing pre- and post-workout habits. Chapter 12 will review habit formation, and habit undoing, but as with the athlete's training programme, it is not knowing what to do – it is actually doing it. Thus, the below topics are presented roughly in order of importance. For example, fatigue management is first. Then, sleep.

As always, what works for one athlete may not work for another. Nutrition provides an opportunity to explore personalizing the recovery nutrition plan. Is jam on white bread, chocolate milk or a banana more appealing? Is it appealing enough that the athlete will remember to take it to training every time? A focused, robust recovery practice will pay big dividends in fatigue management, injury prevention, good health and performance. Without it, adaptation will occur at a suboptimal rate or not at all.

The athlete's recovery programme becomes more important with age, with physiology becoming less efficient over the decades. Recovery times are longer because the restorative physiological processes take longer to complete or metabolization is less thorough. While the training programme may not change much with age, management of recovery becomes increasingly important because of the increasing risk of overreaching and overtraining. When in doubt, undercooked is better than overcooked. A day or two off, focusing on recovery, is time well spent in the long run.

FATIGUE

Fatigue comes in two forms. First, is particular: a muscle, brain cell or neural pathway. For example, when lactic acid builds up, a muscle may fatigue and be unable to perform. This fatigue results from processes at the cellular level. Muscles used intensely will show a progressive decline in performance, then largely recover after a period of rest.[1] Or, a brain cell that has been working to grasp new skills may cognitively overload. A neural pathway may reach the end of its capacity to perform, resulting in clumsiness.

For muscles, the purpose of recovery is to expeditiously resolve fatigue and delayed onset muscle soreness through a variety of recovery strategies such as:

- cool-downs,
- stretching,
- rest and sleep,
- good nutrition and hydration,
- attention to niggles and pains, and
- ancillary approaches such as compression clothing and massage.

Muscle fatigue is a normal part of the athletic training and performance building process. Brain cells and neural pathways recover with rest.

The second type of fatigue is systemic, physiological fatigue: 'physical and mental weariness resulting from exertion, that is, an inability to continue exercise at the same intensity and with a resultant deterioration in performance'.[2] Systemic fatigue is the outcome of total stress. It is the cumulative effect of the particular stresses of training plus other stresses that are part of an athlete's life. Adults have jobs, families and responsibilities. The cumulative physiological impact of all these stresses can erode the body's ability to recover. The athlete feels tired. That feeling does not dissipate over an extended period of time, even with normal training recovery strategies. Systemic stress is

the body's message that its capacity to adapt is comprised, so much so that further training will be unproductive.

Managing fatigue

Fatigue indicates the stress, recovery and adaptation cycle is taking place. It is normal. Rest and recovery management resolve it. Fatigue that does not resolve is a red flag. Allowed to continue, physiological fatigue leads to overreaching, the 'accumulation of training and/ or non-training stress resulting in short-term decrement in performance capacity with or without related physiological and psychological signs and symptoms of maladaptation in which restoration of performance capacity may take from several days to several weeks'.[3] Overreaching, when not addressed, can lead to overtraining syndrome (OTS).

The athlete must balance training and recovery to resolve fatigue. It is not unusual to be tired at the end of a week or of a subphase. The easy week ending each subphase is meant to resolve that fatigue. It is not unusual to be tired at the end of a week. The rest day, and alternating easy days, are meant to resolve it. If the fatigue lingers beyond the rest day, particularly beyond the end of an easy subphase week, an extra day off should fix it. If not, continue with rest days for up to a week. If fatigue and/or enthusiasm for training are then not sorted, it is time to seek medical advice.

Overreaching and overtraining

Let us dissect the overreaching definition to understand what is known about the causation for overreaching (not much) and its symptomology for younger athletes. The observable symptom is a decrease in performance. There may be accompanying physiological and psychological symptoms, such as the athlete feels tired and loses enthusiasm for training.

There may be no symptoms. Table 74 shows overtraining (OTS) possible symptoms, which apply equally to overreaching. Other indicators include an orthostatic heart rate that is significantly higher than the resting heart. This is the indicator powering most mobile applications whose purpose is to provide fatigue information. Cumulative stress involves non-training stress. Thus, moving house, financial difficulties, death of a parent (or one moving in with the athlete), child issues and other stressors all play a significant role in an athlete's total fatigue profile.

Overreaching, when not resolved, can lead to overtraining syndrome (OTS). OTS is a well-known phenomenon that can involve a collapse of the immunosuppressant system. It is very serious. The recovery from OTS is measured in months. Training should not continue. OTS nearly always includes behavioural changes, sleep problems and disrupted mood.

The diagnosis of OTS is made clinically by a physician, although with the lack of specificity in the symptomology it is a difficult diagnosis to make. There are no blood or other laboratory tests that are confirmatory. The athlete who is excessively fatigued may need

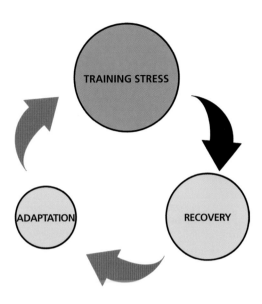

Fig. 114 The process of systemic failure that occurs when recovery practices are insufficient to total stress.

Parasympathetic Alterations	Sympathetic Alterations	Other
Fatigue	Insomnia	Anorexia
Depression	Irritability	Weight loss
Bradycardia	Agitation	Lack of mental concentration
Loss of motivation	Tachycardia	Heavy, sore, stiff muscles
	Hypertension	Anxiety
	Restlessness	Awakening unrefreshed

Table 74 Symptoms of overtraining syndrome (OTS). (Kreher, J.B., Schwartz, J.B.,. 'Overtraining syndrome: a practical guide',. **Sports Health**,. 2012 Mar 4(2): pp. 128-–38)

to offer the possibility of OTS for consideration if their regular physician does not have a sports orientation.

What causes OTS? After seventy years of awareness about it, no definitive answer has been forthcoming. Working possibilities include a variety of hypotheses, all of which attribute the phenomenon to a deficiency in a particular physiological system. The cytokine hypothesis appears to hold the most promise and suggests that OTS is: 'a physiologic adaptation/maladaptation to excess stress initiated by an imbalance between training and recovery'.[4, 5, 6, 7]

Recovery is a crucial component of an adult athlete's training programme, increasing in importance with age. Without proper recovery, the adult athlete's system can just not keep up physiologically with the necessary restorative repairs resulting from training and non-training stress. This suggests that adult athletes may be more at risk of fatigue, overreaching and overtraining than their younger more physiologically resilient counterparts. That's the bad news.

Periodization of training	Ensure adequate calories for training load	Ensure adequate sleep
Tapering for competition	Ensure adequate hydration	Abstinence of training following infection, heat stroke/stress, periods of high stress
Adjust training volume and intensity based on performance and mood	Ensure adequate carbohydrate ingestion during exercise	Rest period of greater than six hours between exercise bouts

Table 75 Preventative measures for non-functional overreaching/overtraining syndrome. (Kreher, J.B., Schwartz, J.B., 'Overtraining syndrome: a practical guide', Sports Health, 2012 Mar 4(2): pp. 128–38)

The good news is that adult athletes have a long athletic career runway. An athlete with a fifty-year runway does not need to rush and can take time off. Thus, physiological fatigue management – rest – becomes an important recovery tool. Other preventative measures for fatigue, overreaching and overtraining have already been identified in this book as an integral part of the athlete's training and recovery programme (see Table 75).

How to tell if an athlete is systemically fatigued? While there are no reliable physiological or psychological markers, some indicators may be:

- A training log that shows measurable jumps in training load and/or deteriorating performance;
- Changes in weight, morning heart rate, maximum heart rate, orthostatic heart rate; and,
- Mood changes

The best evidence-based tool is self-perception. Quite simply, if an athlete feels physiologically fatigued, they probably are. The issue here is athlete self-awareness and feeling empowered. Athletes need to recognize that physiological fatigue, like muscle fatigue, does not respond to 'training harder'. The short-term intervention for fatigue is rest.

How much rest? A good rule of thumb is: a day's rest for every day that performance has deteriorated and the athlete has felt fatigued.

This rule encourages athletes (and coaches) to identify physiological fatigue early and address it quickly. A day or two of rest will not affect fitness. Not resting will exacerbate the fatigue and lengthen the rest needed, or progress the problem to overreaching, then OTS.

Good recovery strategies throughout this rest period are crucial. For athletes who balk at giving up a training day, this is a good time for small work (sitting in a boat and doing technical development), ensuring that the heart rate stays at T0–T1. If after a week of rest the fatigue persists, in whatever manifestation it presents itself for a particular athlete, medical advice should be sought.

Lastly, a comment on the social pressure to 'train harder' and be 'mentally tough'. Training harder and mental toughness have their place as part of the athlete's toolkit in performance development. If performance is not progressing, even though the athlete's thoughtful, periodized training programme and recovery strategies have up to this point been productive, training harder and being mentally tough are not the answer. Rest is. Adult athletes need to adopt a training ethos that they, of all people, know their body best. Each athlete's total recovery package should include 'guilt-free days off' as a tool to achieve their performance goals.

SLEEP

Sleep is the most ignored, underrated and abused recovery strategy. Next to rest, it is the most important. For years, sleep was considered to be a mind/body state that did not have much to offer. Science now understands that sleep is a state of its own, where unique and interesting processes occur. And if some of these processes do not occur, disease or death result. While science is only just delving into the process intricacies, the impact of sleep generically has an excellent research base. Lack of sleep has been confirmed to increase the risk of:

- Hypertension[8]
- Coronary heart disease[9, 10, 11, 12]
- Diabetes[13, 14]
- Alzheimer's [15, 16, 17]
- Cancer[18, 19]
- Death[20]
- Parkinson's [21]
- Mental health issues [22]

The impact of sleep deprivation on an athlete, who is adding additional physiological stress in terms of training, is compounded. The risk of injury for adolescents increases in direct proportion to their chronic sleep deprivation. The average injury risk of approximately 15 per cent for nine hours of sleep climbs steadily, and linearly, to a 75 per cent risk of injury with six hours of sleep.[23] There is no reason to think the same phenomenon will not be replicated for adult athletes since the current research is already pointing in this direction.

Let us look at sleep and one process: brain function. Athletic training puts demands on the brain, both in cognitive and motor skills development. The brain, unlike the body with its lymphatic system, has no unique system for flushing out the wastes created from this neurological activity. The brain accomplishes waste removal through its glial cells, which make up about 50 per cent of brain volume. During sleep, the glial cells shrink in size, creating pathways for the outflow of brain waste. If sleep is inadequate, brain waste removal is inadequate. Of particular note is the resulting build-up of amyloid plaques, linked with Alzheimer's.[24]

In addition, this build-up of plaques and wastes appears to be cumulative, starting as early as the late thirties. Once the system is clogged, it does not unclog. The specific implication for athletes is neurological recovery. The physiological stress of athletic training creates systemic neurological deterioration that can be restored through appropriate recovery strategies. Sleep is crucial.

Another implication for athletes has to do with the acquisition of new information and new motor skills. All sleep is not the same. During the early periods of sleep, the brain shifts short-term declarative memory into long-term storage. Declarative memory is the memory of facts and events. For example, if the athlete was learning new start skills that day, the list of facts associated with the start training are maintained in short-term memory during the day, then transferred to long-term memory during the early sleep cycles. Thus, even if sleep is insufficient there is some chance that the new list of information will be transferred to long-term memory.

Not so with procedural memory. Procedural memory is the memory responsible for motor skills and how to do new things. Procedural memory is transferred to long-term memory primarily during the last 25 per cent of sleep. Thus, if the athlete truncates sleep, the transfer of these new motor skills is impaired. A personal version of *Groundhog Day* where all that work learning starts causes the athlete to have to relearn the skill again, and again, and again.

Because the brain is efficient, constantly seeking ways to clear out long-term memory space, an athlete can get a good night's sleep on the first night and effect the motor skills transfer. However, if that fully restorative sleep pattern is not maintained for at least three consecutive nights (or more), the brain decides that particular long-term memory wasn't really important and deletes it.

Sleep supports the immune function.[25] This is of particular importance since athletic training, which creates systemic physiological stress, tends to undermine that same immune function. Fatigue is resolvable with good recovery practices. Overreaching begins to reach the limits of that recovery. Overtraining leads to the development of a compromised immune system that, from an athletic performance perspective, is unrecoverable in the short term. Sleep has a tendency to act as a protective factor in this escalating process, counteracting some of the immunological effects of athletically induced physiological stress, giving an edge to the athlete with good sleep practices.

Quality of sleep counts, too. The issue for older adult athletes is not that they need significantly less sleep as they age (a myth), it is that the frequent bathroom trips in the middle of the night erode the quality of sleep. For those who party, alcohol can help one to fall asleep more easily, but it disrupts sleep patterns and quality of sleep. Alcohol makes one more prone to snoring and leads to even more night-time bathroom trips. Good quality sleep is defined as: sleeping at least 85 per cent of the time when in bed, falling asleep in thirty minutes or less, waking no more than once a night and being awake for twenty minutes or less after initially falling asleep.[26]

An athlete in training ideally needs ten hours a day available for sleep. This includes preparing for sleep and waking from sleep. Actual sleep ranges from seven to nine hours. It is true that some people need less sleep. These rare people, known as short sleepers, will sleep well under the average seven to nine hours. It is unlikely that you are one of them. How to tell? The condition is primarily genetic. Thus, there will be evidence of other short sleepers in your family to support your claim.

As to how much sleep an individual needs, there is no corroborated test. The best measure is

an individual's perception of how they feel. The social pressure to sleep less is tremendous, with between 33 to 45 per cent of adults in Australia affected by inadequate sleep.[27] Self-perception starts to become unreliable when the social norms are skewed. Perhaps a better approach is to build a pattern of good sleep habits.

- Go to bed at the same time each night.
- In the hour before have a relaxing routine that does not include electronic screens, all of which have been banned from the bedroom.
- Avoid caffeine and alcohol for at least two hours before bed.
- Evening meals should similarly be at least two hours before.
- Minimize the opportunities for night time disruptions. Go to the toilet, make sure the bed is comfortable, find a simple process to turn your mind off and prepare for sleep.
- Stick with the routine.[28]

In addition to the benefits of general health, good sleep contributes to athletic performance. Anything less than eight hours and especially less than six results in a 10 to 30 per cent drop in time to physical exhaustion, with aerobic output reduced significantly.[29] Athletic activity will, conversely, improve the quality of sleep, with morning workouts being preferred. Recognizing that much is happening during sleep, the main objective for each athlete is to embrace sleep as a health and performance benefit and to build good sleep habits into their training programme.

NUTRITION

You are what you eat, and in no case is this truer than for an athlete. Athletic training by its nature tears down the body. Muscles are stressed to the breaking point so that they can rebuild bigger and stronger. Cognitive functions, including motor skills acquisition, are highly active, as is the brain. Wastes are excreted throughout the body and in many forms, including carbon dioxide and sweat. All this activity requires replacement and restorative building blocks. Macronutrients (protein, fats and carbohydrates) are the primary rebuilding components. Micronutrients (vitamins and minerals) are crucial. Add water and the body will repair, replace and improve. The body will repair, replace and improve much more efficiently, and quickly, if the athlete provides the right nutrition at the right time. This speciality is called sports nutrition.

Science now knows that the physiological complexity of the athletic training process is enormous, as is the topic of sports nutrition. Below is some of the emerging Masters' nutritional recovery information. First, a brief overview of day-to-day nutrition and strategies, followed by workout and performance nutrition strategies.

Everyone is busy, busy, busy. Without a great deal of self-discipline, food becomes almost an afterthought in an adult athlete's day. The push towards fast food, pre-packaged and processed foods, as well as eating on the run, all contribute to a very significant challenge. Below are some simple strategies to help guide day-to-day nutrition.

Day-to-day nutrition

Today's adults have been bombarded with general nutrition advice. Below are some general guidelines to simplify the path to improved nutrition.

First, eat good food, preferably as close to its natural condition and place of production as possible. Quality counts in terms of nutritional uptake. For example, the Omega-3 and other nutritional components of chicken eggs that live a more natural life is significantly higher than those in cage-raised eggs.[30] Omega-3 is an essential fat that the human body does not make. It is required for cell membranes to work well. It can be obtained through expensive supplements or, better, by upgrading food quality. Similarly, grass-fed beef has significantly improved fatty acid and antioxidant content than grain-fed beef.[31]

Vegetables and fruits suffer from nutritional deterioration with delivery delays and processing. Their freshness may be disguised because of gamma irradiation, which affects fruit and vegetables no more than processing, but which affects the nutritional content nonetheless. Thus local vegetables and fruit, in season, are a better choice. Frozen fruits and vegetables often have a higher nutritional content than long-delayed, gamma ray-zapped fresh ones. Fat free or reduced fat products are not necessarily better nutritional choices. Reduced fat milk, for instance, has been processed to achieve the low-fat result. The nutritional quality of the resulting product is a bit of a mystery. Consider whole milk, locally produced, instead.

Second, eat proportionately. The rough rule of thumb is a mealtime plate with a quarter protein, a quarter carbohydrate and half vegetables. The carbohydrate should be complex and low GI Index (see Table 76). Another rule of thumb is: good quality fat in moderation is important. The body needs fats for both cell function and nerve repair. Because they are calorie rich, fats should make up a smaller proportion of the plate. Drizzling olive, flaxseed, peanut or other nut-based oil on the vegetables or cooking with same is a good approach.

Third, eat diversely. Try to achieve a Technicolor plate, a plate with every colour of the rainbow. The colour of food is a visible manifestation of its chemical content, announcing the micronutrients contained within. Sprinkling nuts, dried berries, small portions of different coloured fruits and vegetables makes a plate more appealing. If this is difficult to achieve, because it does take some work to chop up all those additions, try to achieve a rainbow day, eating foods of every colour of the rainbow before that full night's sleep. The other diversity rule of thumb has to do with protein intake: try two red meat, two white meat, two fish and one meatless as the meal plan for the week.

Fourth, fibre is important. Fibre in foods is identified by colour. If it is white, it has no or very little fibre, cauliflower being a notable exception. Some of the best sources of fibre are legumes or beans. Other sources include whole grains. Fresh fruits and vegetables are full of fibre. Eating high-quality food close to the source, proportionately and diversely, will naturally take care of this fibre requirement.

The problem with pre-packaged and fast food is that the proportions are all wrong. The nutritional value isn't right, either. Because fast food is a profit-making activity, the athlete's nutritional restoration is not a paramount consideration. Fast and pre-packaged foods are inoculated with fat, cheap fat such as hydrogenated vegetable oil and lard. These foods are full of sugar, cheap sugar that is usually a high glycaemic index. And fillers. And preservatives. This includes canned foods, which have the added problem of high salt content. One way to avoid this dilemma is to create personal pre-packaged foods. For example, cook a meal twice as large as needed. Put leftovers in freezer containers for use as lunches or for those days when creating a proportionate, diverse and Technicolor evening meal is just too daunting.

Strategies for coping with the fast food and the commercial pre-packaged food phenomenon include undermining the fast food industry by ordering your way. Ask for lettuce and tomato, hold the cheese and sauce. Get the salad option. Order a Happy Meal® without fries but with milk and apple slices that, oddly, is a nutritionally appropriate recovery meal with 20g+ of protein and 45g+ of high GI carbohydrates (and you get a toy).

The other pre-emptive strike: become king or queen of the lunchbox. Even a small container of dried fruit and nuts, accompanied by a piece of fruit, carried in the briefcase or car provides a ready antidote. Athletes who embrace organizing their pre- and post-training workout nutrition will need a lunchbox anyway. At a minimum have an emergency supply of nutritional snacks available. Including an emergency bottle of water provides the complete nutritional first aid kit. At best, have a nutritional plan for the day, and week, that has been thoughtfully created in advance.

A final strategy for healthier nutrition involves the approach to grocery shopping. Never shop hungry. Have a list, preferably based on the weekly meal plan and the recovery foods needed. Shop the perimeter first. Supermarkets have the most natural, simple foods located on their edges because that is the most cost-effective place to put the refrigeration. Instead of following the 'up and down aisles' store plan, travel the outside periphery of the store first, which has the added benefit of avoiding the sale displays. Exhaust the impulse buying urge on fruit, vegetables, meat, fish, dairy products and frozen vegetables. Then return to the aisles to stock up on whole grains, dried fruits and nuts, and other lunchbox and recovery items.

Pre-workout and workout nutrition

Because scullers often train in the morning, it is important to have some small amount of food before training: half a banana, a small portion of cereal, toast or whatever high glycaemic food suits. That early morning carbohydrate will be made available to muscles.

During workouts of less than an hour, food is not a requirement for two reasons. The first is that it will not be metabolized in such a short time. Second, is that if carbohydrates are needed, they are more readily obtained through hydration (see below). For workouts of longer than an hour, or for athletes who find the intensity of their workouts is creating low blood sugar symptoms, taking a high-glycaemic food into the boat is a good idea.

Post-workout and recovery nutrition

Training and performance activities create physiological stress. Muscles incur micro-tears. Glycogen in the muscle tissue is depleted. Waste products build up systemically and are excreted at different rates. At the end of training and performance, the athlete's body is fatigued, an indicator of physiological stress.

It is at this time that the body is most ready to recover. The body waits to determine: (a) will the food (and hydration) I need be forthcoming, quickly, so that I can restore and recover or (b) is nothing coming and I need to consider shutting down to prevent the future loss of what is there? This decision happens autonomically and has a profound impact on an athlete's recovery and adaptation.

For example, the process of muscle building is a response to micro-tears in muscles. These micro-tears are a part of athletic training because only through this process can a muscle rebuild bigger and stronger. In order to rebuild, a muscle needs protein. Right away. If immediately after training the athlete consumes protein-rich food, the body takes up that protein and uses it for muscle repair. The result is not only a more efficient muscle adaptation but reduced soreness.

The alternative is to provide no nutritional protein. The body naturally tends toward equilibrium. That is, no muscle cell is stronger than its surrounding muscle cells. For the athlete who does not provide nutritional protein immediately after a workout, the restorative physiologic process for muscular micro-tears is – the affected muscle cannibalizes its neighbours. The affected muscle takes protein from adjacent cells, so that the neighbourhood reaches equilibrium. The adaptation of the muscle with the micro-tear is impaired. The neighbouring muscle cells are degraded (and unhappy about being pillaged). The athlete is often sore, or sore for a longer time, as a result. Fatigue is exacerbated without this

nutritional protein since the myriad of other waste elimination and restorative processes are also affected.

Glycogen is stored in the liver and muscles. Glycogen is used to fuel athletic training and performance. The body's regulatory mechanisms strive to ensure that blood sugar is available and moderated, assisting with how glycogen is released and restored. When that glycogen is depleted, the body develops compensatory mechanisms to sustain itself. In extreme cases of low blood sugar, symptoms such as shaking, light-headedness, confusion and an accelerated heart rate can result.

The athlete who provides a ready intake of high-glycaemic carbohydrate at the end of training assists the body with that glycogen replacement, assisting the body's blood sugar regulatory mechanism. Usually on most adult 'forbidden food' lists, these high-glycaemic carbohydrates are ones that are quickly absorbed and utilized by the body.

After athletic activity, the body recognizes whether recovery is (a) a normal habit or (b) erratic. The body behaves accordingly. That is, anticipating nutritional high-glycaemic carbohydrates and having that anticipation realized results in the body's rapid restoration of glycogen. This repairs the athlete and fosters adaptation.

The body responds differently for the athlete whose glycogen replacement strategies are erratic or non-existent. One way the body responds is to resist engaging in athletic stress that puts it in a depleted state. Another way is when the athlete engages in strenuous activity, the body produces symptoms of low blood sugar. A third, and very interesting one, is the development of a starvation reflex. That is, the body begins metabolically to behave as though no food is coming – ever. The starvation reflex protects the body in that available fuel is used for survival processes, such as brain activity and the protection of protein.[32] None of the former contribute to recovery, adaptation or performance.

Low and high glycaemic levels of foods

The glycaemic index (GI) indicates how quickly a carbohydrate will raise the blood glucose level. High GI carbohydrates do it quickly, low GI do it slowly. For normal nutritional needs, low GI carbohydrates are preferred because they are metabolized more slowly and evenly, assisting the body's regulatory mechanisms to maintain a constant blood sugar level.

For athletes who have depleted their glycogen stores through strenuous exercise, a quick replacement of glycogen through ingestion of high GI carbohydrates is the goal. Preferably as soon as possible after training and within at least two hours.

Examples of high and low GI carbohydrates are in Table 76. Boundless internet resources exist, providing lists and look-up tools for the glycaemic index of foods. The decisions get difficult for foods that are combinations as well as those with hidden sugars. The University of Sydney provides an excellent online GI resource, including a food look-up search.[33]

Low GI	Medium GI	High GI
Most fruits	Pineapple, Cantaloupe	Watermelon
Most vegetables		Parsnips, pumpkins
Most dairy, including flavoured milk and many sweetened yogurts	Plain ice cream	
Whole cereals, whole grains	Wheat bread, pita bread	White bread, processed cereals (including instant oatmeal with sugar), white rice
Fructose, maple syrup, Stevia (natural)	Honey, sucrose	Glucose, Splenda, table sugar

Table 76 Glycaemic Index (GI) of sample groups of foods.

Nutrition needs and timing

Timing is everything in recovery nutrition. The body is receptive to replacement protein and carbohydrate immediately after training. The sooner these foods are available the better, preferably within a half hour. Two hours is the current estimated limit where this receptivity drops off.

Protein consumption is the other key timing-dependent consideration. The body needs increasing amounts of protein as the athlete ages. Beginners also need more. This can range from 1.2g/kg for a younger athlete to 2.0g/kg or more in older athletes. Protein needs increase as training intensity increases,

too. Spreading protein intake throughout the day helps both the recovery process and the efficient uptake of protein. The casein milk drink before bed is a recommended addition to a Masters athlete's diet because emerging research indicates it helps prevent loss in muscle mass and provides a nutritional buffer for the early morning workout.

HYDRATION

Every cell in the body needs water to function. When water is not available, the various physiological processes go awry. Athletic

	Pre-workout	Workout	Post-workout recovery	Before sleep	Daily
Protein	Combined protein-carbohydrate may increase endurance	None needed for workouts less than one hour	15–25g total depending on athlete weight	20–40g casein (milk)	1.2g/kg – 1.6g/kg – 2.0g/kg BW
Carbohydrates	1–4g/kg BW 1–4 hours before	As needed for longer workouts	1–1.2g/kg BW		5–7g/kg BW
Fat					20–35% of daily caloric intake from good fats

Table 77 Nutritional needs and ranges in total grams (g) or grams per kilogram of body weight (g/kg BW).

The miracle of flavoured milk

The first challenge with developing a post-workout nutrition recovery plan is finding portable, digestible and appealing foods that provide 15–25g of protein and 1–1.2g/BW of high-glycaemic carbohydrate. Flavoured milk (chocolate, strawberry or any flavour) is a good place to start. A 600ml carton of reduced fat milk contains 20g of protein and 60g of carbohydrate. Milk is also an effective rehydration drink. Chocolate milk has been studied more, although it is unclear how much the chocolate contributes to the observed effects. Research shows chocolate milk reduces muscle soreness and promotes muscle glycogen recovery, resulting in greater aerobic capacity.

activities produce sweat and water loss through expiration. Without fluid replacement, the athlete's blood gets thicker. Oxygen does not circulate efficiently. An increased heart rate tries to compensate.

All of this is preventable. Because fluids consumed take up to a half hour to begin to be absorbed, hydration planning is important. Another factor for adult athletes is that aging brings about a diminished thirst reflex. By the time the athlete feels thirsty, it is too late. Dehydration has occurred.

Hydration needs to be managed as conscientiously as nutrition. Water is the ideal hydration fluid, up to a point. Here are some other considerations:

• Many athletes do not take on enough fluid. A small amount of sugar or sweetness tends to increase the amount an athlete drinks because of palatability.
• Carbohydrate ingestion during moderate-intensity endurance exercise tends to delay fatigue.
• A small amount of sugar in the fluid replacement tends to improve performance, and the fluid need only be mouth rinsed, not ingested, to obtain that performance benefit. Why this happens is not understood, but the phenomenon has been well replicated.
• The brain uses energy, starting with 20 per cent of total energy and climbing to 40+ per cent when intensely cognitively involved, as when learning technical skills. Even though an athletic may not be exerting themselves muscularly, carbohydrates in the hydration fluid can help delay that 'brain fried' feeling.

- Too much fluid can lead to a dilution of sodium levels (hyponatraemia), headaches, disorientation, coma and death.

Alcohol is not a rehydration fluid. Alcohol reduces reaction time, coordination, balance, judgement, strength, endurance and blood sugar to name a few. It increases water excretion and the risk of dehydration. Alcohol takes precedence over the metabolic process that is associated with endurance. While alcohol jumps the queue, the endurance process and performance are pushed to the back. Save moderate alcohol consumption for non-training days.

Hydration needs and timing

Sports drinks have an evidence base recommending them. They cross over from hydration to nutrition in that they include carbohydrates. Most include electrolytes. Dilution and experimentation is the key to how sports drinks are incorporated into an individual athlete's carbohydrate/hydration replacement plan. Start with a 25 per cent or less dilution. A 25/75 per cent fruit juice/water mix, with optional salt, is an inexpensive option.

Because scullers tend to work out in the morning, night-time dehydration needs to be compensated for by drinking between 350–700ml of liquid well before the planned workout. Preparing two water bottles with diluted sports drink ensures one available for training, to be sipped throughout the workout, and one available immediately thereafter.

The indicator of hydration is the colour of urine, which should be light yellow. Make sure the vitamin B complex in the athlete's multivitamin is not providing a false indicator.

SAMPLE DAILY RECOVERY PLAN

Simply put, when an athlete is not training they are recovering. Having a plan and getting into a routine helps. Table 79 is a sample of a daily recovery plan.

SUMMARY: RECOVERY STRATEGIES

The major components of recovery are rest, sleep, nutrition and hydration. An athlete attending to the recovery process will achieve optimal gains in adaptation. That athlete will have comparatively reduced fatigue, allowing them to train efficiently the next day. As the athlete ages, recovery becomes arguably more important than training. An athlete needs to develop self-awareness about fatigue and self-confidence in managing fatigue, when required, through additional rest. A successful recovery programme is one where training workload increases, adaptation keeps pace and the athlete achieves performance improvements.

The topic of sports nutrition is enormous, and crucially important. Athletes are encouraged to investigate specialist publications that can provide more comprehensive nutrition and hydration information. Anita Bean's *Sports Nutrition* (Bloomsbury, 2017), specifically the eighth edition that includes a chapter on the older athlete, is an excellent option.

Pre-workout	Workout	Post-workout recovery	Before sleep	Daily
5–10 ml/BW 2-4 hours before	At least sips every 15 min	Immediately replace lost fluid		Urine should be light yellow

Table 78 Hydration needs and optimal timings.

2 hours before bed	20–40g of casein-based protein or casein-whey isolate protein shake
7–9 hours	Sleep
1–2 hours before morning training	800ml of liquid and breakfast or low GI pre-workout snack, e.g. half a banana
At training	Two water bottles, one in the boat and one for post-workout hydration, with diluted sports drink. Extra water bottle if longer or high-intensity workout, or higher temperature
At training	Small high GI snack in the boat for longer sessions or high-intensity workouts if needed
During training	Small sips throughout training, approximately 250ml per fifteen minutes
Immediately after training	
Hydration	800ml liquid
Protein	600ml container of flavoured milk or protein shake with 20g+ of protein
Carbohydrate	60g+ high GI contained in the flavoured milk
Post-workout major refuelling	Ensure protein and carb replacement occurs, worst case, within two hours
Every 2–3 hours	Small amount of protein and low GI in meals and snacks throughout the day
Evening meal	Self-check nutritional and hydration intake for the day: adjust dinner as needed to ensure protein and carbohydrates (low GI for dinner) are adequate for the volume and intensity of today's training
Refurbish lunchbox	Refill lunchbox with snacks and recovery items needed for the next day based on tomorrow's training needs

Table 79 Sample of a daily recovery plan.

Endnotes

1 Allen, D.G., Lamb, G.D., Westerblad, H., 'Skeletal muscle fatigue: cellular mechanisms', *Physiol Rev.* 2008 Jan; 88(1): pp.287–332. doi: 10.1152/physrev.00015.2007. Review. PubMed PMID: 18195089.

2 Evans, W.J., Lambert, C.P., 'Physiological basis of fatigue', *Am J. Phys Med Rehabil.* 2007 Jan; 86(1 Suppl): pp.S29–46. Review. PubMed PMID: 17370370.

3 Grivas, G.V., 'Diagnosis of overtraining and overreaching syndrome in athletes', *Sport Exerc Med Open J.* 2018; 4(3): pp.74–76. doi: 10.17140/SEMOJ-4-165.

4 Kreher, J.B., Schwartz, J.B., 'Overtraining syndrome: a practical guide', *Sports Health.* 2012 Mar; 4(2): pp.128–138. doi: 10.1177/1941738111434406. PubMed PMID: 23016079; PubMed Central PMCID: PMC3435910.

5 Robson, P., 'Elucidating the unexplained underperformance syndrome in endurance athletes: the interleukin-6 hypothesis', *Sports Med.* 2003; 33(10): pp.771–781. doi: 10.2165/00007256-200333100-00004. Review. PubMed PMID: 12895132.

6 Smith, L.L., 'Cytokine hypothesis of overtraining: a physiological adaptation to excessive stress?', *Med Sci Sports Exerc.* 2000 Feb; 32(2): pp.317–331. PubMed PMID: 10694113.

7 Lakier Smith, L., 'Overtraining, excessive exercise, and altered immunity: is this a T helper-1 versus T helper-2 lymphocyte response?', *Sports Med.* 2003; 33(5): pp.347–364. doi: 10.2165/00007256-200333050-00002. Review. PubMed PMID: 12696983.

8 Gangwisch, J.E., Heymsfield, S.B., Boden-Albala, B., Buijs, R.M., Kreier, F., Pickering, T.G., Rundle, A.G., Zammit, G.K., Malaspina, D., 'Short sleep duration as a risk factor for hypertension: analyses of the first National Health and Nutrition Examination Survey', *Hypertension.* 2006 May; 47(5): pp.833–839. doi: 10.1161/01.HYP.0000217362.34748.e0. Epub 2006 Apr 3. PubMed PMID: 16585410.

9 Kripke, D.F., Simons, R.N., Garfinkel, L., 'Hammond, E.C., Short and long sleep and sleeping pills. Is increased mortality associated?', *Arch Gen Psychiatry.* 1979 Jan; 36(1): pp.103–116. doi: 10.1001/archpsyc.1979.01780010109014. PubMed PMID: 760693.

10 Wingard, D.L., Berkman, L.F., 'Mortality risk associated with sleeping patterns among adults', *Sleep.* 1983; 6(2): pp.102–107. doi: 10.1093/sleep/6.2.102. PubMed PMID: 6878979.

11 Partinen, M., Putkonen, P.T., Kaprio, J., Koskenvuo, M., Hilakivi, I., 'Sleep disorders in relation to coronary heart disease', *Acta Med Scand Suppl.* 1982; 660: pp.69–83. PubMed PMID: 6982602.

12 Ayas, N.T., White, D.P., Manson, J.E., Stampfer, M.J., Speizer, F.E., Malhotra, A., Hu, F.B., 'A prospective study of sleep duration and coronary heart disease in women', *Arch Intern Med.* 2003 Jan 27; 163(2): pp.205–209. PubMed PMID: 12546611.

13 Gottlieb, D.J., Punjabi, N.M., Newman, A.B., Resnick, H.E., Redline, S., Baldwin, C.M., Nieto, F.J., 'Association of sleep time with diabetes mellitus and impaired glucose tolerance', *Arch Intern Med.* 2005 Apr 25; 165(8): pp.863–867. doi: 10.1001/archinte.165.8.863. PubMed PMID: 15851636.

14 Yaggi, H.K., Araujo, A.B., McKinlay, J.B., 'Sleep duration as a risk factor for the development of type 2 diabetes', *Diabetes Care.* 2006 Mar; 29(3): pp.657–661. doi: 10.2337/diacare.29.03.06.dc05-0879. PubMed PMID: 16505522.

15 Shokri-Kojori, E., Wang, G.J., Wiers, C.E., Demiral, S.B., Guo, M., Kim, S.W., Lindgren, E., Ramirez, V., Zehra, A., Freeman, C., Miller, G., Manza, P., Srivastava, T., De Santi, S., Tomasi, D., Benveniste, H., Volkow, N.D., '-Amyloid accumulation in the human brain after one night of sleep deprivation', *Proc Natl Acad Sci USA.* 2018 Apr 24; 115(17): pp.4483–4488. doi: 10.1073/pnas.1721694115. Epub 2018 Apr 9. PubMed PMID: 29632177; PubMed Central PMCID: PMC5924922.

16 Holth, J.K., Fritschi, S.K., Wang, C., Pedersen, N.P., Cirrito, J.R., Mahan, T.E., Finn, M.B., Manis, M., Geerling, J.C., Fuller, P.M., Lucey, B.P., Holtzman, D.M., 'The sleep-wake cycle regulates brain interstitial fluid tau in mice and CSF tau in humans', *Science.* 2019 Feb 22; 363(6429): pp.880–884. doi: 10.1126/science.aav2546. Epub 2019 Jan 24. PubMed PMID: 30679382; PubMed Central PMCID: PMC6410369.

17 Macedo, A.C., Balouch, S., Tabet, N., 'Is Sleep Disruption a Risk Factor for Alzheimer's Disease?', *J Alzheimers Dis.* 2017; 58(4): pp.993–1002. doi: 10.3233/JAD-161287. Review. PubMed PMID: 28550253.

18 Chen, Y., Tan, F., Wei, L., Li, X., Lyu, Z., Feng, X., Wen, Y., Guo, L., He, J., Dai, M., Li, N., 'Sleep duration and the risk of cancer: a systematic review and meta-analysis including dose-response relationship', *BMC Cancer.* 2018 Nov 21; 18(1): p.1,149. doi: 10.1186/s12885-018-5025-y. PubMed PMID: 30463535; PubMed Central PMCID: PMC6249821.

19 Fang, H.F., Miao, N.F., Chen, C.D., Sithole, T., Chung, M.H., 'Risk of Cancer in Patients with Insomnia, Parasomnia, and Obstructive Sleep Apnea: A Nationwide Nested Case-Control Study', *J Cancer.* 2015 ; 6(11): pp.1,140–1,147. doi: 10.7150/jca.12490. eCollection 2015. PubMed PMID: 26516362; PubMed Central PMCID: PMC4615350.

20 Wingard, D.L., Berkman, L.F., 'Mortality risk associated with sleeping patterns among adults', *Sleep.* 1983; 6(2): pp.102–107. doi: 10.1093/sleep/6.2.102. PubMed PMID: 6878979.

21 Fagotti, J., Targa, A.D.S., Rodrigues, L.S., Noseda, A.C.D., Dorieux, F.W.C., Scarante, F.F., Ilkiw, J.L., Louzada, F.M., Chowdhury, N.R., van der Veen, D.R., Middleton, B., Pennings, J.L.A., Swann, J.R., Skene, D.J., Limamm, S., 'Chronic sleep restriction in the rotenone Parkinson's disease model in rats reveals peripheral early-phase biomarkers', *Sci Rep.* 2019 Feb 13; 9(1): p.1898. doi: 10.1038/s41598-018-37657-6. PubMed PMID: 30760786; PubMed Central PMCID: PMC6374389.

22 Dinges, D.F., Pack, F., Williams, K., Gillen, K.A., Powell, J.W., Ott, G.E., Aptowicz, C., Pack, A.I., 'Cumulative sleepiness, mood disturbance, and psychomotor vigilance performance decrements during a week of sleep restricted to 4-5 hours per night', *Sleep.* 1997 Apr; 20(4): pp.267–277. PubMed PMID: 9231952.

23 Gao, B., Dwivedi, S., Milewski, M.D., Cruz, A.I. Jr, 'Lack of Sleep and Sports Injuries in Adolescents: A Systematic Review and Meta-analysis', *J Pediatr Orthop.* 2019 May/Jun; 39(5): pp.e324–e333. doi: 10.1097/BPO.0000000000001306. PubMed PMID: 30888337.

24 Eugene, A.R., Masiak, J., 'The Neuroprotective Aspects of Sleep', *MEDtube Sci.* 2015 Mar; 3(1): pp.35–40. PubMed PMID: 26594659; PubMed Central PMCID: PMC4651462.

25 Besedovsky, L., Lange, T., Born, J., 'Sleep and immune function', *Pflugers Arch.* 2012 Jan; 463(1): pp.121–137. doi: 10.1007/s00424-011-1044-0. Epub 2011 Nov 10. Review. PubMed PMID: 22071480; PubMed Central PMCID: PMC3256323.

26 National Sleep Foundation (US), *What is Good Quality Sleep?* www.sleepfoundation.org/press-release/what-good-quality-sleep.

27 Sleep Health Foundation (AU). Adams, R., Appleton, S., Taylor, A., McEvoy, D., Antic, N., *Report to the Sleep Health Foundation 2016 Sleep Health Survey of Australians.* www.sleephealthfoundation.org.au/pdfs/surveys/SleepHealthFoundation-Survey.pdf.

28 Sleep Health Foundation (AU). *Good Sleep Habits.* www.sleephealthfoundation.org.au/good-sleep-habits.html.

29 Walker, M., Why We Sleep: The new science of sleep and dreams. Great Britain, Allan Lane; 2018, pp.128–131.

30 Karsten, H.D., Patterson, P.H., Stout, R., Crews, G., 'Vitamins A, E and fatty acid composition of the eggs of caged hens and pastured hens', *Renewable Agriculture and Food Systems* 2010 Jan 25(1): pp.45–54. doi: 10.1017/S1742170509990214.

31 Daley, C.A., Abbott, A., Doyle, P.S., Nader, G.A., Larson, S., 'A review of fatty acid profiles and antioxidant content in grass-fed and grain-fed beef', *Nutr J.* 2010 Mar 10; 9:10. doi: 10.1186/1475-2891-9-10. Review. PubMed PMID: 20219103; PubMed Central PMCID: PMC2846864.

32 Berg, J.M., Tymoczko, J.L., Stryer, L., *Biochemistry.* 5th edition. New York: W H Freeman; 2002. Section 30.3, Food Intake and Starvation Induce Metabolic Changes. Available from: www.ncbi.nlm.nih.gov/books/NBK22414

33 The University of Sydney. *Search for the Glycemic Index.* www.glycemicindex.com

11 | RECOVERY SUPPORT ACTIVITIES

While the primary recovery focus will be on rest, sleep, nutrition and hydration, other opportunities exist for speeding the recovery process along. The purpose of this chapter is to explore some of them.

SUPPLEMENTS

Supplementation is a hotly debated topic, with much popular literature suggesting an individual can obtain all their nutritional needs through a healthy diet. Well, yes, they can. Especially a young, sedentary one. For an adult athlete, particularly one with a high training load aged over forty, the emerging research tends to indicate otherwise. For example, the protein needs for adult athletes increase with age. While the requirement for a twentysomething elite male athlete may be 1.2–2.0 grams per kilogram of weight per day (g/kg/d), the protein requirements for an elite adult athlete aged fifty, male and female, are at the high end (2.0g/kg/d) – or greater. Because of the lack of research, it is unclear how high that protein requirement is. Factors include:

- training history,
- training intensity,
- genetics,
- the natural ageing progression to a less efficient protein metabolism,
- prophylactic needs to stave off osteoporosis and sarcopenia (the gradual loss of muscle mass, strength, and mobility), and
- the increased need for protein in metabolizing carbohydrates in the adult athlete.

All open up the frontiers of research possibilities for adult athletes.

For now, assume a middle figure of 1.6g/kg/d and a 75kg adult athlete aged fifty-plus involved in endurance training with increasing intensity as the season progresses. That elite athlete should expect to consume 120g of protein a day when in training, or more as intensity increases. That is: sixteen eggs, four chicken breasts, almost a gallon of milk, eight slices of red meat or some combination. This amount of protein, which is filling, begins to push other foods off the proportionate, diverse plate. Add to this that appetite and metabolism decrease with age, and that some athletes lose their appetite when they are training hard (and when they most need to consume protein to recover), and protein supplementation provides a possible recovery management strategy.

The real supplementation question is: what works and what doesn't? Sports Australia through the Australian Institute of Sports (AIS) provides the *AIS Sports Supplement Framework* (2019).[1] The framework is based on what supplements have an evidence base and which do not. With its simple ABCD structure, the *Framework* provides supplement guidelines. (The International Olympic Committee has provided a consensus report on supplements that has more detailed information).[2] The issue is, of course, that the evidence-based research base for both reports is younger subjects. Also, the dosage amounts are unspecified although the IOC Consensus has some guidelines.

The AIS 'A list' includes those supplements with strong scientific evidence for use in specific situations in sport using evidence-based protocols. It is a short list with three sub-categories: sports foods, medical supplements and performance supplements. With the stipulation for 'evidence-based protocols', the adult athlete is back to the frontier since adult athlete protocols may be different. The evidence base for younger athletes is quite strong, with their protocols a good place to start.

AIS Group A Sub-category	Examples
Sports foods	Sports drink
	Sports gel
	Sports confectionary
	Sports bar
	Electrolyte supplement
	Isolated protein supplement
	Mixed macronutrient supplement (bar, power, liquid meal)
Medical supplements	Iron supplement
	Calcium supplement
	Multivitamin supplement
	Vitamin D supplement
	Probiotics (yogurt, kefir, tempeh, kimchi, kombucha, etc.)
Performance supplements	Caffeine
	B-alanine
	Bicarbonate
	Beetroot juice/Nitrate
	Creatine
	Glycerol
	Note: best used with individualized and event-specific protocol, with the expert guidance of an Accredited Sports Dietitian.

Table 80 Australian Institute of Sport (AIS) Category A List of evidence-based supplements.

A few observations about the 'Sports foods' category. To use sports food supplements or not, and which to use, is entirely an individual decision. The above sections on workout and recovery nutrition/hydration provide sensible strategies for how the sports food supplements might be used. For athletes who are off season or whose training is not high intensity, the needs for supplementation are less persuasive than for athletes who are involved in a six-month endurance/intensity-based training programme targeting one or more performance events. The best way to determine whether particular supplementation works for an individual athlete is to experiment. The end objective is a feeling of readiness, enthusiasm and well-being the day after a workout.

Next, protein supplementation. The evidence base supports 'isolated protein supplement' which is different from powdered milk and many commercial protein products. Also known as whey protein isolate or whey isolate, this protein is the milk by-product of cheese-making. It is highly bioavailable, is a complete protein including all nine essential amino acids, promotes muscle growth, and may help reduce inflammation. One scoop, dissolved in water or other liquid, usually contains 20g+ of protein.

Whey protein is different from casein protein, the other protein found in cow's milk. Casein protein when consumed prior to sleep has been shown to have a number of benefits including improved muscle synthesis,[3] better post-exercise overnight recovery[4] and increased muscle mass after resistance type training.[5] The first study involved forty-eight men aged average seventy-two plus or minus one year and concluded that the pre-sleep casein drink of 40g casein might provide a novel nutritional strategy to support muscle mass preservation. Thus, the recommendation for adult athletes in training: consume a casein-based protein drink prior to sleep.

With regards to medical supplements, iron, calcium, multivitamin, vitamin D and probiotics all have a strong evidence base for younger athletes. Adult athletes should consider this evidence from the additional perspective of bone loss prevention (see bone health section below), gut health maintenance, ageing's reduced metabolic efficiency for nutrient uptake and the general health research for older adults in relationship to these supplements. In short, the insurance value of multivitamin and mineral supplementation should be considered, especially if training loads or intensity are increasing or high. The recommendation is no more than 100 per cent RDI.

As for performance supplements on List A, there is no comprehensive body of research that supports them for adult athletes. There is no reason to think they are not relevant or that future research on adult athletes might be confirmatory. These performance supplements are intended to improve performance at key events, as opposed to long-term use. AIS recommends supervision by an Accredited Sports Nutritionist. These supplements will not replace hard work. If an athlete chooses to experiment with them, there are protocols for their use that can be obtained from research, starting with the IOC consensus statement. The recommendation is a personal experiment, data based and far in advance of the key performance event, to assess the athlete's reaction to and benefits from the supplement.

The last caution involves cross-contamination. Many supplement manufacturers process a wide range of supplements in the same facility, with cross-contamination by a prohibited substance a real issue. If deciding to use supplements, ensure the manufacturing process is industry standard certified.

Drug Testing and Therapeutic Use Exemptions (TUEs)

Even though athlete anti-doping obligations exist, drug testing has not come to many, if any, Masters sports. But it will, and it will be a surprise when it does. The question is whether the athlete has prepared in advance for this eventuality or is willing to risk losing that hard-won medal?

The issue for Masters is not performance-enhancing drugs, which clearly have no place; the problem is medical drugs, prescribed for a therapeutic reason but that are on the prohibited substance list. When prescribing for Masters athletes, physicians do not as a matter of course assess the performance-enhancing capability of a drug or whether it is a prohibited substance. In addition, some prohibited substances do not require a prescription. The above issue of supplement cross-contamination can arise.

FISA (World Rowing) has comprehensive anti-doping and drug testing guidelines. All athletes competing in sanctioned events are expected to comply with these guidelines. The national sports organizations are responsible for managing their own competitors, with tailored national compliance processes a result.

Each country also has a national anti-doping agency supporting all sports. The Australian Sports Anti-Doping Authority (ASADA) provides an online resource list describing drugs, medications and some supplements. That list states what drugs are prohibited. Most countries' anti-doping agencies have comparable information. ASADA updates annually on 1 January. The competitive athlete of any age is individually responsible for being aware of his or her anti-doping-related responsibilities. Thus, that athlete's checking needs to be annual, too.

If the drug an athlete is taking is on the prohibited list, there is a three-step process to follow. The first is for the athlete and their doctor to review the unintended performance-enhancing consequences of that drug. There may be an equally effective drug that is not on the banned substance list. At the least, it is good to know the unexpected side-effects of a medication.

Barring a change in medication, the athlete can apply for a Therapeutic Use Exemption (TUE). When granted, TUEs allow the athlete to compete while taking the prescribed, prohibited medication. Each country has its own TUE process, which will be aligned with the current Australian process described here. These processes change regularly. Today in Australia, the first step is to determine if the athlete is competing at a level and in a sport for which an 'In-Advance' TUE is required. For example, the Australian Rowing Championship (Senior) competitors are required to apply for 'In-Advance' TUEs. At time of writing, the Australian Masters Rowing Championship competitors are not.

Instead, the Australian Masters Rowing Championship competitors, and those in sanctioned events, are required to apply for a Retroactive TUE. The process is straightforward and available online in Australia through ASADA. Most countries have a similar online TUE application capability. Applying for a TUE will take some time and effort. Applying is far less onerous than losing that hard-won medal when random drug testing makes its eventual surprise appearance at the Masters level.

Stretching and Ancillary Recovery Strategies

Every workout begins with a dynamic (not static) warm-up. The dynamic warm-up is on dry land. It prepares not only the sculling muscles but the ancillary supporting muscles that would not be involved during an on water warm-up, i.e. muscles involved in oblique and lateral movement. It is important that the boat be ready and the athlete move directly from the warm-up to the water. Rowing Australia provides a sample dynamic warm-up on its website.[6]

Age (years)	Male RDI (mg)	Female RDI (mg)
19–30	1,000	1,000
31–50	1,000	1,000
51–70	1,000	1,300
>70	1,300	1,300

Table 81 Recommend Daily Intake (RDI) of calcium.

Age (years)	Male RDI (μg)	Female RDI (μg)
19–30	5	5
31–50	5	5
51–70	10	10
>70	15	15

Table 82 Recommended daily intake of Vitamin D.

What is sarcopenia?

Sarcopenia is the age-related decrease in lean muscle mass. Sarcopenia is a multi-factorial function of age, nutrition, hormones, other medical issues and activity level. As with many age-related physiological phenomena, it is a chicken/egg question where the research is unclear about whether significant lean muscle mass deteriorates because of nutrition and lifestyle changes or is a normal part of aging and, if so, to what degree?[16]

Endurance and resistance training can reverse the loss of lean muscle mass, with adults over sixty in controlled studies experiencing increases similar to what far younger subjects achieve. [17, 18] Better nutrition helps, too, with protein and Vitamin D being key topics for future

calcium, too, with spinach topping the list at 240mg per cooked cup. However, the calcium content of foods is not uniformly predictable or bioavailable. For example, nuts: almonds contain 80mg of calcium per ounce, sesame seeds 280 and sunflower seeds 50.

Next, the uptake of calcium (and protein, too) is affected by Vitamin D, which comes from sunlight-exposed skin and some foods. Nutritional sources alone are insufficient to meet the Vitamin D RDI (Table 82).[13] To complicate matters, the emphasis on skin cancer reduction, sunscreen and sun protection has created a population in Australia where more than 30 per cent of adults now have Vitamin D deficiency. As discussed above in *Supplements*, athletes should consider the insurance benefits of multi-vitamins during training and winter months when vitamin D production might be restricted.

Exercise can help maintain or improve bone density, but it must be regular and osteogenic. Basketball, netball, impact aerobics, dancing, gymnastics, tennis and jump rope, as well as many field sports, are highly osteogenic.

Running, brisk walking, resistance training and stair climbing, moderately so. Swimming and cycling, not at all. Sculling is probably not, either.

The bone health topic is here because it is a cumulative threat. Addressed early, the rate of bone loss can be managed to the athlete's benefit. Not managed, some of the results can be: fractures (including small spinal fractures that result in spinal compression and loss of height), chronic pain including back pain, loss of mobility and premature death. Nutritional recovery, normal nutrition and supplementation should be planned with a view towards optimizing bone health.

Women *and men* over fifty with risk factors (family history, calcium/vitamin D levels, medical history and lifestyle factors) should obtain bone density scans to determine bone health because bone loss can be minimized. The argument here is that a long-term sculler, who has not supplemented their activities with osteogenic ones, is at risk. Bone loss is not reversed, only the rate of loss is attenuated. Thus, self-advocacy with one's physician about assessment, as well as more attention to osteogenic activities, are important.

GUT HEALTH

The lack of diversity in the contemporary diet has seen a steady decline in gut bacteria. Reliance on over-processed foods within this limited diet has resulted in a gut flora that is a virtual desert. Aging contributes to this reduced gut diversity. Science is beginning to identify that the reduction in gut flora has health consequences because, surprisingly, the gut is producing essential chemicals and maintaining a mind-to-gut conversation that affects well-being and performance.

For example, the digestive tract produces 90 per cent of serotonin.[14] Serotonin has been implicated in a broad range of behaviours such as appetitive, emotional, motor, cognitive and autonomic. The level of serotonin is affected by gut health, as is the immune system. Meanwhile, the gut and brain have a continuous and not, as yet, well understood conversation controlling autonomic processes. While one goes about their day, totally unaware, these processes result in mood changes, stress levels and how one sleeps.

Aside from a diverse and balanced diet, with lots of fibre, the gut thrives on having an enriched microbiota. The more alive these microbiota, the better. Research remains unclear as to how much of the live microbiota makes it to the gut through stomach acid. However, populations of peoples who consume comparatively higher volumes of fermented products have better gut health and less bowel cancer. The important factor is live microbiota in such foods as natural yogurt (with live cultures and without sugar), sauerkraut (unprocessed and unpasteurized), kimchi, kombucha, kefir and cheese with mould (blue cheese and others) are all good dietary additions. The benefits of the calcium and protein content in yoghurt and kefir make them good recovery foods.

DENTAL HEALTH

Dental health can impact on training. Poor oral health, particularly poor periodontal (gum) health, is associated with major chronic disease. In those with poor oral health, the acts of chewing or brushing may release toxins, affecting the body's immune response. When the mouth is chronically inflamed, there is potential for systemic inflammation to occur as well.

None of this bodes well for training gains. Indeed, those with periodontitis have been shown to be not as successful as those without gum disease in reducing biological age. A direct link exists between untreated dental problems and missed training sessions, reduced training volume, sleep difficulties and decreased performance. The overall effects of poor dental health are insidious. While the problem may seem small, its cumulative effects over time can be large.

Conversely, training can affect dental health. Remember that section on sports drinks and high glycaemic sugar, every day after training? And sipping acidic, sugary diluted sports drinks during training? The effects on teeth can de destructive, especially when training itself has an effect on saliva production, reducing it and decreasing its buffering capacity. Dehydration can have a similar effect, all setting the stage for dental caries (cavities) or other oral health problems.

Prevention is the key to avoiding dental health problems:

- Regular dental check-ups
- A toothbrush in good order and floss
- Consider fluoride use
- Twice daily brushing
- Brushing or mouth rinsing with water after recovery nutrition/hydration at the end of the workout or consumption of sugary drinks.

Other strategies include eating whole foods. Dairy products may have a protective function, too.

SPORTS PSYCHOLOGY

This topic is ever so important but so totally overlooked for adult athletes. The American Psychological Association defines sports psychology as 'a proficiency that uses psychological knowledge and skills to address optimal performance and well-being of athletes, developmental and social aspects of sports participation, and systemic issues associated with sports setting and organizations'.[15] Sports psychology is an integral component of support services for any performance athlete.

The objective of sports psychology is to provide the athlete with a larger psychological toolkit. This toolkit can include strategies for improving training, recovery and competition. The tools can make the entire training more rewarding and enjoyable, while allowing the athlete to achieve a higher level of performance. Unfortunately, the stigmatization of mental health, both public and self-stigmatization, dissuade many adult athletes from considering the benefits.

When to consider involving a sports psychologist and whom to involve? First, sports psychology is a sub-speciality. Not every psychologist is qualified. In addition to sports psychology accreditation, the provider will be experienced within the performance sporting community. Second, there should be a professional orientation that embraces adult performance sports. Third is that sports psychologists have two skill sets. One skill set is group work that allows for crew skills development and can be engaged in as team-building as well as for performance improvement. The other skill set is individual support. This is best utilized for athletes who are experiencing barriers to improvement, such as disabling or detrimental reactions to, say, competition. Because the adult athlete's career is long, sports participation needs to be rewarding and fun, too. Sports psychology can help when it isn't.

THE SUPPORT TEAM

Younger elite athletes with national and Olympic potential have available to them a support team to facilitate their athletic development. This support team includes, to name a few:

• sports physician
• physiotherapist
• exercise physiologist
• remedial massage therapist
• nutritionist
• sports psychologist.

An adult athlete serious about a long-term, high-performance career needs to assemble a similar team; a credentialed team with, ideally, a credentialed performance coach, as opposed to friends with opinions. This support team development is best done with multiple athletes in mind because, quite frankly, the economic advantages of working with adult athletes is well recognized by savvy providers. Adults have jobs and money. They have very long athletic career runways and long-term service needs. The opportunity for building continuing partnerships with these providers is considerable.

Few providers have significant experience with Masters athletes in general and sculling in particular. Thus, the development of the support team is a longer-term endeavour and involves education, both ways, as well as a provision of services. For example, when consulted, an excellent physiotherapist will discuss the athlete's training programme and collaborate on programme adjustments that will allow the athlete to continue to train. As opposed to 'take four weeks off', the more supportive training advice is, 'No shoulder work for two weeks but cycling, lower body resistance training, high paced walking, and strengthening and mobility work on that shoulder. Then we'll see where we're at.'

The athlete should feel validated in the process of accessing these services. There is nothing more demoralizing than being age-pigeon-holed, especially in sculling where the competition is getting keener every year. Some support team providers are not aware of the serious competitive environment in which many adult athletes operate. It's an important part of that provider's education. In addition, it is ideal if the athlete's support team communicates with one another. We are very fortunate here in Australia to have a sports community that is open-minded and sees the wisdom of high-performance adult sports, as well as a government that is beginning to understand that a healthy adult will live longer but cost the Australian universal health system much, much less.

SUMMARY: RECOVERY SUPPORT ACTIVITIES

Chapter 10 and this one have presented a number of tactics and strategies for improving recovery, leading to improved adaptation. The final issue is implementation and compliance. For convenience, the material in these chapters is in priority order. Start with Chapter 10: fatigue management and rest, then sleep, then nutrition, etc. Pick one and make it a habit. Then, move on to the next. Choose approaches that have a good chance of success. Some approaches, such as finding more time to sleep and improving sleep hygiene, will take significant effort and may lend themselves better to a longer-term, incremental approach. Recovery is 50 per cent of the operative training equation. With aging, it becomes increasingly more important. That container of flavoured milk may contribute more to the total training effect than five more minutes of training time. Creating good recovery practices and sticking to them will go a long way to improving performance and enthusiasm for the sport.

Endnotes

1 The Australian Institute of Sports. *The AIS Sports Supplement Framework. Mar 2019.* www.sportaus.gov.au/__data/assets/pdf_file/0004/698557/AIS_Sports_Supplement_Framework_2019.pdf

2 Maughan, R.J., Burke, L.M., Dvorak, J., Larson-Meyer, D.E., Peeling, P., Phillips, S.M., Rawson, E.S., Walsh, N.P., Garthe, I., Geyer, H., Meeusen, R., van Loon, L., Shirreffs, S.M., Spriet, L.L., Stuart, M., Vernec, A., Currell, K., Ali, V.M., Budgett, R.G.M., Ljungqvist, A., Mountjoy, M., Pitsiladis, Y., Soligard, T., Erdener, U., Engebretsen, L., IOC Consensus Statement: Dietary Supplements and the High-Performance Athlete. *Int J Sport Nutr Exerc Metab.* 2018 Mar 1; 28(2): pp.104–125. doi: 10.1123/ijsnem.2018-0020. Epub 2018 Mar 28. PubMed PMID: 29589768.

3 Kouw, I.W., Holwerda, A.M., Trommelen, J., Kramer, I.F., Bastiaanse, J., Halson, S.L., Wodzig, W.K., Verdijk, L.B., van Loon, L.J., *Protein Ingestion before Sleep Increases Overnight Muscle Protein Synthesis Rates in Healthy Older Men: A Randomized Controlled Trial.* J Nutr. 2017 Dec; 147(12): pp.2252–2261. doi: 10.3945/jn.117.254532. Epub 2017 Aug 30. PubMed PMID: 28855419.

4 Res, P.T., Groen, B., Pennings, B., Beelen, M., Wallis, G.A., Gijsen, A.P., Senden, J.M., Van Loon, L.J., Protein ingestion before sleep improves postexercise overnight recovery. *Med Sci Sports Exerc.* 2012 Aug; 44(8): pp.1560–1569. doi: 10.1249/MSS.0b013e31824cc363. PubMed PMID: 22330017.

5 Snijders, T., Res, P.T., Smeets, J.S., van Vliet, S., van Kranenburg, J., Maase, K., Kies, A.K., Verdijk, L.B., van Loon, L.J., Protein Ingestion before Sleep Increases Muscle Mass and Strength Gains during Prolonged Resistance-Type Exercise Training in Healthy Young Men. *J Nutr.* 2015 Jun; 145(6): pp.1178–1184. doi: 10.3945/jn.114.208371. Epub 2015 Apr 29. PubMed PMID: 25926415.

6 Rowing Australia. *Australian Rowing Team Warm Up Essentials.* 2015. https://rowingaustralia.com.au/wp-content/uploads/2015/10/ROWING-ACTIVE-WARM-UP-EX-POSTER.pdf.

7 Page P. 'Current concepts in muscle stretching for exercise and rehabilitation', *Int J Sports Phys Ther.* 2012 Feb; 7(1): pp.109–119. PubMed PMID: 22319684; PubMed Central PMCID: PMC3273886.

8 Rowing Australia. *Australian Rowing Team Stretch Essentials.* 2015. https://rowingaustralia.com.au/wp-content/uploads/2015/10/ROWING-STRETCHING-EX-POSTER.pdf.

9 Dupuy, O., Douzi, W., Theurot, D., Bosquet, L., Dugué, B., 'An Evidence-Based Approach for Choosing Post-exercise Recovery Techniques to Reduce Markers of Muscle Damage, Soreness, Fatigue, and Inflammation: A Systematic Review With Meta-Analysis', *Front Physiol.* 2018; 9:403. doi: 10.3389/fphys.2018.00403. eCollection 2018. PubMed PMID: 29755363; PubMed Central PMCID: PMC5932411.

10 Holsgaard-Larsen, A., Jensen, K., 'Ergometer rowing with and without slides', *Int J Sports Med.* 2010 Dec; 31(12): pp.870–874. doi: 10.1055/s-0030-1265148. Epub 2010 Sep 8. PubMed PMID: 20827655.

11 Demontiero, O., Vidal, C., Duque, G., Aging and bone loss: new insights for the clinician. *Ther Adv Musculoskelet Dis.* 2012 Apr; 4(2): pp.61–76. doi: 10.1177/1759720X11430858. PubMed PMID: 22870496; PubMed Central PMCID: PMC3383520.

12 Australian Government, National Health and Medical Research Council. *Calcium.* 9 Apr 2014. www.nrv.gov.au/nutrients/calcium.

13 Australian Government, National Health and Medical Research Council. *Vitamin D.* 9 Apr 2014. www.nrv.gov.au/nutrients/vitamin-d.

14 Yano, J.M., Yu, K., Donaldson, G.P., Shastri, G.G., Ann, P., Ma, L., Nagler, C.R., Ismagilov, R.F., Mazmanian, S.K., Hsiao, E.Y., 'Indigenous bacteria from the gut microbiota regulate host serotonin biosynthesis', *Cell.* 2015 Apr 9; 161(2): pp.264–276. doi: 10.1016/j.cell.2015.02.047. PubMed PMID: 25860609; PubMed Central PMCID: PMC4393509.

15 American Psychological Association. *Sports Psychology.* www.apa.org/ed/graduate/specialize/sports

16 Siparsky, P.N., Kirkendall, D.T., Garrett WE Jr. 'Muscle changes in aging: understanding sarcopenia', *Sports Health.* 2014 Jan; 6(1): pp.36–40. doi: 10.1177/1941738113502296. PubMed PMID: 24427440; PubMed Central PMCID: PMC3874224.

12 | TRAINING EFFICIENTLY

This chapter addresses the acquisition of technical skills. Aerobic development is already catered for in the training programme, with the exception of that proportion of aerobic training that the athlete plans to undertake on the water. In this chapter the primary focus will be on technical improvement, later discussing strategies for combined technical/aerobic development. The underlying structure is: connectedness, stability, consistency, versatility and speed. Each builds on the other, the end result being the best performance an athlete can achieve.

Training efficiently requires data. Data speeds the process of assessment and training refinements. Without it, the athlete must rely on other sources of information that are crude and error prone. Training efficiently requires a plan, from the training programme, to weekly plan, to a workout plan. Combined, these are a cumulative map for what skills are being developed as well as the path to achieving the year's training priorities.

SLOW WORK AND PERFORMANCE ANALYSIS USING DATA

If the athlete cannot scull well going slow, they will not scull optimally going fast. While speed can mask a multitude of technical defects, it does not eliminate them.

This section explores performance assessment and standards for slow work. We will consider an athlete who is working on stroke consistency and technical precision, performing a 500m 12/12 piece (12spm and 12m per stroke distance).

The measuring device

To train efficiently requires access to a measuring device. The Nielsen Kellerman (NK) SpeedCoach GPS Model 2 with training pack is the one whose information is used here for exhibits. Another cost-effective option is CrewNerd, a mobile application. There are other apps and devices that may do the job, which is to provide a:

- visible display of
  - stroke rate per minute (spm),
  - speed in metres per second (mps),

- distance (in metres)
- heart rate, and
• capture and download capability for same.

Learning to use the measuring device is a skill in itself but, when learned, the data will provide insight into training performance that expedites skills acquisition exponentially.

How to find metres per second and noise on the NK SpeedCoach GPS Model 2

The manuals for NK devices are available online. To provide a quick answer to this question, the information is included here.

1. Metres per second (mps)

   a. Go to 'Setup', then 'Speed/ Distance Setup', which will display the 'Speed Options Screen'.

   b. Speed mode: Set to 'Speed'.

   c. Units: Set to 'M M/S /500M'.

   d. Return to the main screen and the upper right display will show 'Speed M/S'.

2. Noise

   a. Go to 'Setup', then 'Advanced ...'. 'Advanced ...' is invisible, cleverly hidden below the bottom line. Use the arrows to scroll down and find it.

   b. Go to the next screen and select 'Stroke Rate Setup'.

   c. Noise filtering will appear on the next screen. For slow work, a setting of '2' or '3' is usual, with '3' the default value on the device. A lower number is more sensitive to less acceleration, as happens at 10–14spm.

12/12 sample data

Table 83 is data directly downloaded from an NK SpeedCoach for a 500m piece. (The middle section of the data is deleted.) The summary table of averages and standard deviations at the bottom was created using Excel after the data were downloaded (@average and @ stdev.s functions).

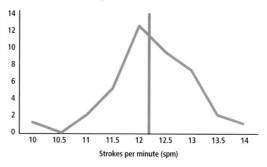

Fig. 115 Sample 12/12 500m piece showing the number of strokes at various ratings, with an average of 12.3spm (green).

Distance (GPS) (Metres)	Speed (GPS) (M/S)	Stroke Rate (SPM)	Distance per Stroke (GPS) (Metres)	Heart Rate (BPM)
15.8	1.97	11.5	11.8	105
27.9	2.4	13	12.1	110
40.6	2.59	12	12.7	112
52.9	2.64	13	12.3	115
66.6	2.69	12	13.7	118
79.7	2.71	13	13.1	122
92.7	2.75	13	13	124
105.3	2.79	12.5	12.6	126
119.1	2.82	12.5	13.8	129
131.9	2.79	12.5	12.8	131
146.2	2.75	11.5	14.3	133
159.9	2.72	12	13.7	134
-	-	-	-	-
390.2	2.65	12.5	12.9	143
403	2.71	12.5	12.8	142
416.3	2.74	12.5	13.3	143
430.1	2.75	12	13.8	143
442	2.78	14	11.9	144
455.3	2.79	12.5	13.4	146
467.9	2.78	13.5	12.6	145
480.9	2.77	12	13	145
493.7	2.76	13.5	12.8	144
505.8	2.73	13	12.1	146
519.7	2.72	12	13.9	144
Average	2.68	12.3	13.2	
Standard deviation w/o start	0.06	0.78		

Table 83 Sample SpeedCoach data 12/12.

		Level 1	Level 2	Level 3	Level 4	Level 5
		Novice		Advanced	Pre-Elite	Elite
10/10	500m test @ T2	X				
11/11	500m test @ T2		X			
12/12	500m test @ T2			X		
12.5/12.5	500m test @ T2				X	
13/13	500m test @ T2					X
Rating Consistency	500m test w/o start (@STDEVA)	1.0+	0.8	0.6	0.4	0.2
Speed Consistency	500m test w/o start (@STDEVA)	0.1+	0.08	0.06	0.04	0.02

Table 84 Performance standards for 10/10 to 14/14 for 500m performance pieces at T2.

Analysis of data

The objective of this performance piece was 500m at 12/12 (12 strokes per minute and 12 metres distance per stroke). The athlete achieved an average of 12.3spm. Fig. 115 plots the distribution of all the strokes. The standard deviation is 0.78, meaning that the strokes cluster fairly well around 12.3. This athlete demonstrates an ability to regulate their rating. They have a good grasp of timing and sequencing. Every stroke is happening at about the same time.

The athlete's rating consistency perfor- mance (0.78 standard deviation without start) achieves Level 2 (intermediate) for rating con- sistency (see Table 84, a subset of the complete skills matrix at the end of the chapter).

The average distance per stroke was 13.2m. The objective for distance per stroke for this exercise is 12m at T2. The 13.2m is a quite high distance per stroke, indicating the athlete either has a high level of technical skills or is exerting themselves beyond T2. This will be assessed below under heart rate. The con- sistency follows the average (Fig. 116). (No distance per stroke standards are provided

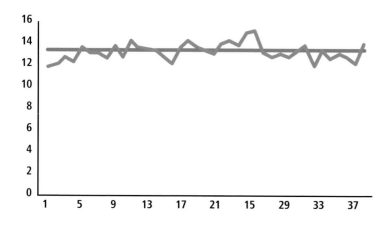

Fig. 116 Sample 12/12 500m piece showing the distance for each stroke with an average of 13.2 metres distance per stroke (green).

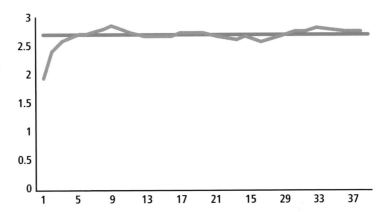

Fig. 117 Sample 12/12 500m showing speed in metres per stroke (mps) with an average of 2.68mps (green).

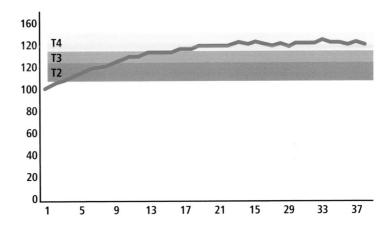

Fig. 118 Sample 12/12 500m showing the athlete's heart rate and training zones.

because these are considered within speed performance.)

The athlete's average speed was 2.68mps with the speed consistency standard deviation at 0.06 (Table 83). The first few start strokes skew the data and are not included in the calculations. The magnitude of this standard deviation is smaller than for stroke rate because the average is smaller, 2.68mps versus 12.3spm. This level of speed consistency is at the advanced level (see Table 84).

Our athlete's heart rate zones are in Table 85. The answer as to whether the athlete is achieving those long distances per stroke through efficiency or muscle is now revealed. The athlete moved into T4 by 250m and stayed there (Fig. 118).

	Bottom	Top
T2	114	129
T3	129	138
T4	138	148
T5	148	153

Table 85 Sample athlete's heart rate training zone.

Summary of analysis

What does all this mean? First, this athlete is new to the dynamic technique but is an experienced sculler. They have already mastered 10/10 and 11/11. This 12/12 performance piece demonstrates that their overall performance

10/10 – try this!

The place to start with slow work is 10/10. It will make obvious whether the athlete is connected. If the athlete is unstable, a section later in the chapter will discuss small work, sequencing and how to improve both.

For now, it's time to play. Turn on the measuring device, ensuring the 'noise' has been set quite low. If high stroke rates such as '47' and '98' appear on the screen, don't worry about them at the moment; erratic readings commonly occur in the early stages of mastering slow work. Try various strategies to get to 10 strokes per minute. It is important not to stare at the measuring device throughout this but to try to develop a sense of timing, a feeling of rhythm. Singing songs, counting to three Mississippi, closing eyes and other tactics help.

Once a couple of '10s' flash on the screen, try to get the same distance for every stroke. This is a function of effort that needs to be consistent. It is also a function of timing. A longer time in the back end will help.

For comparison, Table 86 shows an extract of a 500m piece completed by a sculler new to 10/10. So, don't get discouraged. Be pleased with your willingness to try something new. If 10/10 sounds easy to do, it is definitely not. However, everyone can master 10/10 and launch themselves towards 11/11, 12/12 and beyond.

Speed (GPS) (M/S)	Stroke Rate (SPM)	Distance per Stroke (GPS) (Metres)
2.43	10	13.4
2.20	11	11.1
2.00	12	24.4
2.14	10	13.7
2.31	10	14.1
1.15	12	20.2
0.75	10	15.2
0.83	10	5.8
0.95	18	3.1
1.21	14	6.1
1.60	14	7.9
1.81	14	7.9
1.86	10	10.4
1.81	11	9.9

Table 86 Sample of a 10/10 being executed by a new sculler.

is making good progress into the intermediate and advanced ranges. The issue about high heart rate, when investigated, reveals the athlete has an O'Neill of above average and should be able to accomplish 12/12 in T2 by modulating their effort.

The priority items to work on include (a) performing the piece at T2 to eliminate the effects of fatigue on speed consistency and (b) continuing to work on rating consistency to the advanced level (0.6 standard deviation). The plan would be for the athlete to take their effort down a notch, to T2, which may well allow them to achieve both speed and rating consistency at the advanced level. Taking considerable satisfaction in the speed consistency, this athlete should now start playing with 12.5/12.5 and 13/13.

Other considerations for slow work

For low rating pieces, ensure the 'noise' on the measuring device is set low, say '2', otherwise it may not register. Another caution is that if an athlete is getting very high stroke rate readings doing slow work, especially in the early days, the 'noise' is most likely the athlete's stroke not being smooth. The device will be reading correctly and pick up the 'noise' in the boat. Try to relax and be smooth.

Slow work is done in small bits to start. More on this under the section on learning and habits. In the early days, five minutes of 10/10 is enough and getting five strokes of approximately the same rating in a row is a triumph.

LEARNING AND HABITS

Learning is acquiring skills and information, habits automate them. There are ways to expedite learning and habit formation, speeding the athlete's development. Here are the conceptual approaches. Later, these conceptual approaches will be explored practically using small work.

Incremental, hierarchical and iterative

The notions of incremental and hierarchical were introduced above in slow work. They refer to the skills acquisition process. The athlete starts with a basic performance task, such as 10/10, and works through its elements (rating consistency, speed consistency, distance and heart rate) until a standard is achieved. The athlete breaks skills into their smallest elements, learning each one step at a time. That's incremental.

Hierarchical describes how a series of tasks build one on the other: 10/10, 11/11, 12/12, 13/13, 14/14 and 16–18spm. The athlete needs to do the first task well in order to acquire the skills necessary to begin to do the next one competently. The theory is that each task needs to be mastered in order. Sequence steps, all linked to one another, are a perfect example.

Iterative refers to the fact that these skills and tasks are never abandoned. Each season, an athlete will start with a lower order skills and continue to build competence. Then repeat. That's iteration. In addition, this iteration continues throughout the season, with athletes moving up and down the skills as they master or refine them. Iteration reflects the repetition of learning to form habits.

Hierarchy of efficient training

The entire training process, on a macro scale, is most efficient when it is incremental, hierarchical and iterative. Previously, the discussion has been on skills development, such as slow work. Masters' sculling development at the macro level has a hierarchy of mutually dependent steps, too.

- Connectedness
- Stability
- Consistency
- Versatility
- Speed

The important concept is: an athlete's optimal speed is a function of their versatility, consistency, stability and connectedness. These are hierarchical, with connectedness first. An athlete who masters connectedness, then stability, then consistency, versatility and speed – in that order – will expedite their skills acquisition and performance.

Connectedness and stability are discussed in Chapters 3, 4, 5 and 6. Small work provides the vehicle for acquiring both.

Learning

How the athlete acquires a skill is learning. Already described has been the incremental, hierarchical and iterative approach. This expedites learning since the athlete begins each new skill from a foundation of having mastered a previous one. Proceeding thoughtfully and in this structured way will facilitate learning, scrambling this approach will not.

For example, an athlete who leaps from sequence step to sequence step without linking them will find their sequencing skills acquisition is delayed. The athlete who concentrates on one skill for an extended period of time will find, through cognitive and muscle fatigue, the skill regresses to a prior one.

How athletes choose to learn is important. Rushing through steps will provide less learning than going slow. A behavioural economics book about thinking, learning and choices is *Thinking Fast and Slow* by Nobel Laureate Daniel Kahneman. It describes the choices humans are pre-programmed to make and how the body makes different unconscious decisions when thinking slowly versus rushing, very relevant to Masters skills development.

Habits

How the athlete embeds that new learned skill so that it is performed autonomically describes forming habits. *The Power of Habit* by Charles Duhigg provides a comprehensive discussion of habits and habit formation. The incremental, hierarchical, and iterative approach is the starting point, this time with the emphasis on iterative. Here are some other ways to embed a new skill as a habit:

- Perform it correctly and well, every time. Five repetitions of a new skill is sufficient, working up to ten over time.
- When the skill can be done ten times well, link it to a predecessor skills and/or a subsequent skill that is already established, e.g. sequencing.
- Start with light muscle involvement, then stronger, and only full power after the skills can be executed repeatedly and well. A too

early application of power will result in a quick regression to the older skill.
- Include skills development and repetition into every on water workout.
- For days not on the water, use creative visualization (imagine what the athlete looks like doing the skill correctly) or dry land methods to replicate (sequencing on the ergo).
- If experiencing muscle fatigue or cognitive overload, stop. Drink some carbohydrate. End the workout or wait five to ten minutes to see if the muscular and cognitive fatigues resolve, which they may well do with a brief rest and sugar.
- Find a proprioceptive cue. For example at the catch, knees on the inside of the arms is a terrific cue for all things front end. For those with tight hamstrings, identifying when thighs touch the chest during boat gathering is a good cue to ensure the body is at 25 degrees.
- Use cycling, described below, as a training methodology.

One of the most important things an athlete can do to speed habit forming is ensure a skill was done well the last time they executed it. The brain tends to remember the last new thing and puts that into short-term storage. Then during the athlete's good night sleep, the information is put into long-term storage. For the athlete who is doing a thoughtful skills progression, repeating and developing a new skill every day, the new skill goes into long-term storage night, after night, after night – quickly becoming habit.

Undoing old habits
Old habits are never undone. They are overtaken by a new skill. When the body's stress goes up, the likelihood of regression to the old habit is high. Stress includes physiological fatigue, muscle fatigue or psychological fatigue, say at a race. Regression is the body's way of reverting to behaviours that ensured its

environmental survival. The athlete's new skill may not have been around long enough to satisfy the primitive brain that the athlete will not get eaten by predators when using it.

Thus, one of the ways to stop skills regression is to improve embedding that skill through quality repetition. The second is – keep stress at bay. Regression occurs with fatigue. The athlete should keep new skills sessions short, to the point and successful. Competition and racing bring a different set of stressors, with strategies for dealing with them in the next chapters.

Small work and qualitative performance analysis

Some skills are measured by performance standards, as described in Table 84 and the skills matrix at chapter end. Some skills are measured qualitatively, e.g. wobbles in the boat. Small work is one of those skills sets. Small works refers to technical exercises and activities, usually undertaken when the boat is not moving. Skills such as squaring, feathering and stationary sequencing are examples.

Small work: hands

The athlete should be able to roll a tube in their hand as shown in Figs 63 and 64. The next step is to take this skill into the boat. The oars are angled differently at the catch and release. Thus, the front end and back end hand skills need to be acquired separately. The increments and hierarchy are:

- Oars on the water and at the release, feather and square one blade, then the other.
- Oars on the water and at the release, feather and square both blades at the same time.
- The same at the catch (or in quarter, half, three-quarter slide increments but finally at

the catch). One hand at a time, oars on the water, then both.
- The next hierarchical step is oars off the water, one hand at a time in all the above positions.
- The last hierarchical step is both oars off the water, feathering and squaring both hands at the catch and release.
- All the above performed while the boat is sitting still.

How is performance measured? It is not by the degree of dryness of the sculler, it is the following, and the sculler may look at their hands throughout all this:

- Wrists straight, thumb on the perimeter of the grip, hands relaxed, arms in the correct position, e.g. straight at the catch and level at the release.
- No wobbles.

One might argue that the above is a life's work. One would be correct. But Masters have time to acquire skills incrementally and well. The hands need to function properly for the sculler to achieve their best sculling result. Start small and compete with friends.

The rest of small work uses the same conceptual approach. For sequencing, the iterative steps are the key elements, i.e. release, body flip, hand launch, etc. Then these elements are linked to complete the pre-drive, drive, front-end transition and back-end transition. The hierarchy is:

- Oars on the water
- One oar then the other off the water
- Both oars off the water

Let us try a sequencing progression, starting at the release.

Small work: sequencing example

At a standstill, start at the release. One hand off the oar is a good performance indicator that the athlete is well connected. Two hands off indicates skill mastery of that sequence element (Fig. 26). If there are wobbles, sequencing has another hierarchy to assist. It is the same hierarchy as that described in Chapter 3:

- Group 1 (feet, legs and hips)
- Pelvic girdle
- Group 2 (seat, spine and head)
- Shoulder girdle
- Group 3 (shoulder, arms and hands)

The athlete needs to consciously check, starting with the feet and working progressively up through the body, making sure that all relevant body components are engaged, while those that do not need to be engaged, such as the hands and arms, are not. Usually, the iterative, hierarchical mental check will identify what is not connected. If it doesn't, go through the same hierarchy but consciously tensing and relaxing muscles in each group to identify the possible culprit(s).

If there are still wobbles at the release, rigging is a place to check. Or, that the athlete is in an appropriate boat. A new sculler should have flotation or a very forgiving boat designed for them. That new sculler's hierarchy would be: boat with flotation until all skills mastered, then novice scull with flatter bottom, then performance scull.

The next sequence step is body flip. The athlete flips forward, oars on the water, and checks connectedness and positioning, as described in Chapter 5. Next is hand launch, where the athlete will need to develop a strategy for hand placement so that the launch is smooth.

That is three individual sequence steps at a standstill. The athlete can now do each element wobble free. Next is to link them together. Start at the release, slowly flip and launch hands, ending at the pre-drive transition. The athlete then reverses these three actions to the release and takes one or both hands off the oar. This sounds so easy and simple. It is not. It is very hard work, particularly because in order to be wobble free, the core is engaged throughout, as are many other muscles.

Thus, small work should be done in small quantities. The athlete should do each sequence step slowly and correctly, up to five times. It is crucially important for the last iteration to be done as perfectly as possible because this is the iteration that will go into short-term memory. Thus, fewer done

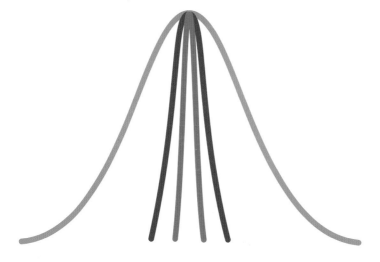

Fig. 119 Example of elite (red), advanced (purple) and novice (light blue) stroke rate spreads (standard deviation).

well will accelerate the learning process faster than many done poorly. Having moved on to another activity and mentally refreshed, the athlete can always return later to this skill and have another five goes, ending perfectly.

When three sequence steps can be done slowly, well, and five times in a row, it is time to start experimenting with continuity, doing them more quickly and increasing the number of repetitions. The caution is that doing steps quickly will hide problems with connectedness and mask wobbles. Wobbles are the boat's way of telling the athlete that their connection is broken.

The athlete starts with individual elements, slowly, then strings three together. When the three are linked successfully with oars on the water, then move through that oar hierarchy, too. Move from a short series of five, to a longer one of ten, and add speed. Then move on to the next sequence step, linking it.

Transitional small work is particularly important because it involves a biomechanical change, say the pulling to pushing motion at the front-end transition. The pre-drive transition and mid-drive transition are also locations where connectedness is more challenging to maintain. The ultimate goal for all sequence steps and links is to execute them absolutely wobble free with oars off the water. While sitting still. Another life's work, but oh so satisfying when each step is mastered and the wobbles stop.

WHY CONSISTENCY IS IMPORTANT

Strokes can be consistent in many ways. Here, we measure stroke consistency through rating and speed because it is easy to do with available measuring devices. Distance per stroke can also be used since it is a function of speed, but it has no specific performance standards. Later, the Empower Gate discussion will review other possible consistency parameters such as catch, slip, wash, release, stroke arc and effective stroke arc. The theory behind the consist-

ent stroke is that subsequent experimental changes applied to a consistent stroke will yield valid and reliable information. Changes to an inconsistent stroke will not.

Consistency is the pathway to performance. When at low ratings an athlete can demonstrate consistency of speed and rating, their sculling system is connected and stable. From that stable platform the possibilities are endless. Let's look at consistency and how it provides the underpinnings of versatility and speed. First, what does consistency look like using data?

There are two ways to assess consistency. One is to 'eyeball' the data. Look at Table 83 and Table 86. Even an athlete new to this approach can see that the Table 83 data show repeated and closely clustered numbers for both rating (spm) and speed (mps). Table 86 is rather different. In the early days, this visual approach is fine for those who are not data inclined.

A more precise way to evaluate the data is through a simple Excel function. The data are downloaded to Excel (or some other spreadsheet programme) easily from most measuring devices. Then, a standard deviation function is used to indicate, essentially, how closely clustered the data are. The function @stdev.s is the proper one but @stdeva will provide the same result, as will @stdev for older Excel versions. Fig. 119 shows the difference in standard deviations for novice (light blue), advanced (purple) and elite (red). All these scullers have the same average. However, the novice's strokes are more varied than the elite, who can repeat the same stroke almost every time.

Consistency is important for experimenting with changes. Our advanced sculler in the slow work section above can now use the experimental approach to identify opportunities that will result in going faster for the same effort. These experimental opportunities can be rigging (move the feet forward), equipment (try Concept2 Fat2 blades or shorter oars), timing change (count to four in the back end instead of three) and so many others. With a consistent stroke, the effect (after multiple on water sessions experimenting with the new change) can be observed through the data. The results may be a little ragged because it is a new change, with the standard deviation less than optimal. If the change had an effect, the average should move. It can move either way, of course.

Our novice sculler does not have this experimental baseline, they have an almost random distribution of stroke ratings and speeds. Any experimental change introduced into this is going to be inconclusive. The athlete's first training objective is to develop the habits that lead to consistency, developing the platform for future experimental change.

The second benefit of consistency is that, in and of itself, consistency makes the boat go faster. Harken back to Chapter 2 and the section on Constant Velocity. A boat whose speed and direction (velocity) are constant will go faster for the same effort than a boat whose velocity is not. Assuming straight directionality, consistency achieves constant velocity.

Last, the physiology of consistency is important. An athlete who is consistent in speed and stroke rate is physiologically consistent as well. Using a certain level of effort, that athlete executes repeated strokes in the same way. Because the effort does not vary, this is physiologically efficient. This physiological consistency provides a foundation for versatility work, discussed next.

VERSATILITY

The relationship between the athlete's various capabilities (fitness, technique, FMB/strength/power and others) describes versatility. Versatility is the gateway to speed. Here, speed is defined as a function of effort and technique. The effort is both muscular (power) and aerobic. Technique refers here to rating, and assumes all the athlete's other technical capabilities are excellent. If they are not, those need to be addressed first. An athlete who can

perform 12/12 at the advanced level would be at an appropriate performance level to benefit from versatility work.

Versatility work is most appropriate for athletes who have demonstrated consistency. It assumes the athlete can achieve a certain speed by modulating their rating or effort. Let's pick a speed, say 3.00mps. The athlete can achieve this by doing very little effort and rating 28spm. Conversely, the athlete can do 12spm and make a significant effort. The boat will still be going 3.00mps.

The challenge with versatility is for the athlete, through a large physical and technical range, to achieve his or her optimum speed. Just trying harder at a presumed rating will not achieve the best outcome. Quite frankly, doing less at higher ratings has a lot to recommend it because the athlete will be able to last longer.

There are two primary versatility exercises and they can be done at any speed:

- Ratings increase and decrease. Using the same effort, preferably measured as T2 in the initial stages of exploring versatility, the athlete raises the rating and observes the speed increase. Over 100–200m increments is useful and with 4spm increments (18spm, 22spm, 26spm, etc.). There will be a point at which the athlete's technique is insufficient, providing information about the next technical focus.
- Effort increase and decrease. At a certain rating, the athlete increases and decreases effort with the same 100–200m increments being useful. The heart rate is indicative of the effort and can be cycled from T2 to T4 and back again.

Then, the two approaches can be mixed and matched to explore different results. As the training season progresses, the athlete needs to identify their optimal technical and physiological capacity, which will define the speed they can achieve at their main event. The constant speed and versatility explorations

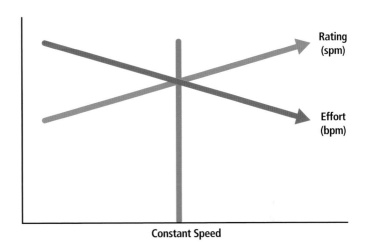

Fig. 120 Versatility means achieving a constant speed through variations in rating and effort.

Constant Speed

will provide the foundation for making the determination of optimal speed, which is the maximum:

- constant speed (mps) the athlete can maintain for 1,000m,
- at a constant effort (bpm),
- retaining the same propulsive force (watts), and
- at a constant rating

There are some redundancies in the above measurements (effort × rating = watts), but the idea is simple. Where is the point at which all the athlete's capacities are exhausted simultaneously, presumably at the end of 1,000m? Fig. 121 is a conceptual representation of the goal: maximum utilization of all the athlete's capabilities to get the fastest time. At some point the heart rate soars, the lungs cannot keep up, muscles don't fire and propulsion drops off. Timing this to occur at 1,001m, not at 500m or 700m, is what exploring versatility is about. Just like the boat performing best at constant velocity, the athlete performs best physiologically at a constant effort. Technical proficiency plays a role, too.

The information above is crucial for race planning and for identifying what the performance limiters are. Is the athlete using too low a rating requiring too high an effort?

What is falling in a heap first: aerobics, muscles or technique? What changes need to be made to optimize each? The constant effort versatility exercises help investigate all of this without the need of repeated 1,000m full-on efforts whose fatigue contaminates the data anyway. Of course, environment, starts and finishes are additional confounding factors discussed in the next chapters. A versatile sculler will have many options available to accommodate them.

SPEED

The sculling system is stable. The athlete's stroke is consistent and versatile. Now is time to talk about speed, starting with 16–18spm. Say what? If the athlete cannot go fast at slow ratings, that athlete cannot go fast at higher ratings. Here is how to go fast and have fun doing it.

An expanded set of prognostics is provided here (Table 87). The similar table in Chapter 7 provided only 18spm data. This table provides the comprehensive set of prognostics and is the one on which speed training is based. Only two significant digits are included because that is how the SpeedCoach screen reads (3.26 versus 3.256 in Table 42).

The athlete's speed training will progress in two directions: low ratings and increasing ratings.

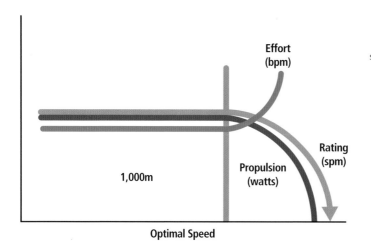

Effort (bpm)

Rating (spm)

Propulsion (watts)

1,000m

Optimal Speed

Fig. 121 Optimal speed as determined by the last sustained point of effort, rating and propulsion.

Low ratings is a progression leftwards on the prognostic chart, along the 16–18spm rating category. The low ratings work is undertaken at T2.

For low ratings, the athlete identifies the speed at which they currently perform 16–18spm. It does not matter what the athlete's actual age grade is. The example athlete from Chapter 7 (Table 49) completed the 1,000m 18spm at a speed of 3.17mps. His HR at the end was 148bpm, which puts him in T4. Ooops. We need 16–18spm completed at T2. So, while the prognostic table shows 3.17 almost at G grade, this athlete needs to take a step or two back. The starting point can be H grade (3.07mps) or I grade (2.89mps). I grade is recommended because of the opportunity for quick success.

Then, the athlete does *not* go out each training session and undertake 1,000m tests. That is for time trials described in the next chapter. The athlete explores consistency, their most likely opportunity for improving their low ratings work. If consistency is missing, stability and connectedness may be the starting point. Thus, slow work and small work will predominate in this athlete's workouts, and in most athletes' workouts early in the season. An athlete who can execute 12/12 can usually do well at 16–18spm because of – versatility; the transition from 12/12 to 16–18spm being the first versatility exercise in reducing effort and increasing rating.

Through the season the athlete continues to target progressions to lower age grades at 16–18spm. This is all load and high load subphase work. With load work continuing for the entire season, the athlete will be working on making 16–18spm improvements for the same period.

For the increasing ratings dimension, the athlete also starts at their 18spm performance. In a different example, a female athlete has completed the 18spm 1,000m at 3.01. In addition to the low rating work, this athlete will now work on increasing ratings, which is a good focus for the low-speed transition, low-speed and high-speed subphases. Rating increase increments of 4spm work well. Thus, this athlete will be targeting 22spm at 3.21 (and can go up to 23spm if needed since that is the category range). An athlete who can perform the 16–18spm prognostic at T2 should be able to do the next level of speed just by increasing the rating.

Which does not always work. Two factors affect the result: fitness and technique. An athlete, with an O'Neill of 'Good' or 'Excellent', should be able to do 22spm at T2 for 1,000m if they are technically proficient. If not, the issue is technical and back to consistency, small work and slow work. If the athlete's O'Neill is 'Above Average' or lower, the issue may be

MEN	1,000m	A	B	C	D	E	F	G	H	I	J	K
75	16–18	3.62	3.61	3.55	3.47	3.39	3.30	3.20	3.07	2.89	2.64	2.33
76	18–19	3.67	3.65	3.59	3.52	3.44	3.34	3.24	3.11	2.93	2.68	2.36
78	20	3.77	3.75	3.69	3.61	3.53	3.43	3.32	3.19	3.01	2.75	2.42
80	21–23	3.86	3.85	3.78	3.71	3.62	3.52	3.41	3.27	3.09	2.82	2.48
83	24–26	4.01	3.99	3.93	3.85	3.75	3.65	3.54	3.40	3.20	2.92	2.58
86	27–29	4.15	4.13	4.07	3.98	3.89	3.78	3.66	3.52	3.32	3.03	2.67
93	33–34	4.49	4.47	4.40	4.31	4.21	4.09	3.96	3.81	3.59	3.28	2.89
96–100	34–36	4.83	4.81	4.73	4.63	4.52	4.40	4.26	4.09	3.86	3.52	3.11

WOMEN	1,000m	A	B	C	D	E	F	G	H	I	J	K
75	16–18	3.21	3.20	3.15	3.08	3.01	2.92	2.83	2.70	2.50	2.20	1.75
76	18–19	3.26	3.24	3.19	3.12	3.05	2.96	2.86	2.73	2.53	2.23	1.78
78	20	3.34	3.33	3.27	3.21	3.13	3.04	2.94	2.80	2.60	2.28	1.82
80	21–23	3.43	3.41	3.36	3.29	3.21	3.12	3.01	2.88	2.67	2.34	1.87
83	24–26	3.56	3.54	3.48	3.41	3.33	3.24	3.13	2.98	2.77	2.43	1.94
86	27–29	3.68	3.67	3.61	3.53	3.45	3.35	3.24	3.09	2.87	2.52	2.01
93	33–34	3.98	3.97	3.90	3.82	3.73	3.63	3.50	3.34	3.10	2.72	2.18
96–100	34–36	4.28	4.27	4.20	4.11	4.01	3.90	3.77	3.60	3.34	2.93	2.34

Table 87 1X prognostic speeds in metres per second (mps) for various age grades and ratings over 1,000m.

fitness. One simple way to determine this is to do a 500m piece instead of 1,000m. Even an athlete with an 'Average' O'Neill who is technically proficient should be able to do the 22spm rating 500m increment at T2.

An athlete successful at 22spm proceeds next to 26spm and so on. During workouts, and while learning these speed skills, the same rules apply as in *Habits* above. High rating work, not thoughtfully progressed, is a recipe for regression. Start with short pieces or intervals, preferably at T2 in the early stages of the season.

Only when the athlete can execute a lower age grade of 16–18spm is the transition to a different higher rating structure made. Our athlete has now moved from 3.01mps to 3.08mps at 16–18mps, a lower age grade (D). She has two training avenues for increasing ratings. One is to continue the higher rating work at the E grade speeds, because this will reinforce good technique. Next is to start at 22spm in D, working towards 3.29. Using both is recommended.

All of this speed work lends itself to consistency assessments as well. The athlete's objective should be same stroke, every time. The rating usually becomes more consistent first, with the speed/effort consistency a somewhat distant second.

CYCLING

With the objective being quick and efficient skills acquisition, as well as improving aerobic fitness through T2 work, the athlete's workout plans need to do two things at once. This is accomplished through cycling in iterative loops through small work, slow work and continuous sculling; or whatever combination incorporates technically intense, but not aerobically demanding, activities while maintaining T2. Thus, the athlete might do some small work (and it might need to be less than five minutes to remain in T2); then practise the skill in motion as slow work; then change to another skill set, say working on 16–18spm even up to the top of T2; and then cycling back. The continuous sculling is at 1,000m increments or an organized subset of same.

Less efficient workout	
Small work	15 minutes
Slow work	15 minutes
Continuous sculling	30 minutes

More efficient workout through cycling	
Small work	5 minutes
Slow work	5 minutes
Continuous sculling	10 minutes
Small work	5 minutes
Slow work	5 minutes
Continuous sculling	10 minutes
Small work	5 minutes
Slow work	5 minutes
Continuous sculling	10 minutes

Table 88 Example of a standard workout compared to one that cycles.

As the season progresses, and the intensity of the work increases, cycling provides good recovery times where small work is undertaken during that time.

BREATHING

Sculling causes a compression in the diaphragm and lungs. At the beginning of the drive sequence, when the sculler is making a large physiological effort, the lungs are squished. Well-oxygenated blood provides a buffer. Well-timed breathing ensures that occurs.

When to breathe at high levels of effort? There are two primary schools of thought. The first involves 'double breathing'. The athlete at the release has expelled air and takes in a deep breath, then during boat gathering takes a small 'top-up' of air. A short pant. Air is expelled during the drive ready for a big breath at the release.

The other option is to take a deep breath at the release, expel that air during the pre-drive sequence and then, during the drive when the air is most needed, the body is opening and providing more pulmonary capacity, to breathe in strongly early, expelling later in the drive.

The issue is coordinating all this in a way that breathing becomes automatic. Initial explorations of both approaches may leave one either dizzy or gasping. An obvious indicator of success is a lower heart rate, which will occur quickly when the blood oxygen levels improve.

Breathing at all becomes an important consideration at a start, where some athletes hold their breath. Hyperventilating right before a start ensures a good supply of oxygen, although too much of a good thing may cause light-headedness.

One method for exploring breathing is during slow work and counting. Some athletes have found that synchronizing their breathing with their counting helps not only their oxygenation but their consistency. The objective for sequencing is that the pre-drive and drive sequence are the same no matter what the rating. Only the back-end transition timing changes. If that is achieved, even the low ratings will provide a good opportunity to investigate what breathing pattern works best.

STARTS

Another life's work, and a deeply controversial topic. The theory is that the catch angle should increase proportional to boat speed, yielding the per cent catch angle increases in Table 89.[1]

Start Stroke Number	Catch Angle (deg)	% of Catch Angle	Actual Catch Angle (deg)
1st	60	62	37
2nd	60	62	37
3rd	60	73	44
4th	60	90	54
5th–9th	60	100	60

Table 89 Start stroke examples using the optimal stroke sequence for a 60-degree catch angle.

Practical advice on starts follows:

- The first stroke is unique. Its purpose is to break the surface tension and move the boat forward in a straight direction. A steady, purposeful, controlled stroke driven through the feet has advantages over an abrupt, massively powered stroke or one driven through the arms. Hands over toes or hands a fist width apart are possible start positioning cues.
- Check the direction of the boat and apply the second stroke accordingly. The second stroke increases acceleration through an even application of effort that is stronger than the first stroke.
- The third through fifth strokes capitalize on the boat run, increasing it by lengthening

the sculler's drive sequence length from approximately half slide (first stroke) to full slide.
- Up to full speed in five strokes is ideal, although directional changes and environmental conditions may require more strokes.

Starts lend themselves particularly well to an incremental experimental approach. Begin by doing just the first stroke, observing direction and the fact that the scull will continue moving forward, and rather quickly, for a very long time. The second stroke needs to occur so as not to interfere with, but to augment, the results of that initial first stroke. Not too soon, not too late. The remaining strokes are longer, from both body position and boat run perspective. There is more time available to capitalize on boat run between start strokes than most athletes think. Those in an overpowering rush just wear themselves out prematurely, as discussed in Chapter 14.

THE WORKOUT PLAN

This is a plan the athlete can either write down or prepare mentally for the day. Some athletes like the structure of knowing exactly what they will do, others like the laissez-faire approach based on conditions and fatigue levels. Whatever the choice, a workout plan helps ensure time is used efficiently. Table 90 is one of an infinite number of types of workout plan. The best workload plan format is one the athlete uses.

OTHER EQUIPMENT

A wide variety of complementary equipment and devices exist. Below are the ones that have proven particularly useful.

Pre-workout nutrition/hydration			
Warm-up			
On water	Cycle 1	Cycle 2	Cycle 3
Small work			
Slow work			
Consistency			
Versatility			
Speed			
Cool down			
Post-workout nutrition/hydration			
Stretching			
Assessment			

Table 90 Sample workout plan template.

Ergometer

The ergo does not replicate sculling. The biomechanical bases for indoor rowing and sculling are different. However, the ergo can be cleverly used to facilitate skills development. In particular, sequencing can be done on the ergo, remembering to take hands off the handle occasionally and mimic the catch extension. Proprioceptive cues can be developed on the ergo, particularly if a mirror is available to provide feedback.

Power (Watts)	Catch (Degrees)	Slip (Degrees)	Finish (Degrees)	Wash (Degrees)	Force Avg (Newtons)	Work (Joules)	Force Max (Newtons)	Max Force Angle (Degrees)
123	-61	9	46	12	229	413	397	-29
124	-62	8	45	12	240	411	396	-26
130	-61	7	46	11	248	438	427	-31
111	-59	7	46	13	202	379	387	-31
128	-57	7	46	13	228	395	406	-25

Table 91 Sample of NK Empower Oarlock data.

Nielsen Kellerman Empower Wireless Oarlock

This device provides information about a large range of technical and performance parameters.

It connects wirelessly to the SpeedCoach GPS Model 2 with Training Pack firmware. Its data elements can be selected to display on the SpeedCoach screen. Table 91 shows a sample of the available data, useful for

		L1	L2	L3	L4	L5
		Novice	Intermediate	Advanced	Pre-Elite	Elite

BIOMECHANICAL

Flexibility	Flexibility Test	20%	40%	60%	80%	100%
Mobility	Mobility Test	20%	40%	60%	80%	100%
Balance	Balance Test	20%	40%	60%	80%	100%
TECHNICAL						
10/10	500m test @ T2	X				
11/11	500m test @ T2		X			
12/12	500m test @ T2			X		
12.5/12.5	500m test @ T2				X	
13/13	500m test @ T2					X
Rating Consistency	500m test w/o start (@stdev.s)	1.0+	0.8	0.6	0.4	0.2
Speed Consistency	500m test w/o start (@stdev.s)	0.1+	0.08	0.06	0.04	0.02

PHYSIOLOGICAL

Aerobic Capacity	O'Neill	Below Average	Average	Above Average	Good	Excellent

PERFORMANCE

Prognostic Performance (1000m)	Rating and HR Zone					
	18@T2	+3 Grades	+2 Grades	+1 Grade	At Grade	At Grade
	22@T2	+3 Grades	+2 Grades	+1 Grade	At Grade	At Grade
	26@T4		+2 Grades	+1 Grade	At Grade	At Grade
	30@T4			+1 Grade	At Grade	At Grade
	34@T4					At Grade
Race Plan		Executed	Executed	Executed	Executed	Executed

Table 92 Skills matrix.

assessing rigging, technique and effort. In this sample, we see an athlete who is well rigged but who may be able to move further forward from their current release (finish) angle of 46 degrees. The wash is quite low with the slip providing an opportunity. Given this is a smaller sculler, the effective stroke length is excellent. The work rate is high and the force is front-end loaded (-29, -26, -31).

Since the data are provided per stroke, for performance pieces the data provide insight into fatigue and where it is happening, for example does the effective stroke arc shorten as the piece progresses?

Randallfoils[2]

Originally created to improve speed performance, which data show they do, the Randallfoils also provide developmental training wheels to reduce oar arcing, as described in Fig. 78. The foils attach to the top of oar blades and provide a distinct proprioceptive cue if the athlete tries to lower the blades too far into the water.

SKILLS MATRIX

The skills matrix in Table 92 provides an athlete with a comparison of their developmental level. With it, an athlete can compete against the international standard and never have to enter a race. For example, a Level 4 or pre-elite athlete would be one who:

- meets 80 per cent of the FMB tests,
- completes 500m of 13/13 at T2,
- has a 'Good' O'Neill, and
- can perform 1,000m at 34spm in T4 at their age grade (or 30spm @ T4 in one lower age grade).

The table helps athletes prioritize training activities and consider which needs the most focus, providing satisfaction through those items that are going well. These are challenging standards. Level 5 is a life's work, but with decades of training ahead, there is time for every athlete to achieve it.

For those who do not want to race, the 'race plan' item on the skills matrix is optional. The hope is that every athlete will give competition a go, even if only time trials or friendly events at their club. For those who decide to compete or race, leave that item in the skills matrix, and for all, read on. Competition and racing are next.

Endnotes

1 Kleshnev, V., *The Biomechanics of Rowing* (Marlborough: The Crowood Press Ltd, 2016), p.129.

2 Randallfoil. https://hydrofoiloar.blogspot.com

13 | COMPETITION AND RACE PLANS

To create a logical pathway from training to racing, this chapter makes an artificial distinction between competition and racing. Here, competition involves the athlete testing his or her adaptation gains in a non-sanctioned activity, such as time trials. Racing involves a sanctioned event. The reality is that the progressive process of self-assessment began with training. That process continues smoothly from training, to competition, to the highest levels of racing – provided the athlete has a plan.

Competition and racing should be about testing the athlete's current adaptation in a different environment. The athlete's capacities and performance times should be predictable. By the time competition and racing occur, the athlete should have executed their current race plan's performance target in training, multiple times. For athletes on the development path to racing, competitions are terrific opportunities to identify and address external factors that can sabotage optimal race day performance.

In competitions, such as time trials or simply sculling a set piece against a mate, athletes can test their sculling progress and their race plan preparation/execution. Did the athlete achieve the expected result in that competition? If not, why not? What training programme or race plan modifications are needed? Alternatively, if the athlete achieved the expected results, the indication is that the training programme is on track and that the race plan works.

Racing takes the process to the next level. Racing is even more about external variables. A time trial on the training lake has some new external variables, such as the format for the time trial. For a sanctioned event, the external variables are considerably more diverse. The race location is novel and may be in a different part of the country, or in a different country entirely. The logistics of equipment, administration and athlete management create a wide range of opportunities for things to go wrong. Discovering how to minimize the external variables and to manage the racing experience to a level comparable to that of a competition or training run are part of what this chapter and the next explore.

At the core of competition and racing is the race plan. The race plan is an outline of both performance and non-performance items. Its objective is to quantify the external variables that can be managed and implement a purposeful approach to deal with them. It recognizes that a documented race plan reduces stress and surprises. The surprises will still happen, but with a race plan, fewer of them.

COMPETITION

The athlete who is assessing their progress is an athlete who is already competing: against themselves. Framing competition in this light is helpful psychologically. A gender difference exists: women shy away from competition, men embrace it, all of which sounds terribly politically incorrect without the research to back it up.[1] Coercion, in terms of quotas, helps increase women's participation. Women appear more likely to sign up to a sporting competition if their participation is necessary for the men to compete.[2] Thus, competitive experiences that are low key, informative and enjoyable are an important development tool, particularly for women.

Another barrier to competition and racing is the stress induced by thinking of both as dramatically unfamiliar. They aren't. They are a logical continuum of the training path with some interesting new factors. Athletes are encouraged to build competitions into their annual training programme. These can be skills competitions, too. Start small, assess, refine and have fun.

Time trials

A time trial, as defined here, is a formatted opportunity that involves two or more scullers. It can be three athletes whose time trial is an informal 1,000m. More likely, it is a set date, time and structure. Time trials are important opportunities for three reasons. First, they test the athlete's performance. Second, they test the athlete's race plan. Third, they introduce a few of the race elements that result in the physiological and psychological changes associated with racing. Time trials are different from training, where creating adaptation is the key. Time trials are for assessing that adaptation, a totally different objective. A good schedule for time trials is bi-weekly or monthly. Athletes should consider time trials as obligatory parts of their training programmes since the resulting desensitization will pay big dividends not only at their target race but over the course of their athletic career.

The Principle of Specificity dictates: the time trial format needs to be the same as the target race. Responsible athlete management dictates that the time trials need to reflect the athlete's training programme at that moment. These two factors, specificity and athlete management, compete for precedence. During the early season, the training programme should prevail.

Thus, a time trial in the first month of training should be at a lower rating and/or lower effort level than race pace. The time trial may be at a shorter distance, although 1,000m is preferred for experienced athletes who intend to race. The level of effort should be consistent with the athlete's training programme as well. For example, an athlete working on aerobic fitness would complete their time trial at T2 since it will complement that aerobic fitness development. Competing at T4 and T5, especially early in the season, will not accomplish this. Most important, the athlete should be clear about how the time trial aligns with that athlete's training programme and target race, using the time trial for their individual benefit.

Late season, the target race should prevail, making the trial as close to the target race as possible. Time trialling at 1,500m when the target race is 1,000m is unhelpful. Physiology can be trained, too, and consistency with the target event helps form a physiological habit. For this reason, recovery between time trial flights is as important as the distance. Late in the season, athletes should be executing race plans either approaching or at race rating and effort. Their recovery should reflect their main event, too. Recovery between 1,000m pieces needs to be complete. The more practice, the more habits are formed and the less stress. These competition experiences temper expectations that, if unrealistic, can get in the way of optimal performance.

	Early season	**Late season**
Distance	Principle of Specificity. The distance should be either a logical subset or the distance of the race being trained for	Principle of Specificity. The distance should be the distance of the race being trained for
Rating	At current training rating	At current training rating which should be approaching or at race rating
Effort	Consistent with training objectives	Consistent with training objectives
Speed	At current training level	At current training level, which should be approaching or at race pace

Table 93 General guidelines for time trial format.

Adaptation assessment is the goal of the time trial. The athlete needs to establish what is being assessed prior to the time trial. Below are a few possible assessment items:

• Race plan execution
• Rating consistency
• Heart rate consistency
• Speed consistency
• Stroke length consistency
• Time to recover between flights
• Start execution

At the conclusion of the time trial, the athlete should identify (a) which chosen assessment items went well, (b) which did not and (c) what changes to the training programme or race plan are needed.

A sample of an early season time trial may be: 1,000m, T2, at 16–18spm. The distance is the same as the target race. The rating is low, which tends to highlight technical opportunities. The training heart rate (T2) limits the athlete's opportunities to muscle their way to a higher performance speed. Because 16–18spm prognostics are available, the athlete's performance can be compared to identify the grade (A, B, C, etc.) at which they are performing.

For example, an athlete performing above grade, for example a D grade athlete performing at an F grade level, most likely has opportunities in both aerobic development and technique. A check of the O'Neill would indicate the level of aerobic fitness. If high, the opportunity is more likely technical. If low, more likely both technical and aerobic development. The training programme should be checked to ensure its objective matches with the observed performance results.

Alternatively, a C grade athlete performing at grade early in the season, such as meeting the prognostic for their grade at 16–18spm in T2, would verify their training programme targets technical improvements that would, next, result in their achieving a B grade prognostic for 16–18spm at T2. That athlete would also begin the process of increasing ratings within that grade, targeting a C grade prognostic at the next higher rating. Because the effort for this early season time trial is at T2, a number of flights (repetitions) would be appropriate and should be well tolerated.

A sample of a later season time trial may be: 1,000m, 50 per cent T4, at 26–32spm, with the athlete self-selecting the rating and heart rate management based on their training programme. This format creates variability so that athletes can refine according to their training needs. For example, an athlete could do high-intensity intervals at different ratings, testing their technical proficiency, or they could cycle between T4 and T5 for a portion to test their anaerobic threshold with lower effort recovery in between. Alternatively, they could do the full 1,000m at one effort and rating, another at different parameters (after recovering), to determine which is faster.

SUBPHASE	Distance	Rating (spm)		EffortT2	Number of Repetitions	Focus
Load	500–1,000m	10-14	16–22	T2	2-5	Technique: stability and consistency at low speed
High Load		14–18	18–24	T2/T3	2-5	Technique (as above) plus prognostic comparison
Low Speed Transition			20–26	T2/T3/T4	2-3 T2 shorter recovery; T4 full recovery	Identifying optimal speed and rating
Low Speed	1,000m		26–32+	T3/T4	2-3 Full recovery	Verifying increase in rating and speed
Speed			28–36	T4/T5	1-3 Mirror race schedule for heats, semis, final	Identifying race plan rating and speed for the main event

Fig. 122 Sample format for time trial progression through the training season.

All of which sounds very much like training, which it should. The main difference with time trials is – there are other people, a format and expectations. This means stress and fatigue, which need to be managed. From the stress perspective, participants with similar training programmes should be grouped and complete a time trial piece appropriate to their training. For very new or stressed athletes, the sole objective for the time trial can be – test out your stress management tools and just complete it. And this can continue to be the noble goal until that athlete decides to change that goal, no matter how long it takes.

From a stress and fatigue management perspective, an athlete's response will usually change from training to competition. It can change considerably for athletes with little competitive experience. Learning to manage stress and fatigue as they escalate is an important skill. Another skill is expectation management; that is, what the athlete 'hopes' to achieve for a performance time and what the athlete should 'expect' to achieve. Competitions are good forums for testing the accuracy of performance time predictions. What an athlete will achieve at a target regatta should be what they have achieved in a time trial, which should be what they have achieved in training. Performance is the result of a predictable, not magical, process.

Excessive, full out 1,000m pieces will not provide a valid or reliable performance assessment. Even if the athlete does their best in the first piece, that first effort is usually tempered by the survival instinct that sees four, five or six 1,000m pieces looming ahead. It's important to differentiate between the purposes of training (aerobic, anaerobic or technique development) and competition (performance assessment). Athletes should feel free to self-select their level of participation, especially when the purpose of the competition (especially time trial) in which they find themselves seems confused. In that case, complete a good first piece, negotiating how to obtain adequate recovery. This may involve ignoring the external format and what everyone else is doing. Then complete a second piece. Being self-focused and acting on the individual athlete's own needs in the face of external pressure is good experience, too.

Electronic regatta (eRegatta)

Electronic regattas are a form of time trial that allow athletes from far-reaching locations to compete against each other. The validity of the results are not as good as for a time trial or sanctioned regatta where conditions are comparable. However, eRegattas do encourage the development of skills that are complementary. For example, the athlete needs to become familiar with their measuring device and be able to obtain accurate 1,000m data from that device. Clever athletes will assess wind conditions and currents to optimize their performance results. Self-management in terms of sleep, nutrition, hydration and other recovery aspects are heightened.

Required for an eRegatta are a season-long schedule, with a Western Australian sample provided in the text box here.

Summary of competition

The purpose of competition, such as time trials, is to assess adaptation. Thus, the format of the time trial needs to be consistent with

where the athlete is in his or her training programme. Later in the season, the format needs to be consistent with the athlete's target race. Each competition provides the athlete with an opportunity to assess different aspects of their training and adaptation. Those target aspects should be identified in advance.

RACE PLANS

The athlete should have a race plan for the time trial (or eRegatta) as well as for a race. Early versions of the race plan will provide a foundation for the more complex race plan needed for a sanctioned regatta. The race plan includes:

- Pre-competitive elements
- Competitive elements
- Post-competitive elements

If the competitive event is conducted at the athlete's training venue, the number of unknowns is fewer. The race plan is smaller. For athletes whose season includes a major race in a different location, creating time trial opportunities in different venues expands the race plan list. Different venues provide good preparatory experience as well. The final shape of the race plan should be a plan, outline or checklist.

The second objective for a race plan is to provide the basis for continuous improvement. The first year of developing a race plan is challenging. On reflection, the number of items needed to encapsulate the competitive experience multiply. This quantity is complicated by the baseline of each element being unknown.

For example, an athlete may have recently integrated a pre-workout and recovery nutrition plan into their training programme, only to discover that what worked in training, when the stress was low, does not work for competition. Athletes evolve and change, as well, with no guarantee that what worked last year will

Electronic Regatta (eRegatta)

The purpose of an eRegatta is to provide an opportunity for all athletes, no matter their experience or where they train, to participate in a competitive event. Required for an eRegatta are a season schedule, with an example provided here, and a volunteer who receives and distributes results. The format and events for this example eRegatta follow the expected training outcomes for athletes targeting the Australian Masters Rowing Championships held in late April/early May. Tables 94 and 95 show the events, categories and grades. Participants can enter two events and choose their grade or a lower one.

Masters Rowing Western Australia Incorporated (not associated with Rowing Australia) manages the eRegatta in Western Australia. After participants' initial trepidation, and concerns about location inequalities in conditions, the end result has been much friendly competition and improved awareness about how to execute a performance piece well. A primary success has been easing the pathway for new scullers into competition and racing, with 100 per cent of those novices involved in the 2019 eRegatta participating in sanctioned events – and enjoying them, too.

9 DECEMBER	500m@14spm or less	1000m <18spm	
20 JANUARY	500m <19spm	1000m <23spm	
17 FEBRUARY	500m <21spm (Novice A/B only)	1000m <25spm	1,000m OPEN
17 MARCH	500m <23spm (Novice A/B only)	1000m <27spm	1,000m OPEN
21 APRIL	500m <25spm (Novice A/B only)	1000m <29spm	1000m OPEN

Table 94 Sample of eRegatta events.

All categories separately for men and women	
Premasters	Ages 24 to <27
Masters	Individual grades: A–M
Novice A	Have not sculled a 1X in a 'real' regatta before. Boat flotation IS allowed. All grades including Premasters.
Novice B	Have not sculled a 1X in a 'real' regatta before (or by permission). Boat flotation NOT allowed. All grades including Premasters.
Masters	Individual grades: A–M

Table 95 eRegatta categories with separate grades for both women and men.

be successful this year. The beneficial process of creating and executing a race plan begins to whittle down the number of unexpected variables. A race plan helps reduce stress and improve perceived control.

The third aspect of a race plan is that it helps form good habits, which function unconsciously. The degree to which there is continuity between the training programme and race plan increases training efficiency. For example, the process of turning on the measuring device should be the same at training and competition. The start sequence during training and competition should be the same. If a particular behaviour or process is achieving good results, its repetition is desired. This repetition creates habits. Automatic behaviours require less of the athlete's conscious awareness. Stress decreases, perceived control improves.

Pre-competitive elements of the race plan

A primary focus of pre-competition is recovery. Recovery should be complete before the competition. The competitive results of a well-recovered athlete will be valid. A poorly recovered athlete's results will only tell the athlete that their performance was depressed because their recovery was incomplete. Both the nutrition and hydration plan should be in place, executed the day before as well as on the day. A prior good night's sleep is important. To ensure that the restorative processes are complete, a rest day before the competitive event is a good idea. If not taking a rest day, the day prior should be easy (E). Equipment should be prepared, including charging the measuring device. All the details of preparation should be identified and noted in the emerging race plan.

Competition, even low key, can raise reactions that are quite unexpected. It is even common for eRegatta participants, who in reality are only doing a training piece by themselves, to report elevated stress levels. There may be physiological stress that disrupts sleep. The athlete may find on the morning of competition that foods eaten prior to training every day for weeks have no appeal. Hydration fluids that seemed perfect may now be unpalatable. Both nutrition and hydration, under stress, can cause a gag reflex that needs to be dealt with to ensure the athlete can achieve adequate nutrition and hydration. Athletes may be unusually short-tempered, talkative or quiet.

The athlete's reaction to the competitive build-up can be evaluated fairly easily by the number of 'flight or fight' symptoms exhibited.

Flight or fight (hyperarousal, acute stress response and the defence cascade)

By any of its names, most athletes have experienced it and unpleasantly so. The only aspect differentiating acute competitive stress from a true psychological pathology is that competitive stress hopefully resolves itself after the event. Flight or fight is a mind/body reaction, with the body starting the cascade. It is a completely normal response. It is completely autonomic, a function of the primitive area of the brain that operates unconsciously to detect threats. Autonomic does not mean realistically proportionate. A range of hormonal and biochemical changes accompany the response, affecting athletic performance. The effect can be debilitating and undermine performance, or it can be performance enhancing. The athlete's approach to managing flight or fight is the determining factor.

Arousal is the first step in activating the defence cascade. Readers who are remembering their own previous races may find themselves, right now, experiencing same. The ensuing flight or fight response then arises.

Cool, pale skin	Fat and glycogen are released for muscular action
Heart and/or breathing rate increases	Sweating
Sphincters react	Digestion slows or stops
The bladder relaxes with frequent urination	Dry mouth
The large bowel empties and diarrhoea occurs	Loss of hearing and peripheral vision

Table 96 Common flight or fight symptoms.

Subsequent reactions can be freezing and immobility in various forms: tonic, collapsed or quiescent. Examples include athletes becoming clumsy, falling to pieces at the slightest provocation, cranky, distracted or hiding from everyone before the event. Different personality types react differently. While animals resume normal behaviours once the danger has passed, humans may find that the symptoms are lingering.[3] The symptoms are systemic and varied. Table 96 shows some of them.

The purpose of flight or fight is to prepare the body for a high level of activity: running away from the sabre-toothed tiger or fighting the other tribe. The bladder and digestive system rid the body of excess weight, then shut down to preserve remaining physiological resources. Blood flow to muscles increases. Heart and breathing rates rise to increase oxygenation. Muscles tense in preparation for extra speed and strength. Reviewed from this perspective, a human body in hyperarousal is perfectly poised for sport performance.

Timing is everything. A high level of stress arousal for hours or days before competition is unhelpful. Aside from the psychological implications of such prolonged stress are the physiological ones: fatigue, constipation, dehydration, accidents, disrupted sleep and illness among others. A period of prolonged acute stress will undermine performance. But with the body on autopilot, what can be done?

Research says: many things. One of the simplest is to ensure a positive, supportive environment where the athlete has an appropriate competitive event and race plan that is achievable, with specific manageable steps throughout. Familiarity with competition can create resilience. Small, informal competitions, whose purpose is experience and fun, can go a long way towards cultivating a long-term delayed arousal response. Athlete self-reflection and awareness of what is happening, its normalcy and the ability to manage it come with experience. These insights should be incorporated into the race plan as well.

On the other hand, entering an event for which the athlete is totally unsupported or unprepared, physically or psychologically, will have the reverse effect. This type of experience has the potential to create real trauma. Unlike animals that recover quickly, the stress for a traumatized athlete can linger and affect general well-being, not to mention dampen their desire to continue in the sport. Certain personality types are more at risk.

This book uses progressive self-assessment, competition and racing as ways for an athlete to build awareness of and coping mechanisms for managing hyperarousal. The timing of how the athlete progresses through these is complicated by experience, age and gender. Younger women appear to have less of a problem with competition, older women more. Experienced athletes who have successfully competed have a skill set that the inexperienced athlete does not. Men have different reactions, usually a function of their personality or experience. Hyperarousal can be managed. Incremental, supportive participation is the first approach to mitigating the flight or fight reaction. For example, an athlete thinking: 'I finished a 500m piece, executed my race plan successfully and was not eaten by the sabre-tooth tiger or chased by the other tribe – maybe I will do this again!'

Having a sense of perceived control over competition, and racing, is important. 'Perceived' control is not necessarily actual control, although it is still helpful. A race plan helps foster a sense of control. Athletes who feel out of control, or perceive themselves to be victims of external forces, exhibit higher levels of stress. Athletes who perceive their situational control to be greater are more effective at coping with stress. Depending on the level of perceived control, the athlete's responses will differ, as will the magnitude and timing of the flight or fight reaction. Those with a greater sense of control are more likely to engage, express emotions and seek social support. Those with a lesser sense of control are more likely to disengage, avoid and only indirectly express negative feelings. Athletes who use tools to assist them in perceiving themselves more in control will have a more positive psychological experience.

For some athletes, the lead-up to an event becomes increasingly distressing and/or the flight or fight does not dissipate at the end. For them, support, assurance, planning and appropriate competition do not help. For these athletes a number of approaches have proven successful in maintaining arousal within a window of tolerance – not too high and not too low.[4] Breathing interventions, mindfulness meditation, biofeedback and cognitive therapy are only some of the interventions with evidence-based success.[5] These are good skills for all athletes to add to their performance toolkits.

Arousal, flight or fight, and its symptoms are normal at a competition and race. The objective is to keep arousal appropriate, preferably within a performance-enhancing magnitude and timeframe. If the athlete is having difficulty in so managing arousal and the flight or fight reaction, and for those athletes who want more tools in their competitive toolkit, a sports psychologist is the perfect resource.

Competitive elements of the race plan

This is the range of activities directly related to the performance piece: warm-up, entering the water, pre-start activities, the race, cool down and leaving the water. Competition is an ideal time to begin to flush out what works, and what does not, with adjustments made accordingly. For example, an athlete who normally warms up on an ergometer may find that none is available because everyone else is using them. Thus, the timing of the ergo warm-up or, perhaps, a switch to a dynamic warm-up that does not involve equipment, may be needed. Did the athlete take a water

bottle into the boat and, if not, was the dry mouth attendant with competitive stress a problem? Were the contents of the water bottle appropriate for before and after? Does it make more sense to turn on the measuring device when the boat goes in the water, letting it run for the entire competitive event, or can starting it be managed at the start line?

For the actual piece, what format has the athlete chosen? What is the start pattern? What is the stroke rate and heart rate for the various subsets of the piece? What are the subsets of the piece (100m, 250m, 500m)? Will the athlete be using the piece to trial different ratings and speeds for their own benefits and, if so, how has that format been developed to accommodate fatigue? What is the psychological preparation to minimize, or eliminate, the athlete's distractibility, understanding that every distraction breaks the habit execution pattern? What are the technique indicators that the athlete has identified in training, for example shortening the stroke at 400m, and what is the plan for addressing them? There are an almost infinite number of competitive elements.

All these questions. No athlete can manage all the above well, which was the point of posing them. Thus, a list. Then, prioritization. Identifying a simple list of prioritized competitive elements, consistent with the current training focus, provides an opportunity for success. The prioritization is simply: what aspects of training, if improved, will yield the best performance result? If the athlete is working on stroke rate consistency during training, that should be a priority item being assessed in competition because this consistency has a major impact on performance. Or, the priority can be heart rate consistency. When progress is made in each, with habits solidifying, it can be both.

A race plan that targets, say, a stroke rate at which the athlete is not working in training, will only provide information that the athlete was not working on this in training. Alternatively, if an athlete is working at 26spm in training, seeing how that athlete performs throughout a 1,000m piece at 26spm will provide information about stroke consistency, effort and fatigue that will help guide future training. Because of the prognostic charts, it will provide an indicator of what the athlete's potential future performance may be with an increased rating.

A race plan helps focus the athlete on what is important to that athlete and what that athlete can control. The athlete cannot control the performance of others. The athlete can control a competitive piece at 26spm and the consistency of same. Thus, a race plan provides an intermediary opportunity for success. Executing the competitive elements of a race plan with precision provides the athlete not only with data but can, likewise, provide a sense of accomplishment.

Last, things go wrong. When they do, it is helpful to realize that this is a good outcome and chance to refine the training programme or race plan. Better these perturbations occur early in the season than during the year's main event.

Post-competitive elements of the race plan

These include, immediately, hydration and nutrition, stretching and the routine that the athlete prefers. One important element is evaluating the athlete's execution of the race plan and the performance results.

Previous chapters have discussed the efficiency benefits of assessment. The training plan's purpose is to produce adaptive results, both physiological and technical. The race plan is in place to evaluate the success of that training plan. An athlete who has been working on stroke consistency for a month at a certain stroke rate should be able to execute, during competition, that level of proficiency. If they can't, the race plan information provides a basis of inquiry for what needs to happen during competition in order for that athlete

to succeed. It may be the pre-competition elements were not well managed. It may be factors related to the competitive elements. Whatever it is, early identification provides the opportunity to address it.

Assessment is helpful in identifying 'what works'. The athlete might not have performed the competitive elements according to plan. However, if sleep, nutrition, hydration and all the pre-competitive elements went well, that is important and a success. Assessment needs to identify those aspects of training that are working. It needs to celebrate successes at many levels, including the new athlete whose noble goal was to complete the competition, and did. It's crucial that competition provide as many, or even more, successes than items for improvement. Continuous improvement can be a soul-destroying quest of personal recrimination, or it can be a pathway to personal satisfaction built from small successes, of which there should be many.

A final post-competitive element is for the athlete to assess how they felt about their performance. If it is relentlessly negative, time to find some new tools from the sports psychologist. If it is relentlessly positive, with a smattering of priority opportunities for improvement, all good.

Example of a race plan

The race plan is a personal tool and very individualized. Both its format and content are those that are most useful to the athlete. Table 97 is a sample of an actual race plan. The experienced sculler (John) who developed this race plan had not used a race plan before. He first created a basic plan for his competitions, evolving this final race plan for his first Australian Masters Rowing Championship 1X participation. John's race plan at 26spm reflected that this was his first year with the dynamic technique and a development year for him.

Monday and Tuesday before
Rest and relax
Consider diet and hydration
Review boat movement map on and off water
Wednesday
Consider diet and hydration
Arrive two hours before start time
Review plan
Sun and warmth protection
Rig boat (I will try to do this earlier)
Check boat and equipment
Obtain bow number (this is usually available one hour before race)
Stretch and warm up
Toilet
Hydrate
Race
Turn on speed coach before leaving beach/pontoon.
Leave beach forty minutes before start.
Practise start and 26spm.
Be prepared to move into starting position when called (boats will be held by stern from the starting pontoon). This will probably require backing into position – stay relaxed.
Hydrate
Be ready to start. Bow may have to keep boat aligned beforehand if any cross wind. Blades buried.
1st stroke three-quarter length slow strong and steady. Keep head in boat.
2nd stroke dynamic technique start. Maintain technique for whole race. 2nd stroke controlled.
Next five strokes build quicker and longer to up rating, length and speed. This is similar to the start we practised. Don't worry if anything goes wrong. Just keep rowing.
Settle at 26spm. Maintain this the whole race with power. 26spm. Slight pause at the end of each drive. Keep thinking 'maintain dynamic form' 26spm.
Finish
Hydrate
Return safely to beach/pontoon
Stretching
Keep warm with suitable layers of clothing. Hot shower if necessary
Food
Review
Before I leave, review the race
Modify plan if needed for the next race

Table 97 Sample of race plan used at the Australian Masters Rowing Championships.

John's pre-race assessment was that he could maintain a high level of technique at 26spm but that at 28spm, with fatigue, that technique deteriorated. The rating of 26spm is mentioned multiple times in his race plan because maintaining a consistent rating was a priority item for him.

John achieved a personal best. He obtained valuable information for his next year's training plan. His average rating was 26.75spm, which was a marked improvement over previous competitive outings and closely matched his race plan. Fig. 123, a simple Excel figure using his SpeedCoach data, shows that there was some variability with his stroke rate ranging from 23.5 to 30 without start strokes. The standard deviation, also derived from Excel and without start strokes, was 1.05. These indicate that John has an opportunity for improving his performance by working on stroke rate consistency.

John's average speed for the race was 3.37mps. The prognostic chart tells us that, at 26.75spm and 3.37mps, he was sculling

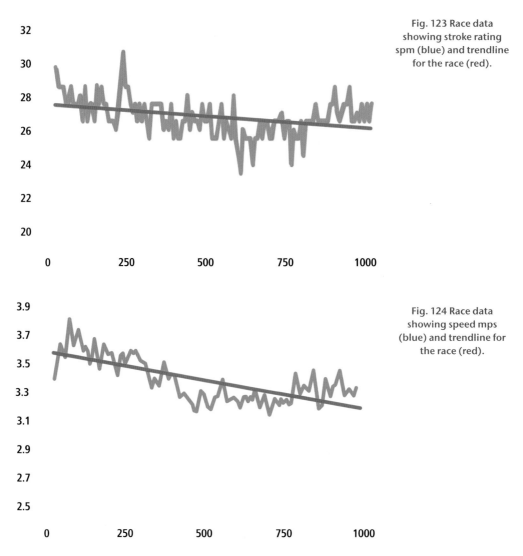

Fig. 123 Race data showing stroke rating spm (blue) and trendline for the race (red).

Fig. 124 Race data showing speed mps (blue) and trendline for the race (red).

about one grade higher than the FISA World Championship time. So, he has improved two grades from the start of his training season and is now only one grade off his age grade. Fig. 124 shows variability in speed. Without start data, John's speed ranges from 3.14mps to 3.8mps. We know this was a development year. Comparing his results to training and prior competitions, we see steady progress.

The trendlines for both Figs 123 and 124 show a downward slope. The explanation for this is fatigue. In John's case, we know one of his biggest opportunities for next year is aerobic development and moving his O'Neill results to the next level of fitness.

In summary, John's race plan provided a platform for him to control the controllables. His race plan addressed the uncontrollables in a way that resonated for him: 'Don't worry if anything goes wrong. Just keep rowing.' He demonstrated measurable progress from the beginning of his training year to his first 1X national race. And, he knows what to work on next year: consistency and aerobic development. Both will help him move down a grade on the prognostic charts when he compares this year's performance to a comparison 26spm performance next year. These training priorities will help him increase his rating and sustain it for 1,000m. With his targeted technical and aerobic training programme, John should be competitive in his grade, nationally and internationally, in the next few years.

Summary of race plans

The race plan is a tool for creating habits around competition and racing. Its purposes are to reduce amorphous stress, increase the perception of control, productively utilize the natural physiological changes that occur with competition and improve performance. Race plans are highly individualized. Early race plans are tested in competitions and further developed for races. They are part of the athlete's process of continuous improvement.

SUMMARY OF COMPETITION AND RACE PLANS

The athlete with a race plan has an advantage over one without. Race plans can improve the competitive experience and improve performance. Now on to racing and the targeted race, which adds even more items for race plan consideration.

Endnotes

1 Niederle, M., Vesterlund, L., 'Do Women Shy Away From Competition? Do Men Compete Too Much', *The Quarterly Journal of Economics*, Volume 122, Issue 3, August 2007, pp.1067–1101, https://doi.org/10.1162/qjec.122.3.1067.

2 Niederle, M., Vesterlund, L., 'Gender Differences in Competition', *Negotiation Journal*, vol. 24, iss. 4, October 2008, pp.447–463.

3 Kozlowska, K., Walker, P., McLean, L., Carrive, P., 'Fear and the Defense Cascade: Clinical Implications and Management', *Harv Rev Psychiatry*. 2015 Jul-Aug; 23(4): pp.263–287. doi: 10.1097/HRP.0000000000000065. Review. PubMed PMID: 26062169; PubMed Central PMCID: PMC4495877.

4 Ogden, P., Minton, K., Pain, C., *Trauma and the Body: a Sensorimotor Approach to Psychotherapy*. New York: Norton, 2006.

5 Kozlowska, K., Walker, P., McLean, L., Carrive, P., 'Fear and the Defense Cascade: Clinical Implications and Management', *Harv Rev Psychiatry*. 2015 Jul-Aug; 23(4): pp.263–287. doi: 10.1097/HRP.0000000000000065. Review. PubMed PMID: 26062169; PubMed Central PMCID: PMC4495877.

14 | RACING A SINGLE SCULL

Racing a single scull is different from multi-seat boats. The sculler is alone with the boat and oars and it is a point of true partnership with the equipment. There is only one propulsive force and for that reason the risk is higher and, for many, the 'flight or fight' response is accentuated. The rewards are accentuated, too. One way to improve the total experience is to control the controllables.

This section will address topics related to single scull racing. Not everyone wants to race, and it is not necessary to race to be an excellent sculler. However, racing is a wonderful way to enjoy the sport, including the goodwill and fellowship that are its hallmark. While single scull racing can be nerve-wracking and take an athlete outside their comfort zone, it is good developmentally. If an athlete can race a single scull well ('well' defined as performance against one's race plan), racing in a bigger boat is a comparative cakewalk. At the finish of a 1X race, there is no confusion about who was responsible for the result, which makes doing well very sweet indeed.

PRE-COMPETITION RACING TIPS

The athlete should have a comprehensive race plan. It should be a race plan that has been successful in competition. The target regatta for the season is not the time to be creative with such plans. For example, if the athlete were interested in exploring the benefits of beetroot for performance enhancement, that beetroot should have been part of a previous training programme and competition race plan, tested and evaluated with supporting data. The same holds true for rigging changes, with the exception of ones that the athlete has trained for, with gate raising for varied weather conditions being one of them. Enough unwelcome unknowns and surprises will present themselves. Here are some of them and how to prepare.

Tapering, equipment and course familiarity

The athlete's training programme should have included a tapering period. That period reduces fatigue, with a disproportionately smaller decrease in fitness. The taper period included in the training programme template

226

Fig. 125 The weather may dictate last minute changes with gate height.

is approximately a week. If the volume and intensity of work, and the athlete's fatigue, have been high and the main event is multi-day, a taper of up to two weeks would be appropriate. If the volume and intensity were low, fatigue moderate to low, and the main event one day with one race, the taper could be a few days. From a fatigue management perspective and for athletes new to tapering, it is wiser to err on the side of a longer taper.

Speed skills diminish quickly. While the volume of work decreases throughout the taper, the athlete needs to continue to maintain speed skills with race pace intensity. Shorter intervals with longer recovery periods continue until almost the end. For a multi-day event with a long taper, the last four days are for rest or, if sculling, only low intensity (T0/T1). A successful taper will find the athlete at their target regatta enthusiastic, full of energy and resilient.

It may also find them at a new venue in a rental boat with oars rigged differently than they were at home. And, with a dictate that nothing can be changed. An important aspect of the race plan is arriving at the venue early enough to become familiar with new equipment, or even the athlete's own equipment that has been in transit, while not undermining the taper period. Training at the venue means shorter outings working up to race pace when training times are offered. The purpose of training at the venue is to retain speed skills and confirm the equipment is in good working condition. Thus, doing 1,000m pieces is counter-indicated and a very limited amount of interval work is appropriate. The

primary objectives are: keep the skills level up, fatigue and stress levels down.

Venue training times provide an opportunity to gain course familiarity, including new starting procedures. At Western Australia regattas, starts are static without starting gates/pontoons. At national events, the starting gates/pontoons are used. While various home-grown solutions help prepare the athlete, true familiarity is acquired during venue training times. Use this training time to assess how long it takes to arrive at the marshalling area; where and when to launch the boat in relationship to the event start time; the direction of prevailing winds and currents; and how to scull on a buoyed course. These skills are often stale or new.

Athlete's schedule of events

The previous chapter on competition discussed time trials and other events over which there was some control. Racing is different. The programme of racing may not be decided until a day or two before. Thus, the athlete needs to enter events based on an indicative schedule, which has no firm heat, semi and final times, making event entry decisions challenging. Most national bodies stipulate a minimum time between race progressions, say an hour and a half. Organizers do not always adhere to it, reducing recovery times even further.

It is indeed difficult to architect a schedule of events when it is unclear whether an athlete will have two races on a given day or six (heats, semis and finals). The athlete should already have a very good idea of what their performance will be. With their training and competition experience, athletes should be able to compare their best efforts against prognostics. If performing at grade or below (a D grade athlete meeting B prognostics), the athlete is likely to be competitive at grade with possible semis and final. If performing several grades higher on the prognostics, probably at the lower end of the field and heat only. Placement at national and regional events usually, but not always, has slower times than the prognostics, which are based on FISA World Championships.

The stress of a regatta that may be in a different time zone (or country), the use of rented equipment and other factors advise a caution here: less is more. The well-trained athlete will have some resilience. That resilience is limited. Scheduling events to optimize recovery will retain that resilience and provide a competitive advantage over those who do not. If the athlete's objective is to perform at their best for a target race or multiple races, his or her schedule of events needs to be well thought out. For multiple-day events, one race a day, with heats, semis and final, is a good place to start. Those with extensive racing experience can adjust accordingly.

Sleep

Good sleep hygiene will help protect the athlete, but some sleep issues related to racing are unavoidable, particularly when travel is involved. If the athlete is not sleeping in their own bed, sleep will be affected. This disruption can be diminished by arriving early and acclimatizing. The first night of sleep in a new location will be disrupted. It is the body's primitive response to unknown threats. This disruption is normal and should be catered for in travel plans.

Other small considerations can provide large dividends. Ear plugs and a sleep mask may help, their use already incorporated for an extended period of time at home. Bringing a pillow from home may seem excessive, but both the famili-

arity and smell can aid sleep. Athletes who have adopted the casein milk drink an hour or two before sleep will find that, in addition to aiding recovery, the cueing helps with sleep. Bunking in with other people creates its own sleep challenges. When an athlete normally goes to bed should be part of the roommate selection process. Snorers have a moral obligation to declare themselves in advance.

Jet lag has physiological, emotional and sports performance implications. If travel involves flying and/or a change in time zones, the body will need additional time to adjust its circadian rhythm. For long-haul transitions, a variety of non-pharmacological interventions can help and include adapting before travel occurs, strategies for how to spend time in flight and post-flight tactics. For example, some airlines have adopted cabin lighting and oxygenation strategies to help ease jet lag for their passengers. Pharmacological interventions include melatonin, caffeine and prescription drugs, all of which bring their own effects, with some on the banned substance list. Non-pharmacological options are preferred. There is a body of evidence-based research to help athletes individualize a time zone management strategy.[1] Athletes should consider this even for shorter flights.

Nutrition and recovery foods

Race planning includes ensuring that the essential foods on which an athlete depends for performance are available. To many this means ensuring food preparation facilities are available. The homogeneity of food distribution in most countries makes this less of a challenge, although regional differentiation may play a role. For example, one state may have a wide range of locally produced flavoured milks readily available. Another may have only one, chocolate, and that may not be the athlete's flavour of choice. Recovery is crucial for multi-day events. A high race plan priority is ensuring that the athlete's normal recovery foods are available.

Familiar foods help with everything from mental health, recovery and digestion. Especially if travelling internationally, consider high-priority foods and either how to obtain them at the location or whether they can be imported in the athlete's baggage. When playing in Asia, the baggage content of Australia's international teams includes large boxes of breakfast cereals. If close to home, replicating the athlete's normal, successful diet will lower total system stress. If far away, finding a successful nutrition alternative for meals will take time, both locating and familiarizing the digestive system. That familiarization segue needs to be built into travel plans.

Hydration

A large percentage of people distinguish a distinct taste in water. Water at home tastes different from water at the race location. This inhibits water uptake and hydration. The simplest solution is a small amount of flavouring added to mask the taste difference. This flavouring should be used at home, preferably in a competitive event when flavour aversion reaches its peak. The flavouring needs to be available at the race location or brought along. Conventional sports drinks in a much diluted form provide an easy solution. For this reason, easily transportable powdered versions have an advantage.

Alcohol. The use of alcohol depends on whether the athlete wants to perform optimally. If they do, alcohol will undermine that quest. Celebratory champagne at the end of the regatta is, of course, the exception.

Warm-up and pre-race preparation

By now the athlete has a warm-up routine, but transporting this to the race venue may present problems. A dynamic warm-up is more versatile but needs a place that is consistent with the athlete's pre-race needs, for example a quiet location away from crowds. Familiarization with the venue prior to race day is helpful in identifying warm-up (and boat launching) locations and how the pre-race plan is going to evolve. To this end, it is advantageous to have multiple warm-up options, for example ergo, dynamic warm-up and on water. These would have been executed at home, the athlete familiar with the benefits and limitations of each.

COMPETITION RACING TIPS

From a pre-race perspective and through competition experience, every athlete finds what works for them. Some like to arrive at the marshalling area early, chat with the other competitors and de-stress. Others like to rush out at the last moment, working themselves into physiological pre-race readiness that segues right into a start. Whatever works to prepare the individual athlete for the race is the objective.

However, some fundamentals of physiology, training principles and the laws of physics apply. Athletes who consider these in their race plan will have a competitive edge.

Constant velocity and constant effort

The boat performs best at constant velocity. The athlete's physiology is most efficient at constant effort. The issue is: what velocity and what effort? The preceding chapter's example race plan and data show a speed (one component of velocity) that is variable. Direction (the other component of velocity) is important, too. In a race fluctuations in direction result in additional drag and may involve clashes with buoys. For discussion purposes here, direction is assumed to be dead straight.

The athlete is more complicated. Pushing the physiological limits is a dance with the devil. Push too far in the beginning, and physiological resources are expended too soon. In the initial stages of intense activity, the body uses two short-term anaerobic energy systems. The first is the ATP – PC (adenosine triphosphate – phosphagen) system that allows for maximal bursts of speed for up to six seconds. The next is the anaerobic glycolytic system. Both operate independent of oxygen.

As fuel, anaerobic glycolysis uses glucose or muscle glycogen, which is broken down into glucose. The process can sustain itself for up to two or three minutes, but with progressively decreasing effectiveness. After thirty seconds it can contribute approximately half of energy output. After two minutes, this output falls considerably. Meanwhile, the waste product of anaerobic glycolysis is ATP (adenosine triphosphate) and lactic acid. This system provides quick energy. It is also inefficient, with the lactic acid produced causing fatigue and preventing further muscle contractions. By three minutes of only aerobic glycolysis, muscles would be unable to contract. The system predominates in sprint sports such as the 400m dash, swimming and badminton.[2]

The problem? Masters races last longer than two minutes. This requires a transition to the aerobic system. An over-reliance on the anaerobic systems at the beginning of a race, as in aggressive starts, will create a surfeit of lactic acid resulting in early onset fatigue. The athlete will be required to reduce their effort considerably while transitioning to the aerobic system. The head start fades, losing its benefit. Then, of course, is the last section of the race. The transition can go from aerobic to anaerobic, depending on whether the athlete has successfully recovered from their lactic acid build-up excesses at the start and has any capacity left.

So, the race plan now becomes more complicated because all three systems are used. What determines their use is the intensity and duration of the effort, as well as the athlete's fundamental fitness and diet. Low glycogen stores undermine performance, high glyco-

gen stores aid it. Modulating the use of these systems is like driving. Envision sitting in a car, one foot on the accelerator. Push down (more effort), the car speeds up but uses more fuel and produces more exhaust. Release (less effort), the car slows down and uses less fuel. Decisively pushing the accelerator to the floor from a dead start creates burning rubber, squeals and noise before reaching cruising speed. It also creates less initial speed than gradually pushing down on the accelerator. That gradual push down uses less fuel, too.

The proposed approach to formulating a competitive race plan is as follows. First, base the race plan on stroke rate and heart rate. Second, designate a stroke rate that can be executed technically well and consistently throughout the race. Third, designate a heart rate that can be maintained throughout and just below the anaerobic threshold. Fourth, use a sensible start with a rating at which the athlete is technically proficient, achieving the athlete's target stroke rate and heart rate as quickly as possible (the warm-up prior to the start should be explored to facilitate this). Five strokes in good weather is a nominal target. Last, sustain this stroke rate and heart rate for the race. The same stroke rate plus the same heart rate should yield the same speed and optimal performance for boat and athlete alike.

When the above is mastered, accessorize with a finishing plan. The ideal finishing plan is: more of the same. Everyone else is behind you. A very refined race plan will have the athlete using a constant effort, at a constant speed, and managing muscle fatigue so that physiological resources are used completely by 1,000m. A good place to verify this approach is to look at the FISA World Championships where race data is available. One will see: constant stroke rate and constant speed for most of the race. Figs 126 and 127 show the 2018 W1X heavyweight winner's data. All other 1X races follow the same theme. Big finishes occur only when needed.

If a scheduled sidelong glance at 700m indicates something else is needed, the

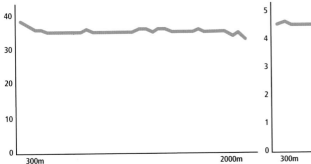

Fig. 126 Stroke rate (spm) for W1X heavyweight 1X winner at FISA 2018 World Rowing Championships, showing constant stroke rate (300–2,000m).

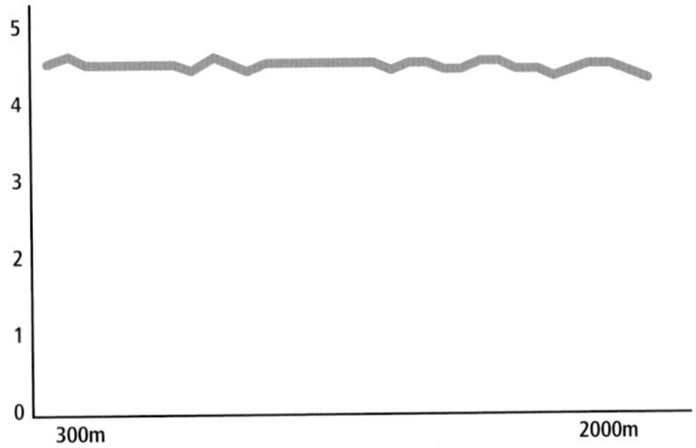

Fig. 127 Speed (mps) of for W1X heavyweight winner at FISA 2018 World Rowing Championships, showing constant speed (300–2,000m).

athlete should have a finish plan. Changes in rating at the end of the race are perilous. Presumably, the athlete has selected the particular stroke rate for their race because they can do it optimally. If a higher rating was not within that athlete's technical grasp when fresh, it is probably not within their technical grasp when fatigued. However, the benefit of a higher rating is that it can increase speed at the same effort level. Alternatively, more effort is less likely to create technical miscues. The timing of that additional effort needs to ensure that the transition to the anaerobic glycolytic system does not result in so much lactic acid that the athlete fizzles at the end. At T5 (>95 per cent of maximum heart rate) a rough rule of thumb is an available forty-five to sixty seconds with lactic acid building up throughout and exponentially decreasing muscular contraction effectiveness. The productive time during this period depends entirely on the athlete's fitness and adaptation to performing at this level.

How to tell what works for a particular athlete, both for static race pace and finishing plans? Practice. Training runs. Competitions. All the above systems are very individual. Some athletes have less capacity and will find their lactic acid building up very quickly. Others will have more resilience. Regardless, the race plan execution should be a function of what the athlete has trained to. An athlete who goes rogue during the start, race or finish will almost certainly undermine their performance. One who executes their plan will outdance the devil, optimizing their performance and getting useful information for further improvements.

Head in the boat

Every time an athlete consciously focuses their attention on a new technical skill, they override an old habit. This phenomenon has been explored in Chapter 12. What has not been explored is that when under stress and distracted, the athlete will regress to the most dominant skill in their motor skill armoury. That is, the skill they have been doing the longest, not necessarily the one they have been learning for the past six months that makes them go faster.

This regressive phenomenon has several implications. First, the race plan should choose a skill level that has been well and truly embedded in training and through competition. This applies to many dimensions of the race plan but, definitely, technical skill. Second, reducing stress helps the athlete be more resilient and less likely to regress to previous skills. The third has to do with distractions during the race.

Every time an athlete breaks from the automatic, the opportunity for skills regression occurs. This break can be focusing on what that athlete is doing in a way that has not been practised. For example, deciding to start looking at how their hands are performing when that has not been part of the priority or routine.

Or, the most common, looking around to see what everyone else is doing. This happens at the start, when stress is high compounding the problem. This happens during the race when an athlete discovers they are behind the rest of the field. It happens during the finish when the boat in the next lane closes in. Every distraction is an opportunity for things to come unstuck. Keeping one's head in the boat and focusing on executing one's race plan will minimize regressive episodes.

Hydration and nutrition between heats, semis, finals and other races

Short turnarounds (one and a half hours between races, or less than one hour on shore) mean focusing on glucose replacement. Hydration should occur as quickly as possible after the first event, at the finish line if possible. Electrolytes and high GI carbohydrates in the hydration fluid are ideal. Some athletes experiment, during training and competitions, with higher concentrations of electrolyte and sugar than they might normally use. For example, a container of undiluted, as opposed to diluted, sports drink. The objective is to replace blood sugar and start the glycogen replacement process as soon as possible, given that absorption may not begin for half an hour. Hydration helps flush out waste products. In order to perform optimally at the next race, full hydration needs to occur prior to it.

Nutritional needs are less during short turnarounds. Protein will not be metabolized in an hour, especially with stress and a digestive system that has shut down. Some foods may create digestive problems, although the ubiquitous banana seems well

tolerated by most. If there is time, and the athlete has been successful with short turnaround food intake, particularly high GI foods, the approach has advantages. Not necessarily for the next race but for finals, where that food intake has had some opportunity to metabolize, providing additional physiological resilience.

For longer turnaround times, the hydration guidelines are the same as above. Nutritionally, normal recovery food is appropriate. An athlete may find that the inter-race recovery nutrition needs to be qualitatively different than normal recovery food. Thus, inter-race nutrition recovery needs to be explored as part of training and competition.

Lightweights

Few lucky lightweight competitors at the Masters level have the opportunity to compete in lightweight categories. For most it is heavyweight and lightweight combined events. In the face of this one size fits all racing, there are strategies to provide a competitive advantage for lightweights.

If well-muscled and fit, the heavyweight sculler will have an advantage in a 2,000m race. However, in a 1,000m race, that advantage is ever so slight. Both equipment and physiology contribute to that slight advantage. The lightweight's job is to gain an even greater advantage by being clever.

First, rigging needs to be optimized. This includes equipment, like oars. The lightweight's boat, oars and rigging should provide the best partnership possible. The lightweight sculler needs to be an outstanding experimenter with a very open mind, exploring the possibilities that work, and don't, while refining these to the best option. Shorter oars, smaller span and different blade types are all good experiments.

Second, most heavyweights depend on their power. A lightweight whose technique is exquisite will find that they can use stroke efficiency to gain an advantage over brute strength that is inefficiently applied.

Third, rate higher. A large, heavyweight competitor usually has longer arms and longer legs. It takes comparably more time for them to complete their stroke than a smaller person with shorter arms and shorter legs. That heavyweight more than likely has a longer stroke arc as a result. Thus, if both scullers are doing the same, the heavyweight will win, but not if the lightweight takes advantage of their inherent capacity to rate higher. Rating higher does not mean taking the same effort at 26spm and applying it to 34–36spm. It means modulating, based on fitness and physiology, to obtain the athlete's best effort at the highest rating (versatility). This higher rating means more constant speed, which the surging heavyweight may not have, obtaining the boat's best effort, too.

Thus the strategic focus of lightweights should be precision and higher ratings, all of which need to be well developed in training.

POST-COMPETITION RACING TIPS

After preparing six months for an event, then executing a well-developed race plan, most athletes are ready to move to off season. These athletes should ensure they undertake a post-competition analysis. Those who plan to compete further need to read on, completing that analysis at the end of their season.

Post-competition analysis

No matter how the athlete captures the information, it is important not only to analyse performance, but to review the other qualitative and quantitative aspects of the main event. Qualitative can be: how did the athlete feel during various stages of their schedule of races? How did they feel about specific aspects of their race plan? What worked and

what changes would help improve the stress management process? From a quantitative perspective one question would be: too many races or not enough? Was the time allotted to get to the start sufficient? It is important to document the experience, through a list or athlete logbook, when that experience is fresh in the athlete's mind so that next year's training programme and race can benefit.

Dual event season

High-performance athletes target a specific event. Sometimes two events are of interest, for example, a regional or state championship that occurs shortly before a national one. If the two events are close together, say a matter of weeks, the athlete needs to target one. That is not to say that performance at the other is non-competitive. The realistic problem is that although tapering will result in improved performance, tapering twice in a row doesn't do the same. The recommended approach is to use the first event as a training experience, but a high-performance one. It may be a good opportunity to trial some short turnaround hydration and nutrition strategies. The second event is the main event, with the taper completed before it.

When more time is available, the athlete can train for a dual event season. The first event includes a taper. After it, a two-week recovery training period is completed at reduced volumes and intensities. Then, if fatigue is managed, the athlete can approach their training in two ways: endurance or high intensity.

The endurance approach involves using the athlete's existing programme with 80 per cent plus of the work at T2. This includes gradual speed work introduction, just like the original training programme. Depending on how much time there is before the second event, the athlete backtracks in their training programme and begins from there. Volumes and intensities may need to be reduced proportionately if the athlete is struggling with fatigue.

The high-intensity programme continues with reduced volumes, say at half the peak week training volumes. The ratio of high intensity work, such as intervals or speed work, is increased to no more than 15–20 per cent of the workload. The limitations of this approach are that it is physiolgically demanding, may have a greater fatigue effect because of the intensity and the athlete may be unfamiliar with how to manage the approach without performance deterioration. The advantages are that it preserves the speed work skills, may have less of a fatigue effect because of the lower volume and is more efficient time-wise.

For athletes new to training with a programme, the endurance approach is recommended. For more experienced athletes, preserving speed work skills has an advantage, as does learning how to incorporate this approach into training for the following year.

OTHER CONSIDERATIONS

The following items are ones that provide food for thought as the athlete continues with his or her athletic career. The sky is the limit in terms of performance potential, provided one first considers the athlete holistically (general health, injury risk prevention) and uses that healthy athlete as the platform for change.

Two weeks after the last target event

The process of recovery includes a gradual training reduction for two weeks after the target event. Athletes should reduce volumes and intensity. Nutrition and hydration have a larger role to play because the training programme, by design, has systemically stressed the athlete, taking their performance beyond their non-systemically stressed range. Monitoring psychological well-being is important, too.

Taking a few days off after the target event is one approach. Then it is important to get back into the training pattern and manage its thoughtful transition to post-season. This is a good time to wrap up the season, writing down notes of what worked in the training programme and race plans, what adaptations were achieved and what the opportunities are for next year.

The recyclable training programme and race plan

Athletes who have completed their first year of using a training programme and race plan are in for a wonderful surprise. If those worked, they can be used again next year with only minor adjustments. With the utility of both fresh in the athlete's mind, now is a good time to tidy them up. Then when the next season comes around, out they come, ready to go.

Next year's programme: chasing the seconds

At the end of the first year, the athlete now has an excellent idea of how they have performed against standards. That athlete knows: their sculling performance against prognostics, aerobic fitness, flexibility, sleep, nutrition, hydration and a range of other information. If the athlete wants to improve performance, the process is simple – chase seconds.

Seconds can come from many places: rigging, improved aerobic fitness, increased anaerobic threshold, more consistency, better recovery, attention to stretching, sleep, nutrition, hydration and more. The continuous improvement plan for next year is to identify those three opportunities with the most potential seconds, then modify next year's training programme to catch them.

Rigging

The past training season has provided much information about the athlete's capacity to perform. If fatigue was a factor in the athlete's performance, it is time to re-evaluate oars and oar rigging, including span changes and shortening the oars.

Off season

As discussed in Chapters 8 and 9, post-season is not 'no season'. The athlete has spent the last six months building up a variety of physiological and technical gains. Aerobic capacities have improved. Finger rolls are fluid. Flexibility gains are obvious. The measuring device provides useful data and is no longer perceived as an invention of the devil. While some regression is to be expected, preserving as much gain as possible should be the goal of off season.

Thematically, the four areas of overall assessment provide a good outline: aerobic, technical, FMB and other. Off season is an opportunity to continue athletic development but in a different way. First, aerobic gains should be preserved by continued aerobic activity, although this should involve other modalities such as hiking, cycling, swimming, team sports and the range of available activities that will help with diverse motor skill and muscle development. The heart rate range to achieve this is T2. The frequency should be at least the minimum for general health.

Preserving technical gains is crucially important because the athlete has most likely made many of them in the past season. These gains range from sequencing, finger rolls, timing and rating. If possible, all of these skills need to be refreshed regularly throughout the off season, or the body will exert its influence. Skills will regress to prior habits, making the beginning of next season very frustrating. Some skills refreshment can be done at home. The athlete can sit on the floor and go through sequencing. Finger rolls can be done in front of the TV. Other skills can be revisited during a low-key scull at T1/T2. The one skill that needs more thoughtful planning is rating.

Speed work does not sustain itself well. Having learned a higher rating, the athlete will find that this capability dissipates rapidly. Thus, athletes who are working on raising their rating are encouraged to build some high rating work into their off season as well as into their early training programme next year. This takes the form of very short pieces at very low effort, say 100–200m with light effort concentrating on technique.

Flexibility, mobility and balance work should progress throughout the off season. Off season is also a good time to target strength and conditioning if the athlete has expended most of their training time in the year on other facets of their development. The whole host of other categories such as sleep and nutrition are places to explore.

SUMMARY OF RACING A SINGLE SCULL

This chapter ends a journey, one that explores the sculling system and the instrument of propulsion, the athlete. Another journey begins. For the athlete whose interests are purely non-competitive, the athlete with international aspirations, and all those athletes in between, a lifetime of exploration is ahead. Many exciting discoveries await each athlete willing to become an experiment of one ... or more.

Endnotes

1 Lee, A., Galvez, J.C., 'Jet lag in athletes', *Sports Health*. 2012 May; 4(3): pp.211–216. doi: 10.1177/1941738112442340. PubMed PMID: 23016089; PubMed Central PMCID: PMC3435929

2 Canadian Academy of Sports Nutrition. *Anaerobic Glycolysis*. www.caasn.com/sports-nutrition/energy-systems/anaerobic-glycolysis.html.

CONCLUSION

Below are topics that provide indicators of where our sport is headed for Masters. The news is good. Information is starting to flow. Each athlete should know that their experiment of one will add to it.

THE FUTURE OF MASTERS SCULLING

The future is bright indeed, particularly for athletes living in countries with national or universal health plans. Governments worldwide, aware of their ageing populations, are developing an acute awareness that a healthy older population costs less than an unhealthy one. In Australia, this has recently seen the Commonwealth direct a portion of its health budget towards increasing physical activity in adults. Where once adult sports participation was of no strategic interest, it is now on the front line.

In the US, the news is also good with US Rowing reporting increasing Masters participation. US Rowing has facilitated this Masters growth by smoothing the transition of rowers from youth to Master, having established an AA grade for ages twenty-one to twenty-six. Other national rowing organizations wishing to grow their Masters membership should give consideration to this very successful AA grade innovation.

The immediate obstacle is that rowing organizations worldwide are not truly aligned strategically with adult sport participation, their focus being primarily on youth and national development. This is a shame because Masters athletes are the lifeblood of most clubs. A well-informed Masters membership, including the large Master coaching contingent, can enhance youth and national development cooperatively along with Masters development. How, or if, the current dichotomy will resolve itself remains to be seen.

MASTERS EQUIPMENT AND RESEARCH

The hope is that athletes who are engaged in their experiment of one will expect equipment suited to them. Footstretchers and shoe plates that are responsive to Masters athletes, particularly women with regards to rake and splay adjustments. Seats that fit wider pelvises – and are comfortable. Oar grips that fit the smaller hand, including the hands of young people, with the size of even the smallest oar grip now available too large for many.

The other hope is that an interest in research about adult athletes, their athletic well-being and performance will begin to snowball, too. Research is, of course, tied to available funding. With the emerging interest in healthy adults, this appears to be on the horizon, too.

ANECDOTAL INDICATORS

Using the Masters development pathway has provided some anecdotal information that, while not scientific, may help other athletes in their experiment of one. First, recovery times appear to increase at particular ages: forty, menopausal and post-menopausal for women, sixty and seventy. The progression may be more linear but athletes should be aware that additional recovery time may be required when they reach these age boundaries. A simple solution has been for the last workout to be Saturday morning with the next on Monday morning, providing two full days, which appears to work well for all athletes.

Another approach has been to embrace T2 training. Many adult scullers are under the impression that their volume and intensity of workload needs to be enormous in order to perform well. The experience with this pathway is that less is more, with small work and slow work, well managed within a T2 workout, bringing significant performance improvements with less fatigue. In addition, all the athletes who pilot-tested this model, including those with prior back injuries and surgeries, have achieved their recent personal best performance improvements injury free.

Protein needs for those sixty-plus appear to increase significantly. This has manifested itself by increased fatigue to the point of overreaching symptoms appearing in those whose workload has not changed from the prior year. For these athletes, rest alone did not resolve the problem. The final solution has been protein supplementation at the higher levels (2+g/kg of body weight). Younger Masters athletes have also reported good results with protein supplementation.

Finally, the implementation of a post-workout nutrition and hydration plan, immediately after training, has shown demonstrable success not only in performance and readiness to train but in mental health. These happy athletes report experiencing less muscle soreness, too.

ROWING MULTI-SEAT BOATS AND THE DYNAMIC TECHNIQUE

The clever reader has figured out that launching hands, gathering the boat, capitalizing on elasticity with a jump and counting to 1–2–3 in the back end may not synchronize well with the traditional technique. It doesn't. But, it does provide more stability and improves performance while reducing injury risk. It also takes time to learn. During that time there is often pushback from the legacy contingent. Scullers who adopt the dynamic technique, aside from being more stable and performing better, are more versatile. They can integrate into a multi-seat boat using any variety of techniques. The reverse has not proven to be true. Persevere. When the time is right, offer to race at 12spm. You'll win.

YOUR EXPERIMENT OF ONE

Decades of discovery await the athlete who embarks on a journey of exploration. May yours be a journey of enrichment, longevity and joy.

FURTHER READING

Ackland, Jon., *The Complete Guide to Endurance Training* (London: Bloomsbury Publishing PLC, 2007)

Baker, J., Horton, S., & Weir, P. (eds), *The Masters Athlete: Understanding the Role of Sport and Exercise in Optimising Aging* (Abingdon [UK]: Taylor & Francis Ltd, 2009)

Bean, A., *The Complete Guide to Sports Nutrition* (London: Bloomsbury Publishing PLC, 2017)

Bean, A., *The Complete Guide to Strength Training* (London: Bloomsbury Publishing PLC, 2008)

Dudhia, A., *Physics of Rowing*. 2019. http://eodg.atm.ox.ac.uk/user/dudhia/rowing/physics/index.html

Duhigg, C., *The Power of Habit: Why We Do What We Do in Life and Business* (New York: Random House, 2012)

Flood, J., & Simpson, C., *The Complete Guide to Indoor Rowing* (London: Bloomsbury Publishing PLC, 2012)

Fritsch, W., *Rowing: Training-Fitness-Leisure* (Oxford: Meyer & Meyer, 2009)

Kleshnev, V., *The Biomechanics of Rowing* (Marlborough: The Crowood Press Ltd, 2016)

Lawrence, M., *The Complete Guide to Core Stability* (London: Bloomsbury Publishing PLC, 2011)

Mayer, E., *Mind-Gut Connection: How the Hidden Conversation Within Our Bodies Impacts Our Mood, Our Choices, and Our Overall Health* (New York: Harper Wave, 2016)

McNeely, E. & Royle, M., *Skillful Rowing: From Juniors to Masters* (Oxford: Meyer & Meyer, 2009)

Nolte, V. (ed), *Rowing Faster* (Leeds [UK]: Human Kinetics Publishers, 2011)

Norris, C., *The Complete Guide to Sports Injuries* (London: Bloomsbury Publishing PLC, 2011)

Norris, C., *The Complete Guide to Stretching* (London: Bloomsbury Publishing PLC, 2015)

Reaburn, P., *The Masters Athlete* (Main Beach, Queensland [AU]: Info Publishing PLC, 2009) and online at www.mastersathlete.com.au

Sayer, W., *Rowing & Sculling: The Complete Manual* (London: Robert Hale Ltd, 2013)

Simpson, C. & Flood, J., *Advanced Rowing* (London: Bloomsbury Publishing PLC, 2017)

Thompson, P., *Sculling: Training, Technique & Performance* (Marlborough: The Crowood Press Ltd, 2005)

Thompson, P. & Wolf, A., *Training for the Complete Rower: A Guide to Improving Performance* (Marlborough: The Crowood Press Ltd, 2016)

Walker, M., *Why We Sleep: The New Science of Sleep and Dreams* (London: Penguin Random House UK, 2017)

INDEX

active training 141, 143, 146
adaptation 115, 132, 137, 138, 139, 140–46, 150, 153, 169, 171, 177, 180, 192, 213, 214, 217, 231
aerobic capacity 13, 15, 115, 146, 159, 161, 162, 179
ageing 13, 14, 15, 16, 17, 140, 141, 183, 185, 236
aspirations 127, 130, 131, 137, 141, 145–50, 146, 235
athlete morphology 61
  feet, legs and hips 41
  flexibility 40, 44, 46, 50, 60, 61, 82, 84
  pelvic girdle 43, 47
  seat, spine, and head 48
  shoulder girdle 47, 49–54, 49, 52, 53, 54, 97, 120
  shoulders, arms and hands 50
available time 127, 135, 146
back end transition 104
balance 49, 60, 61, 109, 111, 120, 121, 134–36, 143, 145, 146, 170, 180, 235
blade path 35–38, 54, 68, 70
boat gathering 83–88, 135, 208
body flip 79, 80–82, 85, 135, 202
body mass 40, 41, 47, 55, 116
body mass index 116, 133
bone density 13, 14, 16, 188, 189
bone health 185, 188, 189
breathing 208
calcium 13, 185, 188–190
cardiac disease 188
catch 29, 43, 56 – 66, 74, 76, 81, 85, 91– 94, 101, 104, 200, 201, 203, 209, 210, 234
  distance 50
  foot position 45
  position of hands and arms 75
catch angle 47, 57–59, 69, 72
centre of mass 26, 32–34, 39, 40, 42, 44
comfort 41, 59, 60, 64, 72, 146, 226
competition 139, 144, 153, 163, 169, 172, 191, 192, 212–214, 216–222, 225–227, 231–233
connectedness 40, 41, 48, 50, 52, 53, 66, 72–75, 77, 78, 84–86, 105, 108, 143, 193, 199, 202, 203
consistency 89, 105, 193, 196, 197, 198, 199, 203, 204, 206, 207, 208, 214, 215, 216, 221–225, 234
constant speed 31, 33, 34, 205, 230, 231, 233
constant velocity 29, 30, 34, 204, 205, 229
  effect of speed variation 30
  effects of roll, pitch and yaw 32

cycling 208
dental health 190
drag 22, 29, 30, 32, 36, 37, 57, 66, 68, 94, 105–107, 114, 125, 126, 229
  factor 29, 32
  form 29, 33, 36, 57, 68, 90
  skin 29, 30, 34
  wave 29
drive sequence 47, 54, 73, 91–108, 208, 209
  catch 91–95
  early mid-drive 97, 98
  initiate body 95–97
  initiate leg drive 93–95
  mid-drive transition 98, 99
  pre-release 99–101
  summary 101
drug testing and tue's 186
dual event season 233
dynamic technique 73–108
  biomechanics 77
  foot position at catch 46
  foot position at catch 44, 45
  foot position at release 46
  how it feels 108
  sequence steps 74
  sequencing 77
effective stroke length 54, 212
electronic regatta 217, 218
fatigue 48, 75, 76, 99, 104, 106, 112, 125, 131, 133, 134, 137, 140, 152, 153, 161– 164, 166, 169–172, 179, 180, 188, 192, 198, 200, 201, 205, 209, 212, 216, 220–227, 230, 233–235, 237
feathering 75, 86, 201
feet, legs and hips 41, 47, 202
finger roll 73, 75, 76, 77, 81, 91, 92
FISA 18–22,25, 34, 40, 42, 119
flexibility 35, 40, 41, 48, 61, 64, 111, 120, 121, 131, 135, 136, 150, 156, 187, 234
flight or fight 219, 220, 221
fluidity 73, 74, 91
FMB 109, 111, 120, 121, 134–136, 145, 149, 150–152, 154, 161–168, 187, 204, 212, 235
front end transition 89
gate 27, 33, 35, 66, 227
glute engagement 95
gluteal inhibition 95
glycogen 13, 16, 139, 177–179, 219, 230, 232
gut health 185, 190
habits 14, 77, 104, 136, 138, 156, 169, 174, 199, 200, 204, 214, 218, 219, 221, 225, 235
hand launch 81, 82, 85, 86, 201, 202
handle speed 58

hydration 16, 126, 139, 165, 170, 172, 176–181, 183, 185, 190, 210, 217, 219, 222, 223, 229, 232–234, 237
  miracle of flavoured milk 179
  timing 180
illness 113, 114, 126, 137, 169, 188, 220
immune function 13, 174
initiate body 96
initiate leg drive 95
injury 42, 43, 48, 50, 51, 52, 53, 55, 59, 60, 71, 99, 106, 112, 117, 120, 125, 130, 137, 138, 145, 150, 154, 169, 173, 187, 234, 237
injury and illness management 106, 187, 188, 191
learning and habits 199
  habits 14, 77, 92, 104, 136, 138, 156, 169, 199, 200, 204, 214, 219, 221, 235
  hierarchical 199, 200–202
  incremental 66, 114, 127, 137, 192, 199, 209
  iterative 199
  learning 12, 23, 101, 106, 132, 135, 154, 173, 179, 199, 200, 203, 207, 231, 234
  sleep 174
  undoing old habits 200
masters scullers 11, 12, 236
maximum heart rate 111, 113–115, 126, 131, 133, 172
mid-drive transition 99, 203
mobility 60, 61, 109, 111, 121, 134–136, 143, 183, 189, 191, 235
muscle mass 13, 15, 16, 178, 183, 185, 189
NK Empower wireless oarlock 211
nutrition 126, 133, 139, 165, 169, 170, 174–176, 179, 180, 183, 185, 189, 190, 192, 210, 217, 219, 222, 229, 232–235, 237
  day-to-day 175
  post-workout and recovery 177
  pre-workout and workout 176
  timing 178
oar handle size 51
oar performance 57
  blade 33, 35–39, 53, 54, 57, 59, 68–70, 86, 90–94, 98, 99–101, 107, 201, 232
  blade path 37, 38
  blade type 54
  tracking 36
oars 27, 34, 35, 38, 45, 54, 57, 58, 60–62, 65, 66, 70, 72, 76, 92, 100, 101, 104, 106, 107, 109, 201–203, 226, 227, 232, 235
  as levers 67

at rest 34
Concept2 Fat2 blade 26, 37, 58, 70, 71, 203
FISA requirements 34
gate connection 33
in motion 35
length 69, 70
other considerations 36
placement timing 92
soft shafts 60
stability 27, 34
off season 133, 137, 138, 141–143, 146, 153, 154, 162–164, 185, 233, 235
off the seat 94
O'Neill test 117, 133
orthostatic heart rate 112, 131, 171, 172
overreaching 13, 112, 114, 116, 121, 126, 136, 169–172
overtraining 13, 112, 113, 116, 136, 142, 145, 169–172
pelvic girdle 47, 49, 95, 98, 99
performance analysis 193
    measuring device 193
    NK Empower wireless oarlock 211
    NK SpeedCoach 193, 194
    skills matrix 212
    slow work 196
periodization 141, 143, 144
phases of training 141–143
pitch, boat 29, 30, 32–35, 39, 40, 62, 87
power test 125, 135
pre-catch 86
pre-drive sequence 74, 78, 80, 82, 84, 87, 89, 91, 208
    boat gathering 83–85
    body flip 80
    concepts and terminology 72, 73
    hand launch 81
    position of hands and arms 73
    pre-catch 85, 86
    pre-drive transition 82, 83
    release 79
    summary 87
pre-drive transition 82–86, 202
pre-release 74, 76, 91, 99, 100, 101, 104
principle of specificity 147, 214
principles of training 137
    adaptation 140
    individuality 23, 137
    overload 138, 142, 170, 200
    progression 135, 137
    recovery 140
    reversibility 138
    specificity 138
prioritization 136
prognostics 19, 20, 119, 205, 206, 215, 222, 228
    1X, 18spm 119
    1X, all ratings 207
    by boat class, age, and gender 21
    developing by rating 22

mps to time conversion 20
Rowing Australia Masters Commission Handicap studies 17
technique measured by on water test 134
time to mps conversion 20
propulsion 25, 34, 36, 41, 52–54, 56–58, 67–69, 72, 96, 98–101, 107, 108, 140, 205, 206
    boat run and free speed 107
    effort through the drive sequence 107
    recommended stroke arc 57
    rigging for 54
    theoretical and practical objectives 56
race plans 214, 217, 225, 234
    competitive elements 221
    example 222
    post-competitive elements 222
    pre-competitive elements 219
    summary 222
racing 160, 201, 212, 213, 214, 218, 220, 225–228, 232
racing, competition 229–233
racing, post-competition 233–234
racing, pre-competition 226–229
rake 42, 43, 44, 45, 46, 56, 93
Randallfoils 211
recovery 15, 72, 126, 131, 132, 137–146, 153, 154, 160–165, 208, 214–219, 227–228, 232, 234, 236, 237
recovery strategies 169-181, 186
recovery support 183-192
release angle 47
research 14–17
resting heart rate 112
rigging 39–72
    catch angle measuring 62, 63
    connection with feet 41
    footstretcher 43, 46, 61
    gate height and offsets 66
    gate pitch 33
    oar inboard 64
    oar length 70
    oar outboard 67, 69
    rake 44
    recommended steps 54, 59, 72
    shoe plate 42
    shoe plate height 43
    shoes 42
    span 64
    technique considerations 59
roll 29, 30, 32, 34, 39, 42, 43, 66, 82, 84, 91, 99, 100, 201
seat, spine and head 41, 47, 49, 202
sequencing 74, 77, 108, 196, 198, 200–202, 208, 210, 235
single scull 25, 26, 29, 33, 40
skills matrix 212
sleep 126–128, 135, 139, 169, 173, 174, 180, 185, 190, 192, 200, 219–222, 228, 234
slip 36–38, 50, 57–60, 67–69, 90, 93, 104, 107, 203, 212
slow work 193, 198

12/12 sample 194
small work 201
    hands 201
    sequencing 202
span 38, 41, 59, 62, 64, 65, 66, 69, 232, 235
speed 25, 29, 30, 32, 34, 37, 70, 74, 94, 100, 101, 104–109, 134, 136, 138, 142, 144, 146, 147, 149–166, 193, 194, 197–209, 212, 215, 216, 220, 223–227, 229, 230–234
splay 42, 43, 84
sports psychology 191
squaring 75, 86, 91
stability 25, 33–35, 39, 42, 52, 59, 62, 66, 70–75, 77, 78, 81, 86, 89, 91–, 96, 105, 109, 135, 143, 159, 193, 199, 206, 216, 237
starts 209
starvation reflex 177
steering 106
stretching 186
stroke arc 57–61, 100–104, 135, 212, 233
supplements 183
support team 191
thirst 13, 179
time available 127
time trials 214, 216
timing 105
training intensity 17, 94, 133, 137, 140, 143–147, 150, 154, 157–164, 170, 172, 176, 178, 179, 181, 183, 185, 187, 208, 215, 227, 230, 233, 234
training program 20, 49, 112-116, 127, 128, 131-143, 145-169, 188, 213-225, 234
    adjusting for vacations 152
    calculating training times by week 147
    cross training 154
    daily workouts 161
    endurance and high intensity 163
    managing 162
    off season 162
    priorities and assessment 161
    relative training intensities 160
    spreading the hours 153
    subphases and intensity 157
    summary 164
    t0/t1 activities 154
    t2 activities 154
training program model 146
training volume 137, 140, 143, 145–147, 150, 157, 164, 172, 173, 181, 190, 227, 234, 237
training zones and ranges 115, 132
versatility 160, 193, 199, 203, 204, 205, 206
vitamin D 13, 185, 189
wash 36, 57, 58, 59, 67, 68, 69, 100, 101, 104, 107, 203, 212
workout plan 209
yaw 29, 30, 32, 33, 34, 41, 42, 66, 106